Spirit&Earth

'Don't think of the Earth as this random rock in space.

It is a living, breathing creature.'

Robert Ballard (Professor of Oceanography)
quote from Alien Deep

Spirit&Earth

Adrian Incledon-Webber
&
Tim Walter

Spiritual Earth

First published in Great Britain in 2018 by Spiritual Earth
an imprint of Dowsing Spirits
Copyright © 2018 by Adrian Incledon-Webber & Tim Walter
Cover Design by Huw Lloyd-Jones

ISBN: 9780995755505

The moral right of the authors has been asserted.

Every effort has been made to obtain the necessary permissions with reference to copyright material, both illustrative and quoted. We apologise for any omissions in this respect and will be pleased to make the appropriate acknowledgements in future editions.

Nothing in this book is to be taken as professional medical advice and is the opinion and experience of the authors. The authors and publisher accept no liability for damage of any nature resulting directly or indirectly from the application or use of any information contained within this book. Any information acted upon from this book is at the reader's sole discretion and risk.

First Edition

Acknowledgements from Adrian

I would like to thank Allyson for her understanding, wonderful breadmaking and for just being a very valuable part of my life.

Annie, the Springer, for her unconditional love and insistence on seeing as much of the Yorkshire countryside as she possibly can.

Alistair and Charles, my two boys, who are both hardworking and honourable people, it is my pleasure to call them sons as well as close friends. Thank you Jess for being there.

My late Mother for passing on her sensitivity and intuition, if it wasn't for her, I wouldn't be doing what I am doing.

My co-author and friend, Tim Walter, without whom this book would not have come about or the filming of the Intuition DVD.

Sara Pryke and Carrie Michael for their support over the years and all those who have attended my talks and courses, plus those thousands of others worldwide who have bought my first book 'Heal your Home', a big thank you.

Andy Roberts, David Telford, Hannah Silcock, Ann and Steve Dawson (Dowsing Anglia), Alison and Gill Bishop, all members of Ridings Dowsers, The British Society of Dowsers and their affiliated local groups. My brother Subash Tamang for opening my eyes to India, Nepal and Tibet, a true living and breathing Buddhist.

Acknowledgements from Tim

I am very grateful to my dear loving wife, Nicky, for her tolerance over the many decades that we have been married. She has accepted all the changes that the Universe has given us with a remarkable intuitive 'knowing'. Her patience shown to me as I questioned, analysed and tested all information imparted from the subtle realms far too deeply and far too often, has been exceptional.

I am truly grateful to both my sons, Oliver and Richard who as youngsters accepted the 'haunted house' more willingly than we could have anticipated and who as young men show more love in this world than I ever did that their age. You are both wonderful.

I am grateful to both Polly and Victoria for being a part of our extended family. They bring more joy to us all than they realise.

I am especially grateful to my brother, Steve, whose battle with mental health at the same time that I was encountering my own mind-boggling experiences showed me that I wasn't going mad. His personal sacrifice, undoubtedly made with a promise in a realm before this one, has been a rock of support that he knows nothing about.

I also thank my departed parents for their creative gifts which have filled my life with wonder and awe. Although I know they are often with me, I miss their physical presence profoundly.

Thanks go to Michelle Gordon and all others who have helped give life to this book, including Dave Barthram, a druid of exemplary conduct and a fine example of a gentleman.

And lastly, my thanks go to Adrian for his many teachings and guidance both in the subtle arts and in those less subtle, often over a welcome pint.

Acknowledgements from Adrian & Tim

Paul Gerry for his individual approach to science and his grounded way of explaining its mysteries. Steve Clark from Vilistus for his Mind Mirror work and patience.

Jane Pryor, Dave Barthram and, of course, Michelle Gordon for their invaluable input into making this book both readable and understandable.

Andrew Sabin, the British sculptor and designer of Coldstones Cut near Pateley Bridge, for giving us his valuable insights.

Mike Dooley for his kind permission for allowing us to use one of Tut's thoughts for the day.

Huw Lloyd-Jones (Full Moon Studio) for his wonderful artwork and ideas.

Contents

Foreword

My own spiritual journey began when a healer I visited (for a bad case of sciatica), got out a crystal pendulum, and began to dowse in front of me. Having only ever read about dowsing in novels, I had never seen it in real life and to be honest, I was in shock. The idea of being able to ask a rock on the end of a chain questions, and receive actual answers, was utterly magical to me.

Soon after that, I found myself holding a homemade pair of rods, trying to find Geopathic Stress in my home that was causing my back pain. The moment the rods swung to pinpoint the stress line, will be ingrained in my memory forever, as it was the moment I finally really understood that we are all connected, that we are all one with this planet, and with the universe. And that finally, I had a way of finding lost objects!

Without the discovery of dowsing, I may not have ended up on my current path, writing books on magical subjects and conversing with spirit. And I certainly wouldn't have met Adrian. Our paths crossed when he was working on his first book, *Heal Your Home,* and his down to earth approach to spirituality was refreshing, because it reinforced my belief that you can bring magic into everyday life. That you can be a 'normal' person, and still chat casually about fairies and angels.

This book Adrian has co-written with his fellow dowsing colleague and friend, Tim, helps to take you further down the magical path of the subtle or unseen realms, that exist within our world. Using dowsing as the link between spirit and earth, this book helps you to explore the subtle realms, and their often interesting inhabitants. Adrian and Tim's combined wealth of experience and knowledge on the subjects of sacred spaces, the elementals and the angelic realms is extensive, and will amuse and intrigue you. From angry gnomes to harassed ginger cats, to trapped pixies and amused angels, this book will encourage and inspire you to research, explore and experience the world in a completely different way.

The spiritual path is not the easiest route to take through this life, and we need all the help and guidance we can get along the way. If you would like to know how to both connect to the earth while enhancing your connection to the universe, then this book will be the perfect guidance for you.

If I have learned anything from my journey so far, it's that it's best to always expect the unexpected. That the moment you think you have it all figured out, something will happen to shift your worldview and possibly your life, moving it in a totally different direction. When I write, I never plot before I begin. I just start with an idea, and a blank page and I start writing. I find out the next part of the story when my characters do, and I am often as shocked as they are by the twists. We cannot prepare for every possibility, so it is best to go with the flow and enjoy ourselves as much as possible. Having said that, learning to dowse, and reading more about the fascinating topics within this book, will certainly help you to deal with whatever happens, and even when it feels like everything is going wrong, it will help you to see that at some point, you will see the silver lining.

Hope your journey is a fun one, and when you meet them, say hello to the fairies (and unicorns!) from me.

Michelle Gordon
Author of *Where's My F**king Unicorn?*
and the *Earth Angel Series*
February 2018

Introduction

Spirit

We have written this book for those who find they want to obtain life-satisfaction from non-material values and self-development, to lead what we would call a modern spiritual life.

To the unaware and the innocent, a word of caution: this path is not always the easiest one to follow and this book will help to take you one gentle step at a time. It is our intention that this book will guide, encourage and support you on your journey.

The New Age Movement, a term coined in the 1970s, has been misunderstood for years. It is looked down upon by those who feel we are on this planet simply to work, eat, procreate and then die, all the while battling to keep up with what our media-led culture extols as worthy.

Sadly, the original New Agers didn't help in creating a good impression. They were viewed as being anti-establishment, because they dared to wear colourful clothes, had long hair and spoke of auras, chakras, angels, and fairies: things that were frowned upon by people living in an increasingly materialistic world.

Adrian recollects, "My father, one day out of the blue, said to me, 'I hate Druids!' I asked him if he knew any, and he said no. He followed that random statement with 'All those long-haired layabouts you read about in the newspapers, causing trouble wherever they go.' I asked him if he believed everything that he read in the papers. Again, he said no. I then asked him if he liked Winston Churchill, and he replied that he did. I explained that Winston Churchill was in fact a Druid. Just as his bank manager might be. That they don't all go around wearing cloaks and carrying a staff. He grumbled but accepted that perhaps it wasn't the Druids that were troublemakers, but perhaps anyone with long hair might have a subversive nature."

To Adrian's father it seemed there was a kind of spiritual uniform that showed others that a person was walking a different pathway. Whether it's long hair, rainbow coloured clothing, or particular jewellery; to him these helped others recognise a fellow traveller, and to instantly trust and welcome them into the fold. Perhaps this uniform also showed a disdain for the 'normal' life that parents, family and friends might expect, or want, one to lead.

Society has always tended to have an issue with anyone who does not quite fit into the 'norm', and New Agers have often found themselves firmly outside the box, often found as Adrian's father believed, in their brightly coloured clothing or long hair. But regardless of how you might dress, it's time to live and breathe your truth. It's now time to "walk the walk and talk the talk". Therefore, it doesn't matter how we dress, it is how we speak and act that matters. To look smart and professional, whilst also living from a deeply spiritual perspective is a good way to bring the paranormal to the normal. It is time for us to establish ourselves by kind deeds and spiritual words, and not to alienate or deter others who may have an interest in what we do, or might want to walk the same path, but don't want to change their wardrobe to do it.

This book is for you, the seeker, the traveller, the ordinary man or woman in the street, who is wanting to change your life. Perhaps you are now starting to look at your life and realise that material goods don't hold true value, that spiritual happiness is important and that life isn't always as it seems.

Earth

If you are not used to seeing 'beyond the veil' then spiritual dowsing will open your mind and change the way you see the world in all its dimensions. You will soon discover that everything seems to be alive and can respond to you if you ask the right questions and trust your results. This applies as much to our dear Mother Earth herself as to anything living on its surface.

Hamish Miller, dowser, author, sculptor always believed, and so do we, that the Earth is a living being in her own right. He was one of the first dowsers to significantly explore the invisible geometric patterns that are found in the energetic layer of Mother Earth and believed it was her way of communicating with humans.

Dowsers are now used to visiting a sacred site and finding various symbolic patterns in and on the Earth, mainly where two energy lines cross. These etheric shapes are usually referred to as manifestations and/or pictograms.

They are basic interference patterns of standing waves similar to those found with interfering magnets or water ripples. The significant thing with these many layered patterns and symbols is that they can respond energetically to the observer or dowser when they begin to work on them. This earthly energy is interacting directly with our minds and shows us that we do have a natural integral link between ourselves and the planet. This is why Hamish was so convinced there was two-way communication going on.

This is hugely significant and is why sites like Avebury and the Thornborough Henges became sacred to our ancestors. They may have been areas where people felt or saw the energy patterns and then started to build temples, stone circles and even churches there.

Some would argue that the intelligence and life spirit found within nature alone is sufficient to call Mother Earth a life form; which is called the Gaia principle. But if we look at how the Earth and the human mind (our inner reality) have evolved then we can also attribute Mother Earth with her own life-force as we are inextricably bound to her for our survival and our collective and individual thought processes.

Like all mothers, she gives of herself usually without question. As you will read later, the Earth plays a major part in our spiritual existence, progress and development. It is a far greater part than we perhaps could have ever imagined.

Universe

The concept of the Universe as a living being has been revitalised in modern Western mainstream thinking though the New Age movement, and in modern self-development programmes such as the *Law of Attraction* or *The Secret.*

The 'Universe' is often used as a label instead of 'God'. While it is an entirely understandable substitution, it does, however, remove the concept of human-like personality from the Creator. As we shall see, this aspect of personality can become very important in our relationship with *all that is* as we progress through healing on our spiritual path.

We hope you enjoy this book. We hope it will assist you in evaluating the role you play in your overall reality and hopefully motivate you to further investigate the influences of the unseen for wellness in your life. Whether you choose to read it from cover to cover or dip into it every now and again, it will be no less effective in helping you master changes in life whether they be big decisions or small actions and thoughts.

We have written this book with you in mind and trust it will remain on your bookshelf and in your mind for a very long time...

...whatever your perception of 'time' may be.

Adrian and Tim
Imbolc, 2018
North Yorkshire
England

Spirit

'Spirituality is not just a belief system, it is a way of life.'

Chapter One

Spirituality & Daily Life

The 'subtle realms' are home to your spiritual self, the aspect of self that is always just a moment away. These realms are referred to as 'subtle' because the methods of using one's intuition to access information from here is not done brashly or with loud announcements. Intuition must be listened for, actively observed and gathered quietly with respect.

There are many ways to access this intuitive information and it can be mastered through practice, patience and perseverance. When one does connect, the rewards are worth the effort. Influence from the subtle realms of spirituality will most likely begin to seep into one's awareness with a delicate light fragrance of honeysuckle on a quiet summer's breeze.

However, this may not always be the case.

For some, their spiritual awakening arrives like a clap of thunder, battering their senses like waves against a small boat in a storm. Such force, often referred to as 'Kundalini Awakening' can overwhelm a person, and cause them chaos, until they know how to ground this new-found energy and begin to appreciate the world with a new sense of wonder.

This can be some time after the initial disturbance has forced them from their quiet normality, as they may find this intrusion can send them into a very lonely and unpleasant place, and the process is sometimes referred to as 'spiritual shock'. This sudden and dramatic intrusion into one's life doesn't occur when the spiritual truth seeker propels their own journey of discovery. It is most likely to happen to those who have ignored the signs pointing to a need for exploration of spirituality for "too long".

The development of a spiritual awareness, that is, the side of one's self which longs for more than just material fulfilment, is usually a gentle process, which often develops with age and perhaps wisdom. It brings with it an awareness of something greater than self, even if that excludes a god-like presence. In most cases, it begins with a need to develop one's intuition to find out if there really is more to life than meets the eye.

Spirituality is not just a belief system, it is a way of life. It is not just buying the latest green product or donating money to charity. It is about understanding, forgiveness and unconditional love.

We have heard many people ask: '*If you are living a spiritual life, why isn't everything perfect?*' The answer to that is that living a spiritual way of life is probably one of the hardest things you can do. Not only do you need to become introspective, (and learning about yourself is not always a pleasant experience), but you also need to look at what you have done in the past; not necessarily to address things that you did wrong in order to put them right, but more to understand why you did them and what effect they had on others.

Spirituality is not just about looking at the world as a sacred place but also believing that you and all other living beings are also sacred. We are all perfect and imperfect at the same time. Some of us act impulsively and some rely on cunning to get through their life. Alexander Pope summed it up quite succinctly in his words: *To err is human and to forgive is divine.* That is very much the spiritual way of life.

The definition of *spiritual* will be different for each person and we use the term to mean aspects of reality that are present in our inner world that can be accessed using our intuition. This inner world is unique to each of us. Many people have gut feelings about situations or people they meet. These reactions are a natural product of the intuitive aspect of the person examining the input that the conscious mind isn't necessarily aware of. We often don't know why we feel uneasy about someone we have just met or why the house we have walked into makes us shiver. The house may look perfect from the outside but the atmosphere within tells a different story. Externally everything says that we should fall in love with the place but our subconscious mind says, 'no'.

The opposite is also true. For example: why do we fall in love with somebody?

We don't fully know what attracts us to another person, but on that initial meeting it can be love at first sight. Intense passion and excitement is generated purely by being close to that person. It is our intuition that has come into play here.

Our emotional reactions to people or places are the result of millions of different stimuli swirling around our body that are processed by the subconscious mind. Our brain reacts to the many hormones and pheromones released by our endocrine system as a result. These flood the neurons in our brain which then react depending on the situation we find ourselves in.

So, our intuition or gut reaction may purely be the result of hormonal stimulation. But does it matter how we label intuition? Is it purely our physiology reacting to chemical changes in the body or does it come from a spiritual connection? If, as we assume, there is indeed a process called intuition, can we use it to help us function more effectively and live a more fulfilled daily life? And, if this is the case, can it only happen if we choose to embrace it fully?

Science has been investigating the way our conscious mind works in conjunction with our subconscious; and the findings are both stunning and significant.

It has been discovered that the subconscious mind operates and makes decisions in advance of the conscious mind. There is a gap of almost a second between the conscious mind and the subconscious mind having the same 'thought'. The conscious mind doesn't register that the decision has already been made and processed by the subconscious.

When we reach for a glass of wine, for instance, our subconscious mind had already made that decision for us and started the process of moving our hand towards the glass. It all happens so naturally that we just don't realise it.

So, what does that say about freewill? What does that say about how we live and function in life? What does that say about the world around us and the nature of reality?

That's what we hope to help you discover.

So, what is spirituality?

We feel that the true definition of being spiritual is beautifully described in the words of Mike Dooley as 'The Universe'© in a recent daily message:

'Being spiritual means a good many things and most of them are misunderstood by a good many people.

So, to clarify, here's how I see "it" and you:

Being spiritual means seeing yourself as divine, not just of the divine; a creator, not just the created. You needn't be saved, forgiven, or fixed.

You've already changed the world, added to its brilliance, and done enough. You're there because, in some long forgotten time, you already earned your wings.

Of course, there are still challenges. You wanted it this way. It is part of your nature and they'll serve to make you even greater.

In spite of these, you are still a winner, you are among the relative few who have been so bold and today is part of your victory lap.'

The Universe (©Mike Dooley @ Tut.com)

And so, if we take a deeper look at the Alexander Pope quote from earlier: *To err is human and to forgive is divine.*

How might this be applied to your life? Can you see yourself and others as divine beings? Even when they are prone to making human mistakes?

In relationships, we can often fail to love and appreciate the other person for who they really are, and instead seek to change them into who we think they should be. This happens a lot in marriages. We fall in love, get married, then spend the next few years trying to change the traits of the person we have married. We want to change the perceived faults we see in our partner, rather than see them as divine beings, perfect in their own way.

In truth, a person's foibles are what makes them special and it was probably what attracted us to them in the first place. As soon as we recognise this, and stop trying to change them, accepting them in all their perfect imperfection, our relationship has the chance to become more loving and harmonious.

We can easily forget that no two people will ever have the same interactions with the outer world. Whilst we understand that every one of the 7 billion people on this planet is unique, we forget that each of those 7 billion people will create their own powerful and unique realities. Looking through our own pair of unique eyes, using our unique brain that has gathered unique perceptions of the world whilst we grew up in unique circumstances, means that everything about us and how we interpret life is utterly individual and only ever available to *us*, never to anyone else.

This is not the place to explore the psychology of this observation, but rather to look at the philosophical implications of it, because for you, setting out on a spiritual path, the implications are immense. In effect, there are 7 billion individuals experiencing 7 billion different worlds of experience all at the same time.

Despite these different worlds, we are all living within a generalised set of 'rules'. But within these rules we react uniquely to everything around us. Our experience of life is a sequence of emotional, intellectual and physiological interactions that are all totally unique to each individual. We are creating a unique energy pattern every time our neurons and cells spark and interact with each other. We send electrical signals that travel along miles of neural pathways through transmitters and receivers within the central nervous system of our individual bodies. These electrical connections and impulses appear to leave a mark or imprint in what Einstein referred to as the 'ether'.

These days, ether, the quantum field of sub-atomic energy that pervades all things in the physical environment, has many names. Probably the most common is 'zero-point field'.

It is the subtle nuances of the atomic field, the zero-point field, that can be sensed by a person's subconscious (intuition) and sometimes seen by sensitives as an aura around the body. Clairvoyants and Seers throughout the ages have been able to interact with the sub-nuclear force in the Human Energy Field or 'Auric Field'. The aura usually appears as a shimmering fog of various colours surrounding the body and there are some photographic processes, Kirlian Photography among them, that purport to capture this amazing energy field.

Just as it is obvious that each person has unique physical features such as hair colour, structure of their face, colour of skin, fingerprints, the size of hands and feet, height, body-type, etc., so it is that they also have individual energetic features, such as colours of their auric field and the unique mental outlook of their individual subjective worlds. These internal energetic features are the unique ways in which we each respond to the external stimuli of situations as we journey through our lives.

When a person has a spiritual encounter, such as an impression of profound peace when sitting in a church, or when they undergo a more startling spiritual awakening, perhaps complete with the vision of an angelic being or bright light, then that experience is totally unique to that person. No other person will encounter or feel the same internalised experience or indeed create the same energetic imprint in the ether.

We feel it is important that we consider that we each relate to the world around us in different ways. It is so easy to ridicule others for their belief systems and religion, because they do not fit our own view of the world. We feel a little compassion would go a long way in our modern world to allow the uniqueness of human individuality to flourish.

Intuition is commonly accepted to be the main process of our inner worlds. No matter what we call our inner voice, one thing that we can be sure of is that the way our intuition works, what it tells us, and how it communicates is very different for each of us. Over the millennia, humanity has tried to enhance intuition using spiritual practices and disciplines, including meditation. Hallucinogenic substances such as peyote or magic mushrooms have also been used especially by shamans and medicine men during ceremonies.

Within our subjective inner world, we can encounter more or less anything we wish. As humans, our brains are programmed to decipher disparate, seemingly random, bits of information and to make sense of the world around us in sequences. This is called 'abstract thinking'. It is the ability of the human brain to relate seemingly unconnected things to each other very quickly and from these relationships, to draw conclusions about what action we should take, that has given us some of our evolutionary advantage.

What is intention?

Intention is simply the way we *intend* an outcome to come about.

So, sitting in meditation with the intention of learning about who you are and your internal energy patterns is one thing. Sitting in meditation with the intention of not falling asleep is something entirely different.

When working with the divine subtle realms, 'intention is everything and everything is intention'. When starting a healing meditation, your intention needs to be as pure and as focused on your healing target as you can possibly make it. Ideally, your vibration should also be as high as you can raise it.

In the past, ceremony was a major part of social practice. Priests and/ or medicine men and women were an integral part of the community. Those holy men and women would have been very careful how often they interacted with the masses.

This is because their energies could have been detrimentally affected by those of the ordinary person. Shamans, traditionally, were also very careful who they chose as friends. They were aware that those around them shared their whole energetic world, with all its positives and all its negatives. They knew that we are all linked energetically.

So, when carrying out distant healing using your intention, you must set that as high as you possibly can, in other words to affect the outcome for the greatest and highest good of your friend or client. The highest possible intention is set by connecting with the Highest of the High. In this way you will be tapping into a healing energy of the archangels and even beyond. As you do so ask (set the intention) that the healing power you are tapping into is used in the most appropriate way and for the greatest good of all things. Often in healing, the intention is to rid a space or person of detrimental energy as this then allows the body's own energy to work on self-healing without the limiting obstacles of the detrimental aspects.

What can intention achieve?

Ceremony is a structured system of movement and plays a huge part in the setting of intention. Ceremony is powerful because, according to Rupert Sheldrake, it latches onto and incorporates the morphic resonance of all the similar ceremonies that have been conducted in the past. That means that all the energies from our ancestors' rituals can enter into our present ceremonies, so long as they are carried out with the same intentions.

Sheldrake posits that this morphic or memory field may be the driver in ensuring that species adapt to environmental change. He also suggests that this morphic energy sends signals to the proteins in our bodies that then change DNA accordingly. These morphic fields are linked to Epigenetics i.e. changes in a chromosome that affect gene activity and expression. And are also linked to the way in which an environment can affect the genes within DNA. It is now well known that the DNA of genes adapts to external stimuli.

We believe meditation and intention can affect your DNA in this manner as demonstrated by research at the Max Planck Institute for Human Cognitive and Brain Sciences in Leipzig (New Scientist 14.10.17) in which mindfulness meditation was proven to promote growth of certain areas of the brain. Both meditation and intention are major tools for creating wellbeing at a cellular level. Even if you do not practice as a healer, you can draw on the power of meditation to bring positive changes into your daily life.

Our freedom of thought and freedom of choice

In order for us to see how we interact with and create the reality around us, it is helpful to become aware of the decisions that we make every day. We are making choices all the time, but we rarely notice, because most of them are habitual and have come from deep within our subconscious mind.

In order to take control of our lives and start to live them differently, we need to become more aware of 'moments of power' when they come to us. A 'moment of power' is the exact time when we can consciously make a different decision from one we have made before, to stop the pattern from repeating. When we do not recognise the moment, we are likely to make the same choice as before, in which case the same result will occur, ad infinitum.

Our subconscious makes twenty million environmental decisions every second, unlike our conscious mind, which only manages around forty per second. *The Biology of Belief,* by Bruce Lipton, is a book we would highly recommend if you wish to gain a greater understanding of this topic. But even with this one statistic, you can begin to question the whole issue of free will.

Science has tried to identify whether we do, actually have free will. Or whether everything is predestined based on our own thought processes and programming. Most notably, neuroscientist Benjamin Libet in the 1980s appeared to demonstrate that subconscious decisions for bodily movements are made before our conscious mind becomes aware of them. Research has been conducted into identifying where conscious thinking actually comes from. Some scientists argue that the self is not the initiator of the original thought because by the time we become conscious of actually thinking a particular thought it has already been created. So where, who and what created that thought?

Fortunately, it is not necessary to know the answer to this to begin our spiritual journey. But what we do need to consider, is that moment of power, in which we appear to make a decision. It is in those moments, that we can seem to exert our own free will, and actively, consciously choose our realities, rather than follow the path that has been predetermined by our past programming.

Spiritual thinkers say that 'everything happens at the right time and for the right reason'. Does this mean that things happen exactly when they are supposed to happen? Or does it just mean that on the spiritual path, we accept everything exactly as it is, because we know that everything is perfect? Why is this useful to us? Why might it be harmful?

It can be useful, in that it says, 'don't worry'. Don't worry about whether you should or should not be making this decision at this juncture in your life. It helps to take the stress out of your life when something that you want to happen, hasn't yet happened. It also proposes that, although we may appear to have free choice, it would seem that we do not. It suggests that, no matter what we do, everything will always happen the way it is 'supposed' to, as if by some pre-destined plan.

But this way of thinking could also be harmful because it stops us from identifying and making the most of those moments of power, in which we can make big shifts and changes in our lives.

We are reality generators, collectively using our thoughts and emotions to co-create, with the guidance from the subtle realms the reality that we each experience. Perhaps our main purpose as humans is to understand our part in this co-creation process? We work alongside the subtle realms and the energy of the Earth in order to create our physical reality, moment by moment. Another less formal term that we use for the subtle realms, is adopted from Tim's mentor, Hamish Miller, as he referred to all beings of the higher dimensions as 'The Management'. It's a term that we enjoy using as it also reflects the huge amount of humour present in the Universe, which when dealing with serious topics, can be forgotten.

If we want the higher realms to actively play a part in our daily lives, we need only to ask for their assistance and this is, perhaps, the point when we can access our free will, in those moments of power. As we will discuss in more detail later, angelic guidance or involvement in our lives only occurs when we ask for it.

People have been praying to a higher power for eons and this is, perhaps, a simple way of formulating your intention into a guided message and asking for help. This is not to say that angelic involvement in our lives will mean that it will be plain sailing, or that we will never face difficulties, problems or issues. Far from it.

In many cases, when we ask for assistance from the higher realms, they expect us to raise our game and they will sometimes test us to ensure we are ready, willing and able to interact with them at this higher level. It is not a matter of ego, however, as it seems important to the dynamics of our relationship, that we don't just continue blindly and stubbornly along the same path, after we have asked for their help.

Angelic assistance will always be in our best interests, but sometimes it is hard for us to see it that way. This is where faith, and trust in the divine comes in. If you trust that the higher realms can see the bigger picture, and can see what is best for you, if you have faith in their nudges, then you will find it easier to make the changes you want to make in your life.

Once you have called on the higher realms to help you, your life may go in a completely different direction than what you expected. This will undoubtedly require your trust. You will be taken out of your comfort zone and shown some unseen aspect of yourself that you will not have experienced previously.

Leaving your comfort zone and heading into the unknown is difficult. Why? Because of the ego. The ego's sole purpose is to keep you safe. To keep you away from harm. And following this new, unknown path could lead to danger, and that is a threat to the ego.

From the ego's point of view, it is better to do what you have always done and not change. And in all honesty, that may certainly be the easiest way to get through life. But perhaps not the most rewarding way. The ego sits within us, biding its time and worrying about death. When we finally do pass over, ego will vanish into the mass of multidimensional energy, perhaps to be reused in the future.

But our soul, the part of us that knows the truth, the fact there is actually something so much greater than our human experiences, will carry on. The soul knows that no harm can really come to us, and so stepping out into the unknown, is not a threat to our existence at all. When we wake from a dream we can sometimes remember the contents of that dream, but it doesn't actually matter whether we do or we don't, as we all know that we dream.

The periods of death, when we are not in the physical reality, are the times when we remember and recount our past and/or parallel lives and then learn from all our experiences. Ironically, it is during these periods when we are, perhaps, truly awake. It is then that we too, are part of the higher realms.

Belief in ourselves as spiritual beings

When on a spiritual path, we need to look at the bigger picture of our existence, which is very different to that of our normal daily life. We have to change our perspective and understand that we are not single human beings living on a planet that is simply a lump of rock hurtling through space, but rather, that everything and everyone is connected and has a purpose. The world of spirit works with a completely different set of rules to the physical world.

We will each experience the world of spirit differently as it is totally unique to each and every one of us. It is our very own inner world, the world of our soul. It is the energy or creative life-spark that sits deep within us, our personal link to the ultimate creator. This means that we are never alone and that we are never working or living in isolation. Everything that we do has a consequence and everything we do is connected in some way to everyone that we interact with.

Following a spiritual path means we need to start seeing ourselves as spiritual beings. Once we begin to look at the world from an energy point of view, we start thinking in a completely different way too. In many respects this is a shift in the philosophical standpoint from which we view our lives and what it means to be human. It demands that we look upon life as allegory, as story, and within the story can be found lessons to be learned, themes to be explored and experiences that can be regarded as symbolic of our life's challenges. Sometimes in order to identify a particular issue we may need to "heal" it is useful to look at our lives as presenting symbolic scenarios to us. What are the common themes we can see being presented to us in different ways, in different things that are happening to us? What emotion do they represent or contain? For example, do they contain anger, fear, exclusion?

To utilise this philosophical viewpoint it helps to focus upon the concept of 'the importance of everything that we react to or observe directly through our senses'. We ask ourselves what is it that we are experiencing in life and what emotion or internal struggle is being reflected to us in this experience? What does it link to elsewhere in our lives, perhaps from many years earlier?

For example, if we find ourselves involved in, say, a demonstration in which we are protesting against drilling for oil in Antarctica, then to look at it from a spiritual perspective we might use this philosophical point of view and ask ourselves what does the drilling represent, what does it symbolise? The drilling could be regarded as a symbol of selfish exploitation. So, we may then wish to examine our life to see where else these symbols of selfish exploitation exist. Perhaps they are in our personal friendships, or maybe in our relationships at work?

It's human nature to deal with external problems rather than our own internal ones as it is often easier to confront a situation like the Antarctic exploitation head on with anger and outrage than it is to sit in quiet contemplation of oneself. From a purely spiritual perspective we should be able to achieve a more effective outcome dealing with our own internal issues before marching out in protest. We are not saying don't choose to take action, we are saying, if we want to find a peace in our own individual worlds then we can use this philosophical viewpoint to analyse what it is in us as reality co-creators that resonates with the external scene and adds to its creation. If we can then "deal" with the internal representation first we will find the external scene "responds" differently.

Don't forget that everything we focus on will react to our focus. If we fight a problem with anger, hatred and other detrimental emotions we will feed that obstacle's energy and it will begin to grow. If we observe the same problem with unconditional love and compassion, staying detached from it, but still taking action there will be less detrimental energy to feed the obstacle and it should in some way start to change.

We all have the ability to see, touch and feel things that are within us. It is a matter of learning how we can relate to what we have found there and how to handle it with care, compassion and suitable intent.

How to be in the 'now'

Once, completely out of the blue, one of Tim's friends said to him 'You know that there is only NOW?' This is the only point in time and space that ever exists and it is happening right now. This issue about there only being a *now* is at the heart of the concept that reality is an illusion built upon the concept of linear time.

Linear time is a construct that enables us to flow through a series of events, which are simply trillions upon trillions of 'nows', all strung together. These nows blend together and give the illusion of time passing.

What is interesting, is that scientists have been researching how the body recognises 'now'. They have been looking at how the brain processes information from the body and starts to form an awareness of its surroundings. They have discovered that the brain accepts a certain amount of time as a 'moment' and it appears to be approximately two to three seconds in duration. New Scientist magazine wrote a feature in January 2015 reporting on the work of Marc Wittmann at the Institute for Frontier Areas of Psychology and Mental Health in Freiburg, Germany. (For the scientifically minded of you, please note, this is nothing directly to do with the scientific definition of 'moments' in connection to forces).

As far as the brain is concerned, everything that happens in that two to three second window will be processed and used to see if the events are connected and therefore of significance. Our brains are programmed to look for connections and we are designed to look for patterns.

As we become more observant and aware of our spiritual connection we will find meaning in the 'something' that has occurred within that three-minute space of *now*. The great psychiatrist and psychotherapist Carl Gustav Jung called the association of seemingly unrelated but somehow connected and significant things, synchronicity. As you work with spirit, you will find that more and more events become synchronistic and the more you meditate the more you will be able to perceive details within this 2 to 3 second time-frame.

Our physical dimension is fed information by the spiritual dimensions, by The Management, who are the main architects and builders of humanity's reality. They can manipulate our perception of our reality and aid our ability to perceive their personalities within the worlds we individually observe.

In order to learn from these spiritual signs and signals we need to be prepared and get out of our own way by at least temporarily clearing the ego. To be in the right frame of mind allows spirit to adjust our inner reality if they deem it necessary to do so.

In the 'now': what it means mentally and physically

We feel that the most effective way to be in the *now* is to meditate. Mentally, this means we must settle our minds, ground ourselves and separate ourselves, through practiced observation, from distracting thought patterns. Meditation creates a space for peace, it helps put everything into perspective. The world doesn't look so bad once you start to connect with your inner spiritual self.

We can use our breath to help us with this connection. Disciplined breathing allows the body to relax; it enables us to focus on our limbs and the various points of tension throughout our body, even down to the tension in the tongue. It is staggering how much tension can be stored in one's mouth.

The Alexander Technique, for example, teaches clients to keep the tongue down inside the mouth to relax the body. When the tongue is up against the roof of the mouth then tension sets in.

Once calm and connected to our inner Universe, we can begin to sense the *now*. The trick is to remember we are only observers, and so just allow things to be. If any thoughts come rushing in, simply acknowledge them and allow them to pass, don't fight them or hang onto them. Simply be in the *now*.

What is meditation?

It seems that as soon as we sit quietly or start to walk with the intent of meditating, our minds suddenly become inundated by daily thoughts that are sent from our conscious 'doing mind'. The 'monkey chatter' of our everyday existence (conscious mind) will always begin to focus on what we are going to be doing in the future or what we have done in the past; anything other than face up to what is actually happening right now, in the present time.

Studies of the brain have shown that the act of processing the 'here and now' is not a common default mode for the neural networks (for thought) in the physical brain of adults. However, in young children, it is a default mode, and in animals even more so.

In adult humans, it is our assessment of images and the association of the patterns in those symbolic images, fed to the brain that enables us to predict what might happen to us in the future. It is how we process the imagery and sensory inputs from our bodies and outer environment that has partly led to our evolutionary superiority. But it has also led to us to becoming more and more separated from our divine nature.

Our good friend and colleague, Paul Gerry is an Advanced Clinical Physiologist at the Royal Devon and Exeter NHS Trust. For over 45 years he has used neurophysiological equipment to measure brain wave patterns to help diagnose various neurological diseases.

Using a specialised electroencephalograph we worked with Paul to carry out a series of experiments to record brainwave patterns when dowsing and healing. In the example below, we illustrate Adrian remotely dowsing a client's house.

Paul's work is by no means unique. However, he brings to the experiment years of practical experience. His unique expert view has resulted in verification of some earlier experiments but also discounted others.

Paul's work confirms that the brain has several bandwidths of frequencies all of which come into play, but for different activities some are more dominant than others.

In simple terms, the bandwidths when in everyday activity are:

Beta: Thinking and doing i.e. the conscious mind linked with everyday activity.

Alpha: Sensory processing within the everyday mind.

Theta: Subconscious activity associated with everyday actions.

Delta: Our connection to the universal mind, the empathic mind, in other words, our psychic connection.

Whereas in meditation, the brainwave patterns change:

Beta frequencies reduce. Beta represents the thinking, conscious mind of everyday activities and thought.

Alpha is amplified, this is our data collecting mode for inputs through our senses, hence our senses are more aware of subtle stimuli.

Theta is a frequency of the subconscious (memory, creativity, insight and spiritual connection) which provides material for meditation when in the deep state as Beta is reduced.

Delta is the empathic mind and our psychic connection.

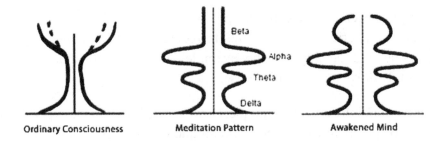

Ordinary Consciousness   Meditation Pattern   Awakened Mind

Brainwave biofeedback patterns
after C Maxwell Cade & Anna Wise
'The High Performance Mind'
1995, Jeremy P.Tarcher/Putnam,
New York, NY, USA

The image above shows representative shapes formed on the Mind Mirrror biofeedback system *(© from Vilistus http://vilistus.com)*. On the left is how the system represents a mind state of ordinary waking consciousness, in the middle is an awakened mind in a meditative state which displays a different pattern of Beta, Alpha and Theta than the representation of ordinary consciousness but retains a similar Delta frequency. The Awakened Mind state shows how the previous two states mix to create a quiet conscious awareness while awake, in sleep or when channelling.

The Awakened Mind state appears to be the first stage of connection to the subtle realms and is required for effective dowsing and all information gathering psychic or healing activity. It is primarily developed through practiced meditation or mindful activity.

Meditation allows us to access our subjective reality inside us, we often become more aware of an inner peace. We can then begin to use that feeling as part of our waking state in our day to day reality. In Chapter Four, we will discuss Meditation in more depth.

Here, Paul Gerry, describes in his own words, two occurrences where he separately connected Adrian and Tim to brainwave monitoring systems to record mind states and brainwave activity for his research.

Paul says, "The first time I recorded Adrian and Tim was using a conventional medical electroencephalograph (EEG) machine, however, although it is used to diagnose such conditions as epilepsy and coma it isn't suitable for the illustration of the subtle mind changes that occur when entering into the dowsing or healing mode.

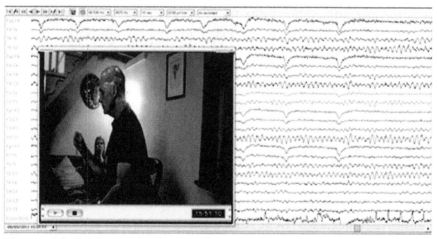

Even with the inconclusive results my interest was piqued in this first instance as brainwave signals from both participants showed a high degree of similarity to each other. This in itself is unusual and they both showed indications of a highly relaxed mind state.

The next time I had the opportunity to record their brains would be using a non-medical piece of equipment, a Mind Mirror © from Vilistus *(http://vilistus.com)*. Before I show you the results of that recording session, I need to say a few words about the system itself.

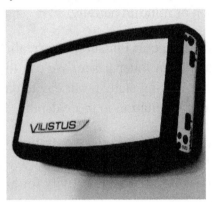

This unit connects up by Bluetooth to a laptop. The software is the latest type of Mind Mirror© which utilizes a compact recording device that can display the various brainwave frequencies in a unique way. This is based upon a system first invented by C Maxwell Cade in the 1970s. *(http://www.mindmirroreeg.com/w/MaxwellCade.htm)*

Brainwaves recorded are a mixture of frequencies mainly from 1 – 30 cycles per second and are traditionally split into five bands:

Delta 1-4 c/s – seen in adults deeply asleep
Theta 4 – 7 c/s – In drowsiness / light sleep
Alpha 8 – 13 c/s – from the visual areas (back of the head) when eyes are closed.
Beta 13 + c/s – anterior and centrally in alert states
Gamma – higher than beta activity.

The Mind Mirror EEG (electroencephalogram) measures all these brainwave frequencies (Beta, Alpha, Theta, and Delta) at the same time. At any moment of time, you have varying amounts of each frequency present.

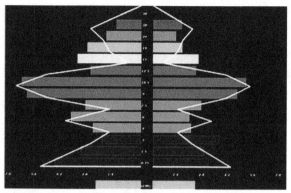

The image above shows a Mind Mirror displaying the frequencies in different coloured bands. Shown here in monochrome, but from the top down: red, orange, yellow, green, blue and purple.

This pattern shows decreased Beta (in yellow, orange, and red) which indicates decreased thinking and thus a quieter mind; increased Alpha (in green), indicating increased imagery; the correct ratio between Alpha (green) and Theta (blue) which gives one access to creativity and memory (ie, the realm of the subconscious mind) and finally at the bottom, Delta (purple) which is the realm of the unconscious mind.

Brainwaves - and what they represent

States of consciousness: a symphony of different brainwaves

The different states of consciousness can be described as combinations of beta, alpha, theta and delta brainwaves. (There is still research being done on gamma brainwaves and their significance). Most of the time we see not only one category of brainwaves but rather a combination of brainwaves interacting in concert.

The meditative descent into higher awareness

ORDINARY CONSCIOUSNESS

The beta waves of random thinking and mind chatter (top of the pattern).

No mid-range alpha or theta.

Delta's radar-like empathy or psychic awareness, present in most people (bottom of the pattern).

CATEGORY 0

Beta begins to reduce (dotted lines).

Intermittent flares of alpha bridge and deeper subconscious theta.

Delta still present.

CATEGORY 1

Reduced beta

Intermittent but stronger flares of alpha, no theta

Delta still present

CATEGORY 2

Highly reduced beta

Continuous alpha

Intermittent theta, possible flashes of imagery related to subconscious memories

CATEGORY 3

Light but relatively stable meditation
Highly reduced beta and continuous alpha
Possibly more continuous theta, with increased mental focus and concentration

CATEGORY 4

Continuing and strengthening meditation state
Highly reduced beta
Continuous alpha, Increased theta

CATEGORY 4 or 5

Meditation pattern
Deep, strong, stable alpha-theta meditation pattern
Little to no beta, with or without the presence of delta
Alpha and theta in proper ratio to each other and the rest of the pattern

CATEGORY 5

The awakened mind of creative flow and peak performance
Meditation pattern with quiet, rounded-in beta for problem-solving
Characterized by strong intuitive insights into questions, issues and
challenges

CATEGORY 6

The evolved mind of oneness, bliss and illumination
As categories unite, self-separation dissolves into universal awareness
Transcendent state of unity consciousness

CATEGORY 6 (7th State of Consciousness) **

Superconscious mind: gamma frequencies (30-64 Hz) over an awakened
mind
Compassion, spiritual ecstasy, mystical transcendence, attentional
awareness
'Aha' insights, super-lucidity, hyper-intuition, kundalini energy
Formation of new brain cells (neurogenesis); rewiring via neuro-
plasticity
Constant flow of creative energy used in compassionate service

CATEGORY 6 (8th State of Consciousness) **

Universal consciousness: gamma frequencies over an evolved mind pattern

Spiritual oneness, mystical union, gamma-induced neurogenesis and neuroplasticity

Joy and bliss in complete spiritual surrender

Let's just remind ourselves of the three fundamental patterns of an average healthy brain in relation to its awareness of self and its immediate environment. There is the Ordinary conscious state, the Meditative state and the Awakened Mind state.

Each in turn created by the following simultaneous frequencies:

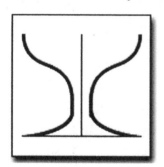

Ordinary conscious state: beta brainwaves alone or in combination with delta (hour glass pattern). Please note that the amplitude is highest at 38 Hz, the curve is open at the top. This splayed beta is another form of beta than the low frequency beta of the awakened mind.

Meditative state: alpha and theta in combination, delta may also be present. Both alpha and theta are necessary here: without alpha we would not be conscious during the meditation or remember its content, if theta is lacking we experience a lively and colourful imagination but without the depth, profundity or insight of theta.

Awakened mind: You will produce an awakened mind pattern first described by Maxwell Cade if you add low frequency beta to the meditation pattern.

You will then be able to tap into the intuition of delta, the creative inspiration, personal insight or spiritual consciousness of theta, the relaxed, detached imagery of alpha and the conscious processing of thoughts in beta, and all of this simultaneously!"

Adrian's and Tim's Mind Mirror patterns

"The following images show the Mind Mirror displays when connecting Adrian and Tim to measure their brain wave activity. We began with Adrian while he dowsed a client's house remotely and then conducted Geomancy healing on that property. The following are shown in chronological order recorded during the session:

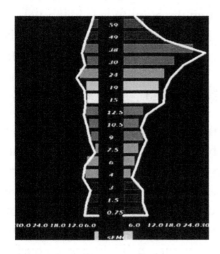

As Adrian settled to begin the remote dowsing, his brainwave pattern showed an asymmetry with the right and left hemispheres initially out of sync.

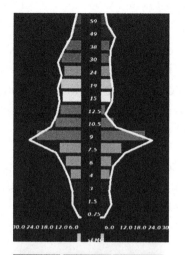

As Adrian begins to dowse and tune in to the home, he enters Category 2 and we can see an increase in alpha in a balanced brain indicating a relaxed state.

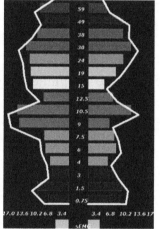

A couple of minutes later and Adrian is displaying Category 4/5 and approaching the Awakened mind state.

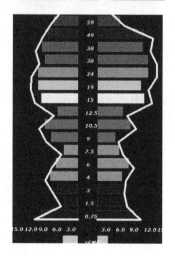

And then on to Category 5/6 as he reaches out for healing to be sent to his client's property. Here his mind shows a distinctive meditative state, which with practice it seems may be maintained for as long as required for remote contact to take effect.

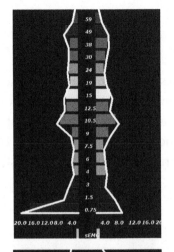

We next connected the Mind Mirror system to Tim and recorded the following images as he entered a trance state to channel his spirit guide:

The first image shows a relaxed but alert wave form with good hemispheric balance.

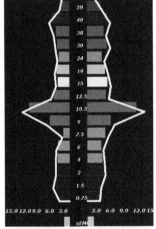

We then see a significant burst of occipital gamma ...

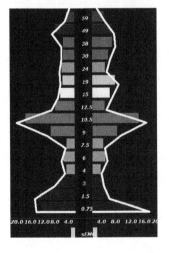

...which cascades down to form a strong dominant Alpha.

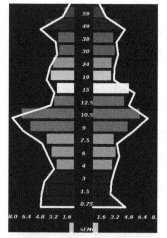

Having established the bridge between the conscious and unconscious, which we may associate with the trance state, which was missing at the start of the recording, the Theta band expands showing that Tim is moving from an outwardly focussed awareness to an internally referenced meditative mind state.

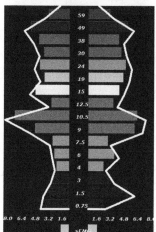

This meditative state is then matched by both a surging beta and …

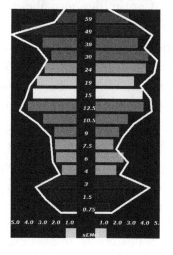

…towards the end of the recording session, a strong gamma frequency.

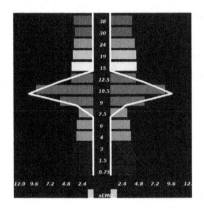

This last image shows the combined average read-out from Tim's session. Throughout the session, the Alpha continued to keep the reflective state active with major Alpha frequencies balanced with delta, theta, beta and gamma. We see little low Delta implying that, while Tim was in a meditative state, his was not falling asleep, but rather maintaining an inwardly alert focus."

Using the Mind Mirror software in the competent hands of experienced clinical neurophysiologist, Paul Gerry was an interesting experience for both Adrian and Tim. We were primarily keen to find out what could be picked up by the computer system inside the brain when people meditate, 'tune in', begin to dowse, and combine it with healing.

The key is that delta frequencies are the brainwaves chiefly associated with meditation.

We were pleased to discover that these results support much that has been said and practiced over the decades (if not millennia), about the necessary conditions of the individual to enact remote or hands-on healing and other so-called psychic phenomena. It would seem that the brain has several modes of operation resulting from a combination of different brainwave patterns, i.e. different relationships between the alpha, beta, delta and theta wavelengths. This supports what sensitives and others who have routinely experienced mystical or esoteric experiences have felt in the past – that they tune into a different state of awareness in order to access the intuitive information and power accessible to us all. The brain needs to settle into a combination of frequencies which are synonymous with a relaxed state (of mind).

Day to day stress and general activity does not create the necessary brainwave patterns to facilitate a good connection to the intuitive state of awareness. Hence the advantageous power of meditation to train the brain to gently become familiar with this state of being. It would seem that, just as many "mind over matter" disciplines have advocated over the ages, there is much power to be harnessed through consciously controlling our brainwave frequencies and hence our state of mind.

Subconscious mind versus conscious mind

The subconscious mind is what enables us to function. As mentioned earlier, it does far more work than our conscious mind. The subconscious processes around twenty million environmental stimuli per second, versus just forty environmental stimuli interpreted by the conscious mind. We are therefore only consciously aware of a very small amount of the information we are receiving.

In order for us to process the massive amount of data we are receiving, the subconscious relies upon the most energetically efficient route for survival. It relies upon on a tried and tested system so that it doesn't have to keep creating new neural networks or pathways each time it faces a similar situation to one it has experienced before.

The main problem with this is that our subconscious is largely programmed during early childhood, meaning that we are functioning on outdated programming. As adults, it's like we all need to run an anti-memory programme and then install upgrades for our subconscious.

The good news, is that we can all change our subconscious reactions to threatening situations, but we need to be aware of what our current default reactions are. Once we have that awareness, created through being mindful, we can start to change them. We have to programme new neural pathways that can overwrite the old habitual ones.

Bruce Lipton and others involved in Epigenetics say that our very DNA responds directly to the external environment that we find ourselves in. The proteins conduct these interactions at a cellular level, they change and adapt depending on the stimuli and perceived need, resulting from the external inputs.

It is a very clever system, but in order to allow the cells to function as they should, the environment for those cells needs to be balanced and harmonious.

For most of us, that is far from the environment we have created for our physical selves because we fret, worry and create stress. Stress fundamentally affects our potential to be healthy at a cellular level and the root cause of most stress is the use of outdated subconscious processes that are trying to remedy what we perceive as unpleasant situations.

Observed with a philosophical eye, stress, it seems, is primarily created by fear. It is that which separates us from the spiritual every second of the day. Our subconscious beliefs keep us tied to habitual thought patterns and tied to the same reactions to trauma, and it will continue that way until we consciously start to do something about them.

This concept of what makes us conscious beings is at the centre of current consciousness studies by scientists and philosophers. It is known as 'The Hard Problem', a term coined by David Chalmers in the United States to describe the central issue of 'what is consciousness?' By the term 'consciousness', he means the feeling of being inside your head and looking out. The conscious mind is our busy 'doing mind'. It is the mind that thrives on monkey chatter and mulls over everything and nothing. In working with the subtle realms it needs to be controlled and focused, which may take some practice, but is achievable by us all.

Chapter Two

Higher Realms

Archangels, angels & your Higher Self

What are angels and archangels? We believe that they are anthropomorphised energy. Anthropomorphism is the process of giving human characteristics to non-human things or form. It is simply a way of explaining how we may perceive them. When we say the angelic realms are anthropomorphised energy, we are not in any way denigrating their presence, far from it.

We refer to archangels and angels as being of the same broad spectrum of energy as a way of keeping things simple and distinguishing them from other subtle energy forms such as elementals or other non-human forms, therefore we often interchange the labels, archangel and angel.

Scientific exploration and research is running at such a pace that new information is being published all the time about the way humanity functions and the way reality is perceived. Relatively new fields of research such as Quantum Biology are revealing how incredibly complex we humans are as informational processors within our own environment. The beginning of the 21st century is a rapidly changing and potentially challenging era.

'Potentially challenging' because many of us are beginning to look at and question our core beliefs. Just what does it mean to be human?

To call angels anthropomorphised energy is to embark upon the thought that everything we encounter in life (and we mean EVERYTHING) is at its most basic level, simply energy and information.

We are surrounded, indeed, we are immersed in, a sea of energy from which it is our task to identify and collate all the relevant information into sensible sequences. If in one moment we become briefly open to the influence of a particularly high level of energy that manifests itself (in our vision) as a bright light accompanied by an overwhelming feeling of love, then we could well be in the presence of an angel.

Equally, we could tune in on a slightly different level of perception, in which that same energy may take the form of a human figure, not just a shining light, who would be emanating great love. This too, could be referred to as an angel, although an angelic presence is rarely experienced this way. It is far easier to experience an angel within our mind's eye, the result of an energetic shift, rather than to experience one in physical form. We often experience the presence of angels in other ways too, for they will commonly manifest physical objects for us, instead of appearing as the archetypal feather-winged vision.

How to access the higher realms

The higher realms are the dimensions in which the architects of this world live, namely the angels and all those who we refer to as spirit guides and protectors. The higher realms are accessible to everybody and their influence can impact our outer, physical world during healing or meditation.

Our Earth, the physical dimension, may have been established at the same time as the higher realms and dimensions or it may have come later. It isn't really significant *when* it was created. What is significant about the higher realms is their ability to see the 'bigger picture'.

We on Earth are very focused on the things we see as important and, even if we side-step the issue of how important *money* is, for example, we are still focused on staying alive and trying to do the best we can for ourselves and for those we love.

The higher realms, those with the bigger picture, regard time differently. They can see how events, that we perceive to be unimportant, fit into events that are yet to come or have already occurred, and how this will affect our lives. Because we perceive time as being linear, it is difficult for us to see the overall tapestry, and how each event is linked to another. It is our perception of time that limits us in this dimension.

It would seem that the angelic realm inhabits a dimension slightly 'higher' than the realm to which our souls pass when we die. Their higher vibrations can come down through many layers to our levels, just as energy travels from the crown chakra to our heart chakra, but we believe we are unable to move upwards to be fully immersed in their dimension. When we make contact with angels and archangels, we are doing so in a different dimension of reality, but not necessarily the one from which they originate. Whether we meet them exactly half-way is open to question.

All the beings from the higher realms are incredibly important and it is a privilege for anyone who connects with them to be in their presence or even just to feel their presence in their lives. One of the most difficult things for many to understand is that, although these beings are incredibly powerful, they don't have an ego. Anger, envy, jealousy and all the other emotions of a low vibration are part of being human. The angels do not have these emotions, and when we are stuck in these emotional states, they stop us connecting to the higher realms. These emotions keep us in the lower human vibration.

We all have the potential to connect to these higher realms in sacredness, joy, love and compassion. To do so, we have to still our human emotions and alter our mindset or attitude to enable this connection to happen repeatedly using mindfulness and meditation. The angels themselves understand our plight as humans and they accept us, with all our faults, without judgement. They endeavour to help us to reach them and make conscious contact. This is what many people's journeys of self-discovery are about.

Often, Tim sees very sensitive people amongst his clients who refuse to believe they can connect to these higher realms, because they feel they are not worthy. But these feelings are misplaced. It is never a question of worthiness, as the angels see all human beings as worthy and deserving, and will strive to help us to connect with them. So, if we, as humans, put in a bit of extra hard work and effort to clear our minds and raise our vibrations as much as possible then we would *all* have angelic guidance and influence in our daily lives.

The angelic realms

Many people who may not have yet considered the spiritual side of the world in which we live, are beginning to wake up and look at the spiritual aspects of their existence. They have probably spent the first few decades of their lives busily earning a living in a world that was built upon corporate capitalism. There is nothing wrong with that, and can often be an important step in personal evolution, indeed Tim and Adrian have both run successful businesses in the past, before being approached by spirit and encouraged to change their lives.

Encountering the different and influencing energies that can suddenly appear and begin to encroach upon our realities, can be an unsettling and confusing experience. As you should now be aware, the influx of these new energy patterns demands that we examine our belief systems and look closely at our prejudices.

Angels are one aspect of a changing reality that we may need to accommodate at some point on our path. Both Tim and Adrian have encountered angels in their lives and in quite different ways and both had spent many years in total denial of their existence.

Here is Tim's story:

"I spent many years ignoring angels as I couldn't equate the images of angelic beings, encountered during my Church of England upbringing, with the experiences I was now having with the other aspects of spiritual activity. Those golden beings with halos around their heads just simply didn't seem to fit.

"Gradually I was assisted to see that these angelic intelligent beings were, in fact, an aspect of the intelligent ether, the quantum field of existence that permeates everything in this and other dimensions.

"I went through a period accepting that calling upon angelic forces was purely an interaction with a form of energy that we don't yet fully understand. Eventually, though, I was forced to accept that the most logical explanation for the effects and feeling of the interactions was to consider them as discreet personalities."

As we have mentioned earlier in the book, there comes a time when you learn to accept that the world is not what it seems and understand that what we have been taught as we grow up about reality actually takes us further from what we are here to achieve. The power and effects of this realisation magnifies the effectiveness of us as spiritual beings and the healing results increase exponentially.

How can we work with the angels?

In the early days of your spiritual awakening, one of the first experiences you may have with angels is with the 'parking angel'. For those of you who aren't yet aware of the parking angel, it is a great phase of your development and wonderful to experiment with. It is an active and instant way of you manifesting an outcome. With so many cars on the road, it can be very difficult to find suitable parking spaces, especially the free ones. This is how it works:

Ideally, you will have a parking space in mind and you picture yourself parking the car there. You really do need to concentrate on that space. Think of the person who has parked there getting into the car as you drive towards that space and moving away just as you get there. Ask the angels to assist. The more you concentrate, the better you become at it and you will be amazed by the results. Don't forget to thank the angels, (even before the space is yours).

Admittedly, attributing parking spaces to an angel is a little trite but they don't mind. It serves as a way for humans to begin to interact with this new found energy of creation. As you progress along your spiritual pathway, you will come to acknowledge what is commonly known as your guardian angel, a specific personality helping with your spiritual growth. They are there to guide and protect you as you develop.

On a global scale, we feel we may now be on the verge of seeing the three worlds of humanity, elementals and angels converging into one as we continue to evolve.

Different vibrational energies

When learning to interact with spirit, some of us will need extensive training, slowly developing the belief and awareness of how to make successful, safe and rewarding contact. This can be done through training courses, self-development classes, or mentoring as well as reading books.

When working with the subtle influences of the angels, archangels and higher realms, it is helpful, and also important, to *feel* the changes as they happen.

When Tim was learning from his spiritual teachers, they all emphasised how important it was to actually *feel* the presence of spirit as well as see and/or hear them. When using the term *spirit* we are including all beings in the subtle realms: angels, archangels, elementals, and all other non-physical souls.

When Tim works with his spirit guide, Myrddin, he feels his presence strongly at the right-hand side of his body. It is very much an earthly connection and a feeling that Tim has finally got used to after several years of working closely with Myrddin. However, after training with Adrian for an intensive period, learning more about house-healing, and the role of archangels in that process, Tim decided that it would be really helpful if he had a better connection with the archangels rather than "just" spirit guides. As far as he was concerned, it was the archangels that were responsible for clearing and the re-balancing work being done as part of the spiritual house-clearing. Which is why Tim thought it would be a good idea to get to know the archangels better.

"I believed, at the time, that one had to be at an advanced stage in one's spiritual development before one could connect or work with these, higher beings," explains Tim. However, the archangels, angels and all in spirit are always willing to connect with us so long as we are genuine. The effectiveness of the connection is not about how advanced we are, or how spiritually aware we have become, it is mainly down to our own individual willingness to connect and to perceive their contact.

In other words, if we don't feel we are worthy of that angelic contact, we won't feel their presence, even though they are still around us. Tim sums it up like this, "The effectiveness of the angelic connection is really down to our own self-image, our own awareness and opinion of self, and I guess that reflects our own self-development and healing."

In order to connect with these wonderful beings, Tim decided that meditation was the answer. After several intensive sessions in which nothing happened, one day, he suddenly felt a temperature change above his head. Usually, if this was on the right-hand side of his body it would indicate Myrddin's presence, but this was different. This new connection came from straight above and into his crown chakra. It was a completely new, wondrous feeling which felt very different from earlier experiences with other guides.

"The energy went straight down through my central core," Tim says. "It was a warm feeling like a glowing golden bliss! It was complete acceptance, but this connection didn't come as a character or personality, in the same way as my connection to Myrddin had always been right from the start."

It seems the angels and archangels have a very different energy signature from an earthly spirit guide such as Myrddin. They will always connect with us if we ask them to, but it is up to us to recognise their presence. When first making contact with the angelic realms, the feelings can be very intense and over time the intensity may change. Don't expect the intensity of your first experience to necessarily continue, as in all cases, it is very much down to each individual how they experience each connection.

Before this connection happened, Tim was not prepared to accept the idea of angels and archangels existing as distinct personalities. He felt that they were just a different form of universal energy, that it wasn't necessary to separate them into personalities that represented their individual characteristics. He has since rescinded this view as it seems that they do, indeed, have very distinct characters and personalities, aligned to their chosen ways of helping humanity. But these individual traits can take a little time for a person to assimilate and distinguish.

These angelic energies are always present and, over the ages, not only have their individual personalities been recognised but they also have their own names as you will see when we explore them more later.

We live in times of great transformation and in terms of humanity's relationship with the Earth, we are in total turmoil and a global crisis is upon us. As a species we are in a time of great need and require help. So it makes sense that all the archangels, angels and elementals are part of the rescue plan for humanity. Humanity appears to be disconnected and has lost its relationship with these important aspects of harmonious reality. Regaining and maintaining that connection is what is likely to save us, and that will be done through individual actions. It is our individual ability to connect with these other realms, and to enlist their help which will enable the necessary shift in global perception to take place. Perhaps this sounds a little grand, but we believe that is what needs to happen and it needs to happen on a personal and individual level to start with. It will then begin to spread; as more and more spiritual teachers appear, many of whom are considered old souls, here to bring lessons and new energies to our planet.

Time and time again we have been told by spirit and those in the subtle realms that 'everything will work out well in the end.' We are told not to fear death and to consider it to be a natural part of life. If we can achieve this, there is no fear. If we are not afraid of death what else is there to be afraid of? And once there is no fear what is there in life? Just things to be observed, in which we can find joy, and for which we can express gratitude.

Perhaps humanity's role, during life on Earth, is to observe and to work with the elementals and angels to enable the global energetic shift in experience to occur.

To help the concept of unity between these aspects of reality, let's look at how we can integrate the angelic realms of those of the elementals into our human experience of reality. To start with, let us consider the following statement, that 'angels are to humans, as elementals are to the Earth.'

It is known that at least two archangels, Metatron and Sandalphon, have lived here on Earth and reincarnated several times. This has given them first-hand experience of what it's like to be human, having learned about our frailties, the ups and downs of life on this planet: the enjoyment and the heartaches. Because of this knowledge they are two fantastic archangels to work with and have on your side.

Perhaps, like therapists, the most helpful angels seem to be those that have been through the mill and have seen physical life in all its glory. They are there to help us, but the angels won't interfere with us unless we ask them to. Be careful what you wish for, as you will often get what you want, but not quite in the way that you expect.

The table below shows how archangels are linked with both humans and Elementals:

Archangel	Human Chakra	Elemental Aspect
Feriel	Base	Earth
Sammuel	Sacral	Water
Uriel	Solar Plexus	Fire
Raphael	Heart	Air
Michael	Throat	Air
Gabriel	Third Eye (Brow)	Ether
Zakiel	Crown	Ether
Metatron	Above the Crown	Ether

We feel that even from ancient times and the early stages of mankind's development chakras were a part of the subtle makeup of the physical realm. As humanity evolved, the higher chakras have activated while at the same time, archangels and elementals have also evolved as part of the overall development surrounding Mother Earth. It seems that we are guided and protected both as human beings and as a planet by the angelic realms.

Humanity and the Earth, seem so important to the Universe as a whole that we are administered, nurtured and cared for, although it may not seem like it as the higher realms guide us, but also allow us to make some mistakes. All of which is part of our learning process as a species.

In regards specifically to geomancy healing, "I used to sit and wonder why, if the Management were so big and clever, did they need us to tell them if something was wrong and needed healing down here on Earth," recounts Tim.

Perhaps the answer is in the way the different realms are connected and the way we conduct ourselves here on Earth. When Tim asked the Management about the above situation with specific reference to earth energy lines, the answer was that the healing wasn't so much about the Management not being aware but about the act of asking for attention to be focused on the issue that required healing. It wasn't so much that the Management needed to know about it in order to make the changes required for wellness, but the act of asking and the energy exchange in asking, the desire and willingness to ask for action and change was the important part. The interconnectedness of all things being so significant that anything we do is never an action in isolation.

But there are of course different levels of awareness for different circumstances just like there are in all *human* relationships. A mother is always aware of what her toddler is up to, and sometimes she will allow that toddler to make mistakes in order that it learns. Other times she will step in to protect her child from danger. We believe that the angels, in particular, seem to react to our circumstance when we ask them directly for their help, even if this request had been made many years beforehand when a person initially asked for guidance. Asking for that help created a connection to the angelic realm and made them on hand for further assistance. Also, there are times when the angelic realms will step in and their help appear to come from nowhere. But just like that mother watching her toddler there was an awareness of what could be about to happen.

When conducting geomancy healing which is primarily based upon working with different levels of intention, the issue is not about the Management being unaware, it is about the human beings involved focussing their intent on the need for change and asking for the appropriate assistance to enable that change to occur. The Management has always been aware of the circumstances throughout but wants us to be the conduit for change.

When asking for help with specific situations we suggest that you ask out loud three times to ensure that the angelic realms fully understand that your request isn't just a passing thought.

The angelic realms are aware of us as a species because we are a part of them in some way. Another way to look at it is that it is rather like our awareness of our kidneys, liver and lungs. We don't need to do anything with them until they start calling for help and when they do it is usually because they are damaged in some way and need our assistance, to get relief from the pain. It is possible that our emotions work this way too.

Perhaps the angelic realms maintain us, as the elementals do for Mother Nature, often interacting when we dream and meditate. Not only that, but when we pass over at the end of our lives, there is still a lot of angelic maintenance carried out for us too. When we pass over, the angels seem to assist us to make decisions for our soul's advancement before we return to a new life on Earth, (if that is our choice).

The elementals and angels are always there and we can call upon them whenever we need their help. Even if you request help from one specific angel, you may be surprised by who actually turns up to assist in your plight. Even those you haven't directly requested may come to your aid.

On one occasion, when Tim was calling in his usual angelic healing team of Raphael, Gabriel, Michael and Uriel, to assist him with a client, he was amazed that a new presence made itself known to him, in the form of a powerful symbol. It was Archangel Metatron, who appeared in Tim's awareness as an amazing geometric cube, a complex spinning 3D structure, helping to bring healing. 'I hadn't called on Metatron, but it is wonderful to know these beings are there to help us whenever we need them'.

Interaction with angels

Having worked and connected with the angels for several years, we can say with confidence that they are here for us all, not just the chosen people or believers, but everyone.

As you begin to walk your spiritual pathway, you will become more aware of their angelic presence. During a healing, for instance, evoke the help of one or more archangels (as appropriate) to help guide and assist you. The result can be very interesting.

With their help, it can enable you to focus very deeply and achieve a greater understanding of what you are doing. This can lead you to having greater insights into the spiritual and healing world.

Angels are everywhere. We just don't always notice them. Always ask for signs that you will recognise when connecting with the angelic realms. They may respond with a white feather suddenly appearing from nowhere, even when indoors, or perhaps unusual shaped clouds in the sky. It could be anything, but you will know when you see it that it is meant for you.

It's suggested that during meditation, if you want an archangel to be with you, simply try blinking with your eyelids closed, you may see a defined colour appear and this can tell you which of the archangels is present. For instance, Archangel Michael is often associated with blue and Archangel Gabriel, green. You can either research it on line, look through a book or dowse to see which archangel is working with you.

It is so easy to dismiss these amazing beings, but please put disbelief to one side for the moment and sit quietly, use the exercise at the end of this chapter and then see who or what comes through. Notice if there is a change of energies around you: do you feel warmer? Calmer? Cosseted? Loved? The list is endless. But never be afraid to ask for help, in any circumstances. The help might not arrive in the manner you expect but it will happen in some way.

How to be more aware of angels around us

The more sensitive you are, the more you will feel the connection with the angelic realm. Sensitivity is your openness, awareness and willingness to accept there is a power greater than yourself in the Universe. Once this is accepted, you may begin to open up and to channel many of the energy patterns that are around you; commonly referred to as spirit. Often this awareness comes during or after a spiritual healing session, during the search for a cure to an illness via complementary medicine, yoga, meditation or even sometimes through psychological trauma.

There are many spiritual courses and/or workshops that you can attend, such as those held by the authors and by doing so can lead you to a greater understanding of the subtle energies around us and as this awareness grows, so will your ability to tune in.

Many, if not all of us, carry stress patterns, trauma, and unhappy memories around with us and these can manifest themselves in our subconscious. Unless we can shift these emotional blockages or deal with these life issues, we can remain trapped by this deep emotional conditioning and the habitual practices that they produce within us. We won't necessarily know what is holding us back, but it is usually an old belief or behaviour pattern learned from parents.

For example, there was a lady, a sensitive, who believed that she should not use the Tarot to give readings to people. When she was pressed to do so, as she was talented, she always ended up, shortly afterwards, having some form of disaster in her life. She linked the two together and attributed it to spirit who, she thought, was punishing her for using the cards.

A more likely cause was that she was self-sabotaging her work through her deep-seated belief system. We do not believe that spirit would ever allow a disaster to be linked to her work, assuming that it was being carried out in the other person's best interest or higher good. No angelic being would operate from that judgemental level. It is therefore likely that, during her work, she had picked up a mischievous entity or attachment and it was that which was manipulating her emotions, or she may not have felt worthy of the gifts that she had been given.

This had a knock-on effect with her daughter who also became fearful about what might happen if she used the Tarot. Like her mother, she is a very sensitive and tuned in woman, but unfortunately her belief system stopped her from accessing and developing her talent.

Our belief systems can sometimes hinder our development, but with awareness, we can change that.

Why would the higher realms work with us?

All the dimensions are interlinked, so whatever happens in one dimension will affect all the others. Reality is multi-dimensional, and every action has a consequence in our multiverse. Hamish Miller, a well-known dowser and author, always felt that humanity's role in the grand scheme, or plan, must be very important, as we seem to be the lynchpin that connects the higher and lower realms.

Picture a tree, for example, with its roots buried deep in the ground and its branches reaching into the air. We are just like that, able to communicate with elemental beings and those that vibrate at a much higher level, such as the angelic realms. The communication between realms can be verbal but is not usually, it's often based more on emotion and feelings.

We are emotional processors and there is no greater or more powerful emotion than love. The higher realms are built on love and, it seems, very little else. The authors' experience says that once we journey beyond the astral plane, we soon move into the higher dimensions where love is all-pervading. The higher we go, the deeper and more all-absorbing that love is likely to be. Down on the earthly plane, however, it is not like that. We *aspire* to love unconditionally and we *aspire* to be compassionate, but although it sounds cynical, more often than not, what is usually exhibited is every other emotion but love that is unconditional.

Here on Earth, we rate being of service and the emotional 'vibration' of that act as being one of the highest possible we can achieve - unconditional love. People like Mother Teresa, The Dalai Lama and, perhaps, Gandhi come to mind as role-models for their service to humanity. But there are many other amazing human beings that selflessly also exhibit the same behaviour in their daily lives. It is just that we rarely hear of them.

The angelic realms and psychic protection

Archangels are, in the simplest of terms, more commanding versions of angels. Heaven, like planet Earth, has a structure and a hierarchy in place; we consider archangels to be superior to other angels, because of their knowledge and experience.

It is through working with archangels, and assisting others in this world, that everyone can become more familiar with the inter-dimensionality of creation. Humanity has an important part to play in that overall creation and structure just as the angelic realms do.

There are a great many significant beings in other dimensions, some of whom impinge on our reality more than others. Elementals for example, are probably closer to the "density" of our dimension.

In our view, archangels are amazing beings to work with, and they will do what they can to protect you. However, they do appreciate it when people help themselves. Psychic protection is an example of this. Psychic protection is required whether you are a dowser, a healer or just leading a normal life. For general day-to-day dowsing we would say that protection is not always necessary, as the hobby dowser probably won't be going into places where detrimental energies are concentrated.

As professional dowsers, both Tim and Adrian will psychically protect themselves before any healing or dowsing sessions. In a similar way the Shaman would use it during their trance journeying between worlds. There are many different types of psychic protection, but the one that we recommend, is a chakra-based protection visualisation given to us by Adrian's early mentor and well-known healer based in Surrey, Andy Roberts.

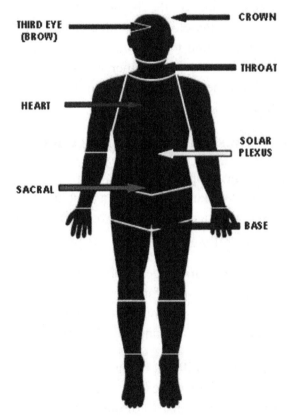

Psychic Protection Visualisation

Sit quietly and take a few deep breaths to calm yourself and focus on the task.

Breathe in red light through your base chakra. Imagine it filling up your body. At the top of your breath exhale, cleansing your body of all detrimental energy patterns. This will form a 2" layer of red around your physical body. You might like to say the words, 'cleanse' as the coloured light enters the body and 'protect' as it wraps around the outside of your body.

Next breathe in orange through your sacral chakra, filling up your body. Then exhale, cleansing the body of all detrimental energy patterns and forming a second layer around you, outside the red.

Breathe in yellow through your solar plexus chakra to fill your body. Then breathe out, cleansing the body of all detrimental energy patterns and forming a third layer around you, outside of the orange.

Through your heart chakra, breathe in green and breathe out, cleansing the body of all detrimental energy patterns. It forms a fourth layer around you.

Breathe in light blue through your throat chakra, cleansing the body of all detrimental energy patterns on the out breath. This forms a fifth layer.

Through your third eye or brow chakra breathe in dark blue and then exhale, cleansing the body of all detrimental energy patterns, to form a sixth layer.

Through your crown chakra, breathe in purple and then out, cleansing the body of all detrimental energy patterns, to form a seventh layer around you.

Staying with your crown chakra, breathe in a silver light. Visualise it filling your body. Then breathe out, cleansing the body of all detrimental energy patterns, to form an eighth layer.

Then breathe in gold through your crown chakra and out, cleansing the body of all detrimental energy patterns, to form a ninth and final layer.

Finally breathe in divine white light filling up your body from the tips of your toes to the top of your head.

Ask that any detrimental energy that has been dislodged be taken to the light.

You are now fully protected

It is easy and very straightforward to use and we both use it on a daily basis. In addition to this, we call upon a number of angels, archangels, protectors and guides to help us while we are working, whether dowsing or healing. The most obvious archangel we call upon is the great Archangel Michael with his sword of Truth. Archangel Michael is the great protector. He oversees the human race and our planet, along with other heavenly beings. As one of the warrior archangels, his protection is consummate. It is literally the power of love. Archangel Michael is always there to respond to your call for help. He transcends all religion, as his love is all enveloping and he is an all-powerful protector against the detrimental energies on this planet.

People have created many different types of 'boxes' in which to place spirituality, called religions. These different boxes very often form the basis of conflict between countries, certainly this is the picture if we look at how the media presents the current situations. However, it has been our personal experience that virtually every spiritual believer, no matter what their faith, understands that love is at the heart of all religions. Unfortunately, most inter-faith conflicts come about by those in power (governments etc) diverting people away from the original foundations of their religion.

The energy that forms Archangel Michael could well be the same energy that is used by other faiths to create beings of similar magnitude and compassion. It is simply the label that differentiates the being, but this does not dilute his power for good. Calling on Archangel Michael for help and protection, if nothing else, will ensure that you have put some of the basic foundations of protection in place.

Connecting with your Higher Self

Do we all have a Higher Self? The Higher Self is often thought of as the essence of you: the sum total of all your lives and experiences. Some liken it to the Akashic Records, but we consider it to be much more personal to each individual. The most simplistic way of looking at the Higher Self would be to liken it to a heavenly mainframe computer; it holds all that you have been, all that you are today and all that you will be in the future.

It is thought that we come to Earth to learn lessons, which can be anything from responsibility to freedom, from trust to poverty and so much more in between. These lessons, learned over many lifetimes, are supposed to bring us to a final stage of enlightenment. In Buddhism, it is called Bodhisattva, where one makes a vow or promise to work for the complete enlightenment of all sentient beings. We believe that our Higher Self contains the sum of our knowledge built up over millennia, throughout all of these lifetimes.

So, our Higher Self is the aspect of us that contains all the information about our past lives and it knows far more about the 'bigger picture' than we do once we have reincarnated back on Earth, because we are given a clean slate, in which to create a new reality for ourselves in each new lifetime. We often refer to all our other lives as being in the past, however, it is possible as far as the other dimensions are concerned, that we are living all of our lives at the same time, in parallel universes.

Hamish Miller was certainly under this impression during and after his Near-Death Experience (NDE). During his 'clinically dead period' in hospital, he met the angelic beings that he then referred to as the Management. They showed him evidence and gave him information from all his 'parallel lives'. From this, he could decide whether to return to the Earth plane and continue his current life or stay there. Luckily for us, he decided to return for a short spell.

When we are born, we retain an energetic connection to the 'hereafter'. Perhaps those who have had a Near Death Experience are more aware of this connection than those who have not. After his NDE, Hamish said that he felt very close to The Management, almost as though he had left a piece of himself behind when he returned to this dimension. Between our incarnations on Earth, it seems that we are given the opportunity to evaluate the life we have just lived. But we are not judged by some deity, the only judgement that might occur is when we judge ourselves for things we did, or didn't do, thought, or said. We are not judged by anybody except ourselves.

We believe we are meant to live many lives and we will evaluate each one as we pass over. If we have fulfilled our plans in them, we may choose other plans for other lives, and this will bring further enlightenment to us. If not, we may have to come back and live the same plan all over again, but we always have a choice.

Just as with the angels, our Higher Self can give us guidance and help - but only if we ask for it. We have some free will here on Earth, and aside from gentle nudges and signs, our Higher Self and angels cannot step in to help without permission. It is a good idea to say your request out loud and even to repeat it three times.

If you want confirmation that your request has been heard, and action will be taken, ask for a sign. But do remember to ask for one that you will recognise and please don't forget they also have a sense of humour, so expect the unexpected. We can connect with our Higher Self at any time, anywhere, but meditation is considered the best way to do so. It stills the mind and allows two-way communication to more easily occur. Don't expect a complete message the first time you try, though it is possible, meditation, like everything, takes practice and patience.

Connecting to our Higher Self on a regular basis can bring greater clarity into our life and can help to answer our questions and remedy some of the self-doubts that we all have. It can also help us to see that the lessons we learn are important, particularly the hard ones. The more you connect, the more help you can expect: typically, that inner voice we call intuition will get louder and you may begin to look at life and the people you meet in different ways. You may also feel more protected and loved. Your Higher Self is your connection to the divine, don't be afraid to utilise it.

What can we learn from our Higher Self?

Patience, respect for one's mortal self, enlightenment, love, wisdom... there is no end to the knowledge that our Higher Self can impart to us. But though we can learn much from connecting with the higher realms and to our Higher Self, it is worth remembering that much of our learning is often achieved through interaction with others, whether they are family, friends, work colleagues or just people we casually meet.

Self-awareness is critical here, because without becoming self-aware, how can we be aware of our Higher Self? To not value yourself and the unique part that you play in life on Earth is rather like watching a film only to find the scenes involving the leading man or woman have all been deleted; it would make the whole thing pointless and nonsensical. You need to be aware of how you fit into life on Earth, including how you have influenced others, perhaps changed their lives in some way and how you have loved and been loved by parents, siblings and friends. By embracing self-awareness, you will begin to feel your connection to the divine and the connection to your Higher Self becoming stronger.

Accepting that you have a Higher Self that you can access at any time, should mean you never again feel alone. The Higher Self is what is referred to as your 'other half', your spiritual twin if you like, the one that knows you better than you know yourself and who loves you unconditionally. Which means that, you love yourself unconditionally. But often, many souls do not put this into practice, with loving words and intentions toward themselves. These actions of self-love are a huge part of your spiritual growth.

Our Higher Self knows what is good for us and what we should avoid during our time here on Earth. As humans, we more often than not, tend to ignore these inner feelings (our gut reaction or intuition) and stumble blindly onwards, determined to choose our own path, ignoring all the signs telling us to stop. Our Higher Self is screaming 'No, no, no', but our conscious mind totally ignores it, adamant that everything will, hopefully, be okay.

It is therefore imperative to become more aware of this inner knowing or intuition, doing so can help keep you on the right path, steering you around the rapids. Now, we are not saying that your life won't have its challenges or difficulties but once you have become familiar with, and actually listen to, your Higher Self, you can start to take control of the situation before it becomes untenable. For instance, if you find yourself in an awkward position or begin to feel uneasy about a particular person the inner alarm bells will begin to ring, and you can react before anything bad happens.

This is not your ego (or self) talking to you this is the Universe. For example, how many times have you known something bad (or good) was about to happen? Whether you stopped the car just as another driver came around a blind bend on your side of the road or decided to take a different way home only to find that an accident had occurred on the normal route. In extreme cases listening to this inner knowing can save your life, but in most cases it can help steer you through the day to day problems that affect many people.

Remember, you are receiving messages from your Higher Self and these potentially important lessons should not be ignored. If you are unsure whether a message you are receiving is from your Higher Self or not, ask yourself – is this message coming from love or fear? Your Higher Self and the angelic realms always come from love.

If it's suggesting you do something you are not comfortable with, always feel free to question it. Don't be afraid of stepping out of your comfort zone but they will never suggest anything too dangerous to begin with or something that could cause harm to others. That is not to say that the dangers could be there in the future as you live and learn, moving truly out of your comfort zone.

Is a spirit guide the same as our Higher Self?

A spirit guide is the energy of someone that you have chosen to work with or who has volunteered to be your guide during your time here on Earth. They have elected to stay in the higher realms to assist and protect you. They will know you firstly as a spiritual being but also in your mortal guise. It appears that, before we reincarnate, much goes on between us and those who will end up being our spirit guides.

We all have a spirit guide or guides. Some will be with you from birth and stay with you through your incarnation on Earth. Other guides will come in at different points during your life, but there will always be a special one who will be with you for the duration. Some people consider this their guardian angel.

Myrddin, Tim's main spirit guide, has told him on many occasions that a long time ago they both agreed to have a partnership in this lifetime. He has also said that he is as much a part of Tim as any spirit is. He is also very careful to point out that as human beings we don't have the language or the concepts to understand the way the interconnected nature of reality works. Myrddin expressed surprise at Tim's reluctance to accept him when they first started working together.

You will often find that youngsters are more aware of spirit guides than adults and can not only see them, but also talk with them. In many cases, they are referred to as the child's 'imaginary friend'.

Adrian had one that he called Bangkinks. Luckily, his parents went along with what they felt was a child's fantasy. Bangkinks went everywhere with Adrian, a space was always left for him in the car, he sat at the dining table, went upstairs to bed at the same time and even to school. Sadly, Adrian grew out of seeing his 'friend' and this interaction was lost during the educational years of his life. However, he re-established contact in his late 30s when a spirit medium told him that this 'imaginary friend' was in fact his spiritual brother and that they'd had many lives together. This time, the medium continued, Bangkinks had chosen to remain in the higher realms to help Adrian develop his healing techniques and strengthen his connection to the divine.

We need to accept that during the early years of a child's life they can experience a world which is very different from ours. They might see spirits and talk to them, as they haven't yet been told that ghosts don't exist. Children's minds are uncluttered, they have yet to undergo the indoctrination that we call schooling, and science has not yet clouded their open mindedness. Scepticism is not a word in their vocabulary.

We can only wonder at the damage caused when a parent tells the child that their friend does not actually exist. Imagine the confusion as the child can see their friend standing beside them. As Adrian says, Bangkinks was real; he was dark skinned, spoke with a very soft voice, unless he was being ignored, and their conversations were very real. For

Adrian to find out much later in life who he was, was a very humbling experience.

So, if your child has an imaginary friend, we suggest you choose to go with the flow. Ask the child questions about who it is, what they look like and why they are here. A word of caution though, please be aware there are false guides as well as mischievous spirits out there. If your child does things that are unexpected, out of character, gets upset with their 'friend' or they blame them for making them do something they shouldn't then please contact either Tim or Adrian for advice.

What is a spirit guide and where do they come from?

As we have said, spirit guides are usually a friend or loved one that you have incarnated with in the past. You will have spent several or many lifetimes together forming a special bond of love, trust and friendship. For this life, they may have decided upon a very selfless, loving act and vowed to remain in Heaven whilst you come down to Earth for your next life-lesson. If you don't encounter your guide as a child, then it is possible that later in life they may appear in your dreams or whilst meditating. You might hear their voice or receive a message sent to you via a sign.

They will always be with you, sometimes despairing of your behaviour and, perhaps, sometimes cheering and 'shouting' encouragement, just like a human parent.

It can be said that all spirit guides are a part of us, in the same way that everything in the universe is a part of us. Spirit guides assist and can give information to us through dowsing, meditation or during a healing session. However, if you are to work with them regularly, you will need to set your intention accordingly and practice tuning in to their energy often.

It seems that we can each have several or many guides with us at the same time. Though we may not be aware of them all. Usually one is more dominant and this is especially true in the early stages of your development. As you become more proficient at tuning in, they will start to appear as individuals. You can also call others in to help with specific tasks, like writing a book for instance.

Buddhist monks consider it rude to ask a spirit guide their name; you are supposed to simply acknowledge their existence and work with them. We suspect this is in recognition of the Oneness and interconnectedness of all. Perhaps unsurprisingly, many people have past historical spiritual leaders as their guides. Statistically, science says that we could all have a few atoms of famous leaders from the past in our physical make-up, such as Napoleon or Julius Caesar. So, it is likely that others such as Gandhi, Jesus or the Buddha may also be present inside us.

If we apply the mind-set of the energy principles of homeopathy to the above, then we can see that it is entirely possible that each of us could be influenced by all of humanity that has existed in the past.

Homeopathy suggests that the tiniest amounts of energy transference can affect an individual. Some homeopathic remedies are made with a dilution of less than an atom's worth of energy contained in them. This is partly why the scientific community won't accept Homeopathy as being of any practical use, despite so many of us having had experience of it working.

In addition to our spirit guides, we will also have deceased members of our family visiting us to see how we are getting on. Specific ancestors, like a grandparent for instance, can be with us much of the time. It is unusual not to have at least one ancestor looking out for current members of their family. These ancestors are not normally referred to as spirit guides.

We will be looking at how powerful our ancestors can be when called in for ceremonial purposes and how they are all still very close to us even when they have passed away a little later in the book.

How many spirit guides do we have?

It seems that usually we can have up to three main spirit guides, although other specialist guides will be on hand to help during healing etc. As we have seen, one guide will normally stay with us for the duration of our life on Earth. Your guides may change as you change. For instance, as you begin to move away from the materialistic or commercial way of life, start walking a more spiritual path or begin healing people or places, different guides will come in to assist you on your new pathway.

At these times, you may find protective guides coming in to help you on your journey, to protect you during the transformation you are gently, or not so gently, experiencing. Spirit guides can move on; most of them are not here for any set period of time.

It is up to you how fast you wish to progress. If you prefer to move ahead slowly then you will probably have the same guide for a longer period. However, if you want to 'fast-track' then a succession of guides will come and go. You, to a certain extent, have your feet on the spiritual accelerator and brake.

In the first stages of transformation, when you are waking up to the fact that there is more to life than you have so far encountered, you can be vulnerable. Your light is beginning to shine brighter and, if you haven't learned about psychic protection, you will need someone in the spirit world to watch your back and keep you safe.

Should you begin to work in the complementary therapy or holistic field, then you will find a wise spirit guide coming in to help you; it will be they who gently (or sometimes not so gently) steer you in the right direction. They may appear to you in the form of a Shaman, an Indian medicine man/woman or Druid priest. However, they don't necessarily have to have come from this background. It is perhaps our perception of what a spirit guide should look like that will influence how they reveal themselves to us. Keep an open mind and allow them to appear as they are, not how you imagine them to be.

How can you become more aware of them?

First of all, you need to acknowledge their existence. Once you truly believe they are with you, you can start to communicate with them to build up your relationship and develop trust with each other.

Meditation is the best way to begin, to still the mind and then tune in to your spirit guide. Don't be surprised if you hear a sigh of relief when you do so as they have probably been waiting years for this connection, or re-connection, to happen.

Doubt is the biggest obstacle to adults seeing or feeling their guides. We need to try to rid ourselves of that doubt using whatever means possible. Often the spirit world (The Divine) will help with this, giving us hints and perhaps a glimpse at what lies beyond the veil to pique our curiosity, without scaring us away.

As adults, we are taught to question everything and this complicates our lives because we rarely accept anything at face value. If you do suddenly get a vision of your spirit guide, your automatic response probably will be to question what you saw, maybe think about it for a few minutes and then dismiss it.

Please don't stop questioning, but do so in a constructive, open-minded way. Spirit guides are so willing to connect with us but we, as adults, put up the barriers, mostly as a result of scepticism, suspicion and closed-mindedness. Take off the blinkers, leave the logical thinking behind for a few minutes (or hours) and be in the now. Clear the mind of as many unwanted and unnecessary thoughts as possible, close your eyes, concentrate on your breath and then start to listen.

Tim's main spirit guide is Myrddin, but Tim has also worked with his late grandfather. They had never met as he passed away a long time before Tim was born. Tim's late father is often with him too, for protection.

Whilst Tim was learning to work with and trust Myrddin, his father became a safety line and knowing that he was there, helped Tim to feel safe and protected. His paternal grandfather had elected himself as gate keeper during Tim's developing trance mediumship work. This, therefore, is an instance in which an ancestor has, in fact, taken the role of spirit guide.

Myrddin is the guide that Tim now regularly interacts with and is the most likely energy to come through when Tim is sitting in trance. During his geomancy work and remote healing, there is also a Chinese Guide, called Chiện, who is there to help Tim with that aspect of his work.

For those of you who would like to connect with your spirit guide or strengthen your link, this next practical lesson will help. In time, you will be able to communicate with them, but be patient.

Who is my spirit guide?

Spirit guides are there for everybody as they are a part of the human experience on Earth. Not all of us connect to spirit in the same way. Some will do so clairvoyantly, some clairaudiently, some clairsentiently. Not all connections to spirit are received in a flamboyant or dazzling way. Most experiences tend to be subtle and fleeting, especially when one is learning to develop their own connection. Nobody should dismiss their own abilities or experiences, based upon what they think *should* happen in comparison to somebody else's experience.

Through our working with individuals on tutoring courses and in workshops, we have found that people are very often in contact with their spirit guide already but they simply haven't recognised the fact. They have often set the bar so high and built up their expectations of what a spiritual encounter might be like, that they couldn't see what was around them already.

How to connect with your spirit guide using meditation

When following this meditation, it is good to have a pen and paper ready to make notes afterwards.

Before starting, please make sure you have followed the coloured chakra protection exercise. Then sit with both feet flat on the floor, get comfortable, switch off your mobile phone and make sure that you won't be disturbed.

Begin to quieten the mind and body, take a few deep breaths, start to relax and feel the breath within your body. Continue counting your breaths for as long as you need in order to quieten your mind. Gradually you will feel the calmness within. As you do so, picture yourself walking along a pathway, it doesn't matter what type of pathway, make it one of your choice.

Feel the air around you, become aware of the sounds around you, perhaps the birds are singing, bees buzzing or there is a gentle murmur of faraway traffic. Feel the ground underneath your feet. How does it feel? Rough or smooth? Is it a pavement or an unmade pathway? Just concentrate on walking along it. Feel the sunshine on your back and the natural warmth of the day.

A short way off you see a woodland and the path you are on takes you into it. As you walk amongst the trees, the leaves cast dappled shadows on the ground. These shadows become more pronounced the deeper into the woodland you go, until there is nothing but darkness. Do not worry as you are fully protected.

In the distance, you see a tiny pinprick of light. You walk towards it, gradually becoming aware that the sun is once again shining through the leaves and then suddenly you walk out of the woodland into a lush green meadow.

You stop and take your shoes and socks off. Instantly you feel the connection to Mother Earth. You feel grounded. You become aware of the healing energy moving up your legs, passing through your base and sacral chakras and into your solar plexus chakra where it is held as a glowing ball of light.

Then become aware of a magnificent light shining from above, entering your crown chakra, passing through your third eye (brow) chakra, throat and heart entering your solar plexus where it mixes with the healing light from Mother Earth.

The Sun's energy then enters from the front and back of your solar plexus chakra meeting and mixing with the other healing energies stored there. Finally, the Moon sends down her heavenly light which envelopes your whole body and then condenses into the solar plexus where all the energies merge together.

The glowing ball of light starts to expand, through your cells, bloodstream, major organs, skin, chakras and so on until it has completely cleared your body of all detrimental energies. It continues to move through your aura until it has reached its extremity.

Once it is there, ask that all the detrimental energies that have been dislodged be taken into the light and disposed of in the most appropriate way.

Now that you are clear of all unwanted and unneeded energies you are ready to meet your spirit guide.

Look around you.

There, a few steps away, you see a wooden bench with two cushions placed on it. Walk towards it and sit. Once seated, slowly become aware of how peaceful you feel, how much a part of the whole you have become.

You then become conscious of an energetic presence somewhere in front of you. As you focus your attention in that direction you see your spirit guide beginning to grow from the ground upwards and in a few moments take solid form.

You are now in the presence of an amazing being. You might recognise them from childhood. They sit beside you and take hold of your hand. Feel the connection and allow it to move through your body. As you do so you may hear a voice. They may also give you a gift to bring back.

Stay for as long as you wish, the energies here will be very beneficial to you.

Once you decide to leave your spirit guide and return to the room in which you are meditating, put your hands together as if in prayer, bow and thank them for being with you today and thank them for the help they have given you over the years.

Walk back along the meadow, stopping to put your socks and shoes back on, before you enter the woodland once again. At the edge of the meadow and just before the woodland, on your right hand side, you see a 'spiritual wheelie bin'. Open it and dump any old thoughts, worries, and stresses into it. Leave behind in that wheelie bin anything you don't want to bring back home with you.

Re-enter the woodland, noticing once again the dappled shadows on the pathway. Keep walking as it gets darker and darker until you reach almost pitch black. Then, again in the distance, you see a pinprick of light and you walk towards it. Your surroundings become lighter and lighter until you find yourself back in the sunshine and on your original pathway. Follow this until you are back in your room.

Take some time to 'come to', then when you are ready, open your eyes.

In this first meeting with your spirit guide you might not see, hear or feel anything at all but don't give up. Repeat this process as soon as you can and as often as you can. The more you do it, the easier it will become for you both to make meaningful contact.

Write down your experience, remembering any little thing that you can about your travels and the visit to see your spirit guide. Make a note of their appearance, what they might have said and what gift they may have given you.

Add to this each time you meditate. By doing so you will be able to see how your connection is changing and improving each time you meet up.

Chapter Three

Chakras

Our chakras and our earthly connection

Our ancestors were very much of the Earth. In the very early days of mankind's development they had no need for a higher understanding, as their lower chakras were linked to their welfare on the planet, providing such aspects as safety, reproduction, power and strength. As they evolved, they had a total understanding of the flora and fauna around them and knew the seasons intimately. As they became more aware (conscious) of themselves and the world they lived in, their higher chakras began to develop. They began to look upwards, towards the heavens, and see patterns of animals in the stars; The Great Bear (Ursa Major), Taurus the Bull, Alpha Draconis (The head of the snake) and so on. Many of the paintings found in caves at Lascaux in France and Altamira in Spain are now thought to be star maps stylised as animals.

Early Homo Sapiens had the same size brain cavity as Neanderthals but what seems to have been different was the way the brain had evolved to develop a greater capacity for higher social thinking and less focus on daily physiological survival skills. It's almost as though as Homo Sapiens became more and more aware of the 'bigger picture'; their minds and brains literally began to expand. We believe their consciousness moved or shifted upwards into their heart, throat, third eye and crown chakras.

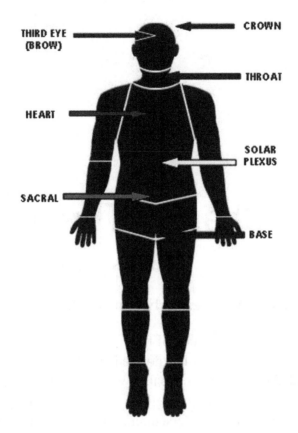

THIRD EYE (BROW)

CROWN

THROAT

HEART

SOLAR PLEXUS

SACRAL

BASE

Crown: Heaven connection

The crown chakra is associated with spirituality, it is our link to the heavens or the Creator. It is our spiritual communication chakra, and through it we connect with spirit, channel information and/or receive messages from above.

The crown chakra is opened during meditation and helps to clear muddled and confusing daily thoughts before connecting us with the heavenly realms. It is therefore imperative that we practice psychic protection in order to keep those messages free from external interference.

Connecting through the crown is a way of being able to experience unconditional love from the Universe. It is about connecting to and trusting the Divine, a surrender or letting go of the dense material world, allowing your spiritual self to breathe and expand its knowledge.

A purple (or violet) shaft of light is often seen above people's heads. Purple is supposedly the highest of the chakra colours and used in many religions, in Christianity, for instance, with priests wearing purple robes and hats.

Other chakras positioned outside our body, found above the crown, have been written about by mediums and psychics in recent years and there may be further chakras formed as we all become more spiritually aware.

Third Eye: Heaven connection

This chakra is often called the brow chakra and is the all-seeing eye/ third eye. It is through this energy centre that we receive visions of the divine or see the future. This is the external link to our pineal gland which produces melatonin (connected to sleep and meditation), perhaps allowing us to see beyond space and time. Meditating helps us to 'open' this chakra, to become more psychically developed, and to develop a deeper intuition leading to spiritual enlightenment. It is usually associated with indigo.

Throat: Heaven and Earth connection

Perhaps the first of our chakras that starts to touch upon more 'Earthly' issues, the crown and third eye being linked to spirituality and the heavens. The power of speech or communication with those around us, this chakra allows us to connect with people across the world.

Early man probably communicated with sign language or perhaps, in certain cases, psychically, as is known to be the case with the Australian Aborigines and other indigenous people living on and with the land. Speech can be very helpful, but also a hindrance to our spiritual development. Being quiet and still is so important when tuning in to spirit or meditating. However, many people find silence difficult to achieve as they are unable to still their chattering minds. This chakra is often out of alignment or blocked in those who find it difficult to speak their truth.

Asking questions (the right questions) leads to a greater understanding of the world and people around us. It is a necessary part of our life here on Earth, to gain knowledge both spiritually and mentally, linking our hearts to our heads. This chakra is usually considered to be blue.

Heart: human connection

'Are you ruled by your head or your heart?' It's a question heard many times over the years, but what does it mean? The head (mind), signifies logic, rationality, reason and thinking, perhaps all pointing to a certain amount of coldness and lack of feeling. The heart, on the other hand, indicates softness, love, intuition, psychic sensitivity, affection, friendliness and openness.

Adrian would say that in his early days his head ruled, but as he got older and wiser his heart began to take over. He feels that perhaps being a parent helped him to see life differently.

A closed heart can lead to severe problems in many aspects of life, but opening your heart too far too soon can also leave you in a vulnerable state. We would suggest that a certain amount of self-development, including nurturing self-belief, has to be carried out before it is safe to open yourself fully. You will need to be very certain of your friendship base too.

As the power of the heart chakra became more prevalent through natural development, attitudes started to change. Perhaps the psychically-sensitive are showing the others the way forward, opening the heart chakra when you are ready will help you to connect with the Universe. The heart chakra is usually considered to be green.

Solar plexus: Earth and human connection

The solar plexus chakra is the central point of the body, it links us to the Earth as well as spirit. It can be viewed as the power house of the body. It can utilise the sun's energy to boost our body and energise the mind and spirit.

This is where much of our healing power can be channelled through. This chakra enables us to connect the Earth with the Sun, Moon and universe, giving the person inner strength and potential. It can be used to increase the healing power of intent and, like a muscle, the more you use it the stronger it gets. The solar plexus chakra is usually shown as being yellow.

Sacral: Earth connection

In Sufi writings, the sacral chakra is said to incorporate all the elements of man's 'lower self', the sexual drive and physical strength needed to survive in a hostile world. It is usually illustrated as being fiery orange.

It is about living an Earthly existence, not necessarily a spiritual one although its connection to sexuality can also be used in a sacred way. It does, however, show Mankind becoming aware of its own existence, developing from being centred on the self to a more community orientated focus.

Base: Earth connection

The first of our chakras, this is the one that keeps us grounded and joined to Mother Earth and governs anything related to basic survival. It also gives us a connection to the elementals or nature spirits.

This strong connection to Mother Earth gives humanity foundations to survive and grow. Attributes of basic life survival such as securing sustenance from food and competing for heat from fires are required less in the modern world than in the past. Today's struggles are less basic and more about adapting to our current social structures and associated mindsets. So although this predominantly red lower chakra is still present it exists almost as a legacy, especially in some people who have practiced deep spirituality.

Chapter Four

Meditation

Meditation - how long for and when?

We have mentioned meditation a few times already, but in this chapter, we will give you more tips and ideas on how to bring it into your daily routine, if it is not already a part of it. If you are used to meditating, then around twenty or thirty minutes a day is a reasonable length of time to sit. It is long enough for you to go deeper within yourself, to contact your subconscious and to get some benefit from the session.

If you are not familiar with meditating, then it is useful to start with just a few minutes each day, to practice focusing your mind and concentrating on clearing it of the 'monkey chatter'. This practice is also something that will help your dowsing. The more you can focus, the better your dowsing accuracy will be.

Also, as you clear your head of daily noise and start to bring quiet into your mind, you may find you develop an improved ability to focus on just one thing, as the depth of your concentration improves. As this occurs, so too might you notice that your perception of everything around you becomes enhanced at all times, not just in meditation. Quite possibly, you will start to see colours with greater depth, hear things with a detail that you had not previously noticed and see and feel everything in nature with a sort of clarity that you hadn't been aware of before.

In their explorations of energy channels in New Zealand, and the relationship that the ancient Waitaha people had with the Earth, Hamish Miller and Barry Brailsford used to cite the meditative practice of the spiritual elders who had, from an early age, been selected as medicine men or women.

The Waitaha shamans were mostly women, and they practiced intense meditation to fine tune their powers of concentration and connection. It is said they could pick out, and feel in harmony with, a single shell amongst the millions on the sea-shore whilst sitting high up on a cliff overlooking the beach. They had the ability to focus so precisely on this one, minute speck amongst so many, this individual shell, they could tune in to it and "feel" it as part of themselves and so be in perfect harmony with it.

When meditating, we are adjusting our brainwave patterns and that, of course, will change our experience of our own reality as described above. It gives us greater clarity, greater focus of concentration and improved empathy, so we can feel more aligned and in tune with all in the natural world, the flows and rhythms of nature and its plants and creatures become more accessible. As this change is a physical process, the neural networks and pathways will take time to develop. When we first start to meditate, it can feel like a frustrating exercise; a seemingly slow and tedious one. But if you are patient and persist with daily practice, meditation can reap a great many rewards both in terms of exploring the world within us for peace balance and harmony as well as the outer world as our senses seem to develop more sensitivity.

For many, the best time to meditate is first thing in the morning. The longer you leave it, the more your day begins to fill with other mundane matters; you feel guilty about taking 'me time', you start to procrastinate and then you find that your day has completely disappeared. Days quickly roll into weeks and there comes a point where you realise your good intentions have faded. So, begin either first thing or just before you start your working day. However, this does depend on how slow you are to wake up and 'come to' in the mornings.

It is good to get into the habit of meditating in the same place each day, as the energy of that location will begin to change over time. It is also good to dowse for the best location in your home to sit and meditate, as you may find a special place or 'hot spot' where several energy lines cross in a very beneficial way. As you meditate, you will encourage a feeling of peace in this place. You could further enhance this 'sacred space' by using crystals and other meaningful objects that you have a connection with, placed in various positions that your intuition suggests as appropriate.

Some people are tempted to meditate in bed before they get up in the mornings, and that is fine if it suits you, however it's worth being aware that different practices will suit different people and you may just find if you try this that you will be too tired and not able to concentrate or clear your mind. Try different techniques and times of day and see what best suits you.

Meditation underlies development of the self, both internally and externally and it is really helpful if you can take the daily practice seriously. Making a connection to the divine and your subconscious *will* take time, effort and practice but the rewards are infinite and although it's helpful to be serious about your determined efforts, try not to be too serious in the endeavour. There is always fun to be found, even in the most sacred of acts.

How to meditate

There are many ways to meditate. The important thing is to find the right way for you. One way is to sit quietly with your eyes open and stare at an object in front of you. Really scrutinise and analyse it, imagine yourself as that object, immerse your whole self within it.

Another way is an outdoor or walking meditation. In this practice you simply switch off but remain very aware of all that you are. The idea being that you merge with your surroundings as in 'the forest is aware of me, I am aware of the forest and I am part of the forest'.

Then there is meditation in which one sits quietly in contemplation, waiting for inspiration or the answer to arrive to a particular problem that you are wanting to solve. The most popular and commonly held view of meditation is connected to mindfulness. In this, one would sit comfortably, as described, in quiet observation and allow the stresses, strains and general chit-chat of daily life to dissipate, letting your whole self relax.

Meditation and mindfulness give you the opportunity to step away from the frantic chaos of everyday life in the 21st century. They enable you to find peace and contentment in solitude, which ironically should not be called solitude at all, as it is the connection to your Higher Self and the heavenly realms.

Meditation is the tool that will help you to become the best version of yourself, but you will need constant practice to master it. Eventually this will involve the ability to slip quickly into your quiet space at any time, allowing the day to day stress and worries to dissipate, instead of allowing them to pervade and interrupt your thoughts.

Gentle observation will then allow your brain to move easily to the next frequency level. As you become more aware internally, you should begin to observe the chaos in your mind in a more detached way. By remaining detached, you should be able to feel when the turmoil quietens and settles inside you. You will find the peace within your being.

From this position of self-control, you will start to see everything around you differently, including how you live your daily life when you are not in a meditative state. For those who suffer with low self-esteem or are inclined to be hard on themselves, daily meditation is perfect. The more you meditate, the greater the awareness of self becomes.

You will soon become aware when you are beginning to slip back into those old, unwanted habits and you can, by stilling the mind, stop yourself going there. You are in control and can start to make changes, choose a different path and alter your reaction to old stressful trigger points as they occur.

Therefore meditation, particularly mindful meditation, is a great way to help ease stress, anxiety and self-doubt. It gives you the strength and inner resolve to step in and take charge before those old unwanted habitual responses kick in.

Mindful meditations can be practiced when pursuing creative activities such as writing or drawing too, so for those of you who feel unable to commit to what may initially seem intense traditional meditations, mindful pursuits that encourage the seed of an inner connection to the subtle realms are also valuable.

How to clear your mind of superfluous clutter

Those of you who practice yoga will appreciate how the breath holds the key to accessing much of your inner universe. Combining a focused awareness of the breath with a visual inner awareness is probably the easiest way to get into a meditative state.

Try this exercise: while sitting comfortably, close your eyes and take a few deep breaths, inhale through the nose and exhale through the mouth, then use the chakra protection exercise from chapter two, going through each chakra, with its designated colour, cleansing your physical body and aura.

As you work through the chakras, from the base up to the crown, you may feel a slight sensation where the chakra emanates from the body. Don't forget that many of these points are also situated at the back of your body, so do spend a moment or two focussing your awareness searching for those subtle feelings of connection at the back of the spine as well as the front. This is not to say that everybody will definitely feel the connection, you might or you might not, it doesn't matter, you will find the way it works for you. It's worth spending a little time trying to feel the connection so that you become familiar with the way your body and energy system works. Once you are more familiar with that then you will be more confident in detecting the very subtle energies around you in daily life when you want to.

The physical sensation of feeling your chakra connection (if you can) may also help you to see, through your mind's eye, the energy system of your body as you work through the exercise. As you get to the higher chakras, you may find that you pick up stronger physical sensations and the closer you get to the brow or crown chakra, you might feel more tingling in your body. This can be evidence that a connection to spirit (the subtle realm) is taking place.

Make sure you have a strong, grounded connection to Mother Earth before you use this exercise to explore the subtle realms further. You may choose to do this at the beginning of the exercise when you are working with the base chakra. Become aware of it, as described above, then send the energy from your base chakra down into the centre of the Earth. Visualise the energy flowing down to the centre of the Earth where you can wrap it tightly around a massive crystal like a root of a tree. This anchor point will keep your energy firmly connected to the Earth so that if your awareness starts to wander it will always be able to get back into your body when you want it to. Bear in mind, that this is not what is referred to as astral travelling or remote viewing, you are not trying to go exploring with your awareness away from your body, but rather you are being aware of changes within your energy field through which you may connect to aspects of the subtle realms.

Once you have completed the whole chakra protection exercise and filled your physical body with white light, focus your attention on your crown chakra, using that as the direct link to the higher realms.

You may feel you are travelling away from the Earth plane or perhaps into a whiteness, if so then this is when the grounding practice may help you feel more confident about allowing these changes to occur. Usually it is sufficient to just allow images and possibly your feelings to start to change and if you are looking to connect to an angelic guide or seeking information from a spirit guide, then this is when it may happen. This could be a conversation or purely an exchange of images, feelings or thoughts. If you suddenly find the monkey chatter returning, as your conscious mind tries to take control again, go back to your breath and inhale and exhale carefully and mindfully.

Become aware of the air moving in through your nose, down into your torso, passing through the heart chakra, solar plexus and sacral chakras to your base chakra. Then, as you breathe out, notice the energy of that same breath moving up your spine, through the back of your chakras and then out through your mouth or nose as you exhale.

Allow some of this breath to remain in your body for the next circulation. Carry out the same exercise with a new intake of breath until peace returns.

You may find it helpful to visualise the monkey chatter. How would you characterise it if you were to picture it in your mind's eye? Perhaps it is like an ocean: the waves appear choppier one day than the next. Or perhaps it is like a cloudy sky, as you clear your mind the sun begins to shine. As you become aware of specific thoughts, such as anger or frustration, simply acknowledge them, identify what they are and say to yourself 'Hello anger, here you are again today' and simply watch as your focused attention allows that energy to dissipate. Try not to get attached to the thought, but rather observe the fact you are having a thought. With practice you will find the difference between these two states of mind and be able to use it successfully.

Imagination

The dictionary definition of Imagination is - *the faculty or action of forming new ideas, images or concepts of external objects not present to the senses.*

When working on their self-development, we have assisted many clients who fear they are 'making it all up' and that the responses they receive (in meditation or dowsing, for example) are purely in their imagination.

With practice, and by ignoring the judgement of others (and your own sceptical conscious mind), you will achieve a genuine interaction with all the different aspects of reality. Every time you question or query what you have seen or felt during a meditation or healing session, your logical brain is likely to step in and dismiss the vision or feeling as being purely down to your imagination.

The more you do this and the more you listen to your logical, sensible self, the further away a genuine connection to the subtle realms will be. Meditating and imagination go hand in hand and are by far the most sensible and effective way of starting to develop a connection with, for example, elementals, who are often one of the first aspects of personality within the subtle realms to make an approach to humans.

Just observe and get to know what your imagination actually feels like. It is a conduit through which you create (imagine) responses and reactions from the unseen realms. Gradually over time, with practice, you will realise that you are *receiving* snippets of information rather than *creating* them. Having realised what using your imagination to create feels like, you will begin to feel the difference as you start to receive the information instead.

Receiving information in this manner uses the same physiological process that is used in the creation process: it is the same conduit. However, when you receive information, the traffic is going in the opposite direction to when you are creating it.

An example meditation

Find a comfortable position and relax your arms and legs and shoulders.

Be aware of your body, make sure you are as relaxed as possible, don't forget to relax the muscles around your head, neck and face including your tongue, if it is pressed up against the roof of the mouth it will indicate stress.

Close your eyes and take several deep breaths: in through your nose and out through your mouth.

Keeping your eyes closed start to find that quiet space within you. A sequence of three or so deep breaths will start to separate you from the chatter inside your head.

Sit and breathe, nice and deep, slow and rhythmically, a natural relaxed state. In through your nose and out through your mouth.

You may feel your heart beating or become more aware of your body: allow these feeling to disappear as you relax back into the rhythm of your breathing.

Don't dismiss any aches and pains in your body, just accept them for what they are.

As you continue breathing you may become aware of tension in your limbs or around the face, head and shoulders. Focus on those areas to see if you can release the pressure.

Come back to the breath again, feel it, for it is your life force.

Feel the weight of your legs, continue down to your feet and focus on them. Notice how they feel on the floor or in the slippers or shoes that you might be wearing.

Then on to the soles of your feet, they may feel warm or cold but that doesn't matter. Just sit and focus on how important your feet are, they not only carry the full weight of your body but connect you to Mother Earth, to Gaia, an amazing being that we are all a part of.

Your feet are the human connection to the nurturing Earth, a solid mass of rock beneath your feet, your connection to nature and all its wonders.

Become aware of your connection to Mother Earth and send your loving feeling down through the Earth beneath your feet, push, and push and push, sending your love deep into the planet.

Don't fight the feeling and don't allow negative thoughts to come in.

Simply feel your feet and the awareness of the Earth beneath your feet.

The floor is the Earth, the floor beneath your feet.

Now take your mind down, down past your feet, down into Mother Earth.

Send your love down into the Earth, it doesn't matter what you perceive as you do so, just keep pushing.

Concentrate on the Earth's centre many miles beneath your feet and feel its density, the density that is the Earth mother, the heart at the Earth's centre: always there for you.

Connect to it in whatever way you wish, to that centre of the Earth.

Feel your feet on the Earth, move that awareness to your legs, then to your hips, spine and upper body.

Listen to the beat of your heart.

Move your awareness up to your shoulders and arms, feel the weight of your head.

Sit for as long as you wish. Experience this new connectedness to Mother Earth, be aware of any new feelings or thoughts that may come in as they are important for your onward journey.

Now turn your attention back to your breath as it flows, in through your nose and out through your mouth, stay that way for a few minutes and then when you are ready open your eyes and gently come back into the room.

A meditation to make contact with your spirit guide can be found here on Tim's YouTube channel: *https://youtu.be/9nClFlLUTCA*

Walking meditation

It feels like it's very difficult here in the West to find spare time; time that we can use just for ourselves. This is, perhaps, why people go on pilgrimages, treks, short walks or retreats; to be by themselves, away from their family, work and the daily pressures of life. We all need thinking time, to look inward at who we are, who we have become; to have genuine 'me time'.

This 'me time' is so important to our development as humans and spiritual beings. It is only by being introspective and experiencing an inner learning journey, that we will eventually be led to look *outward*, to connect with the Universe. We know that meditation is the key to a better connection with the spiritual realms. We also know that it is very difficult to clear our minds of unwanted clutter. There will always be something, to occupy our thoughts if we let it. So why not try meditating whilst out walking? This answers all the above problems in one go. You can do this when walking to work, for instance. That way you don't have to find any spare time, and it can easily become part of your daily routine. Ideally, when deciding to do this, switch off your mobile phone as you won't benefit from the distraction of it. Try it, but you may find it harder than you think to sever the need to be socially available at all times.

In your walking meditation you may follow a well-known path, pre-plan a route or just see where your journey takes you. Getting lost can be a good thing. It means that you have freed yourself from the shackles and the need to be in control at all times. As you walk, become aware of the rhythms of movement within your body: the air moving in and out of your lungs, your arms moving at your sides, the weight of your legs and the way they swing forward supporting your whole body above them while allowing you to constantly move forwards. Feel the way your feet hit the ground within your footwear and how they react to different surfaces. Be mindful of everything around you using all your senses. For example, listen to the different sounds that you make and those from the surroundings as you walk. Maybe it's your own footsteps or the surface on which you tread, or your clothes rustling, maybe the occasional bird overhead. Whatever it is, be observant, but don't let each observation take your mind away from where you are now. Don't get caught on a train of thought that takes you back in time to a memory or forward to something you might want to do later. Allow yourself to stay present, in the here and now.

Ideally, this form of walking meditation should take place in the countryside. If walking in woodland, once you've got accustomed to the mindfulness exercise above, try adding in this affirmation as part of your meditation: "I am aware of the trees… and the trees are aware of me… I am a part of the trees… the trees are a part of me." See how you feel after a while of repeating this affirmation over and over gently in your head and paying attention to *how* you are seeing the trees. Is your vision changing at all, do the trees change the way they look to you? Do your feelings about them or your awareness of them shift at all?

Walking is good for you, physically, mentally and spiritually. It exercises the body and meditating while walking helps to clear the mind of daily stress, worry and anxiety. It allows us to connect with the whole, the Universal energy that is so important to us and our spiritual journey as human beings.

Walking can be relaxing; it allows the spirit to feel alive as well as providing a connection to nature.

Grounding and the 'Now'

Grounding is sometimes called 'earthing'. When our lives become too centred on our thoughts, rather than producing actions in the external or physical world, we simply live our lives vicariously in our heads. Living for prolonged periods in one's head and not being grounded can be detrimental. It can, as Tim knows from experience, in some circumstances, lead to anxiety attacks, which are usually associated with hyperventilation (not breathing properly), a feeling of isolation and some forms of depression.

There are several simple ways to ground yourself the first is simply to stand on your tip-toes and gently stretch or bounce up and down. It will feel strange to begin with, but it will get you back in touch with your physicality quickly.

The other way is one favoured by Hamish Miller who would simply say 'Go and dig your garden!' This form of physical exercise allows you to get in touch with your muscles and also the Earth. But this only works if you have a garden! Otherwise, take off your shoes and socks and stand on the bare earth or grass for five to ten minutes and allow yourself some perspective on life.

One from the heart

In modern societies we step into adulthood so quickly and, as we do, we leave so much behind us. Including wonderment, the ability to daydream, fantasy, imaginary friends, contemplation and FUN. If you ask people why they leave such things behind, their first response is probably, *'I haven't got time for them anymore'*.

We need to start looking at our lives very closely and decide what is truly important to us. Is it really money, work, new clothes, a new car, a bigger house and so on? Do these things truly make us happy?

It would serve us well to find the time to appreciate the things in life that are free: a beautiful view, a river, trees, birds, rainbows, the company of people, and so on. Become aware of the rustling of leaves as you walk past a tree, the noise from a waterfall, and the crackling of a fire. We just need to open our eyes, ears, hearts and minds to see and feel the wonders that are truly all around us. These gifts from nature are far more rewarding in the long term than anything money can buy, like cars and shiny trinkets.

We are not naïve. Money is important. But, really, how much do we actually need to live in abundance and be happy? Be open to the unknown and never before experienced. Rejoice in what is around you, the seen and unseen. By being restful in yourself, you will attract likeminded souls to you and that may include inquisitive nature spirits too.

Operating from the heart and not the head is the beginning of your spiritual journey. It means giving rather than just receiving, being kind to others and being considerate enough to yourself to take time to listen.

The creation of reality

Now, a quick word on quantum science and meditation. This entire book is about how we interact with the world around us and these days that really has to include some of the basic bones of quantum science. This science is the study of the very, very, small and how it interacts with the macro-scale world of 'ordinary' physics that we are used to.

Theories of quantum physics don't make much sense in traditional Newtonian scientific terms, but there are recognised attributes of actions at the quantum, (subatomic), scale of existence which affect our experience of reality.

The Creation of Reality occurs in every moment, so says one of the many aspects of quantum physics. Reality demands an observer to materialise the *possible* into the *probable* then into *actuality*. It's a process that scientists refer to as the collapse of the quantum wave function. It's one of the foundation propositions of quantum physics and describes how packets of energy at the very smallest level of existence (quanta) display properties of waves (like light) and particles (like electrons) but they can never do so at the same time. They only behave as particles once they have been *observed*. There are various theories as to whether it takes *human* observation to collapse the wave form into particle existence or not.

Scientists realised some decades ago, that the *experimenter affects the outcome of the experiment.* It has led to many a conundrum in science, but the role of quantum processes in our natural world is now accepted.

Quantum biology is now a recognised area of learning, whereas previously anything to do with the quantum was the sole preserve of physics.

We now know from quantum biologists that many animals use quantum processes to achieve some amazing feats that we have hitherto found inexplicable. For example, the European Robin, has now been found to have a quantum compass in their eye that is sensitive to the Earth's magnetic field and therefore helps them to navigate (*Biophysical Journal, DOI: 10.1016/j.bpj.2008.11.072*). Quantum biology has also discovered quantum processes within plants involved in photosynthesis (*Gregory Scholes, the University of Toronto, Nature DOI: 10.1038/nature08811*).

The likelihood is therefore that humans will also have quantum processes within their physiology. Often the sorts of things these quantum processes might be involved in are in the realms of pseudo-science. Until very recently, 'real' scientists could not get the necessary funding to evaluate possibilities. Those that research areas such as telepathy and, dare we say it, dowsing, are still only considered to be at the very fringes of acceptable scientific study by their peers. But times are slowly changing.

When doing remote healing on houses or people, we believe humans use as yet unidentified quantum processes. Those of us who are in these fields are at a disadvantage when it comes to being perceived as sane, worthy folk by much of the scientific community at large, however, both authors have enough experience to testify that many things that come under the 'spiritual' heading occur with regular frequency when working for clients, despite being seen as impossible by science. Not the least of which is being able to identify specific information about objects in a person's house on the other side of the world.

We think it is only a matter of time before science starts to believe too. There are already signs of acceptance, with informative articles on quantum processes and research into the nature of consciousness in journals like *The New Scientist.*

Consciousness and earth energy lines

Tim's introduction to the subtle realms was through buying a house that had two earth energy lines crossing within it, which had formed a special sacred place in the back section of the property. He and his family were then approached by the guardian energy of that space, who they came to know as simply 'Jane', who informed them that she wanted to be considered 'part of the family'.

Tim lived in the house for fifteen years, and during that time he had plenty of opportunity to talk with Jane about the crossing earth energy lines, the nature of life after death and so on. He also began to ask questions of the guardians and spirits he encountered when visiting sacred sites.

Here, Tim relays some of what he learned during this time. These conversations affected his view of earth energies and their role in the creation of our reality.

"When I first started out, I had not heard of *The Law of Attraction* or *The Secret* and had no idea that we, as humans, are co-creators of our reality. Jane, the guardian, said that she was there to assist the flow of spirits using the earth energy lines.

"Early in my 'awakening' I visited many different sacred sites and stone circles. When there, I would ask the guardians why there were so many insects around, as on one occasion I saw literally hundreds of money spiders. They were everywhere! The answer? It was due to a combination of my energy and thoughts plus the energies of the site. This intrigued me, and I began to wonder about the possibility that my thoughts could actually interact with the energies found at sacred sites in some way.

"When visiting one stone circle I was greeted by waves of voices saying 'welcome'. This was because of my growing clairaudience. It made me think that all stone circles had actual spirits of once living souls attached to them. But I have since learned that is not necessarily the case. One incident, in particular, has stayed with me for many years, as it was a big lesson for me. Hamish (Miller) and I were, travelling in a car together, looking for a particular stone circle and, as is quite common, we couldn't find it as most are now in isolated or out of the way places and are rarely signposted.

"As we drove around the village, supposedly near the stones, I casually said out loud, 'They must be around here somewhere!' and, just as I uttered those words, a very obvious signpost appeared, pointing us to the location of the circle. I smugly said, 'There you go!!' Hamish just smiled knowingly and said, 'Ah, so you think you manifested that sign then, eh?'

"That was the first time I had ever heard the word 'manifested' used in the sense of humans actually being able to create material things in their own reality. At the same time as I was receiving this spiritual input, I was reading about quantum science, trying to get my head around the developing theories of consciousness and awareness. Luckily, I came across the book *The Self Aware Universe* by Amit Goswami, which is written in a down to earth sort of way for the non-science minded.

"Gradually the concept of probability and the potentiality of everything around us came to me; the notion that everything around us sits in a state of potential, waiting for us to decide what to think and then it creates it for us. This is based upon the quantum theory of the collapsing waveform, used to describe the way in which the potential of the sub atomic structure of everything exists in a state of 'undefined-ness' as a wave of potential, until it is observed, then it collapses into particles, hence taking a solid manifested form. I communicated with spirit on various occasions about the idea that God is right here, right now, all the time. 'God' in this sense being like a process: a process of creation. It seemed to me that earth energy held the key, as it is part of the structure of the universe at the quantum level.

"I don't understand quantum physics fully, but the notion of 'everything being potential until it is observed, at which point it turns to probability and then actuality' did strike a very deep chord with me. I resonate with the idea that earth energy lines are an integral part of the fabric of reality and are a part of our dimensional structure. They are the spider's web of possibility and we interact with them to manifest what is in our hearts, moment to moment. The work of our friend, Jim Lyons, develops this philosophy much further. Jim has many theories about how we connect with this earth energy and how the manifesting process itself works.

"Many ancient sacred sites are integral to the process of combining earth energies, humanity and spirit into a system whereby manifestation can be achieved rapidly and we have no doubt this is a key part of their purpose in being built. Humanity, The Management and earth energies combine to create form in the material physical sense. We are, in fact, above all else, reality co-creators."

During another day with Hamish, Tim encountered something else that brought him further understanding about the structure of the spiritual communication we can have at sacred sites.

As Tim explains, "Hamish and I were reconnoitring some of the many stone circles found in Cornwall. As we approached each stone circle, I would hear wave upon wave of human voices welcoming us and inviting us into the site. The key here is the wave-like nature of these collective voices and I remembered that Jane had spoken to me like that in the past."

Waves are the structure of everything in the physical world: absolutely everything is built from waves created by vortices, some so infinitesimally small we cannot perceive their scale because they exist within the quantum world. And some are so massively huge that they can span the solar system.

Jim Lyons would say that the earth energy lines we find are set up as 'torsion fields' that carry information in packets, with our brains acting as receivers, picking up the information in waves. At the moment, however, torsion fields are not an accepted part of science, although there's much to support their existence. As science develops new theories will emerge about all of this over the coming years, so, watch this space.

What we wish to get across to you in this section, is that for all of us, how we expect the world to behave around us, is the way the world will behave around us. The individual observer collapses reality around him or herself into the form they are expecting and anticipating it to take. Each person can be described as a reality co-creator, in that they receive and transmit signals about what they expect to experience every moment of every day.

Those signals are picked up by other transmitters and receivers (humans) and combined with the receptive aspect of earth energy where it crosses into the spiritual dimension. The Management will interact in all this too. The result of this three-stage input from human, earth and the Divine is that a new reality is constantly being created.

This means that creation is occurring in every moment of every day. This, the authors feel, is how so-called miracles can happen: it only takes a few unpredicted energetic exchanges to form a whole new, unexpected reality.

The picture painted above suggests that reality is based upon a human-centred universe as we each live in the worlds we have co-created or brought into existence. We are all provided with the exact same fundamental particles (or waves), with which to create the experience we call life. It's up to us, to a large extent, what we do with it.

There are currently some seven and a half billion human souls on this planet and each person has an effect on the others i.e. the human collective, but this happens even more directly when those human experiences overlap, or two or more people share the same space and time.

It is difficult for many of us to comprehend this process and it is not helped by another common feature of quantum science, in that it seems at the quantum level time is not linear. This theory indicates that something we might do in the *future*, can have a direct effect on our existence *today*. So, something that you did at forty years old, for instance, may well have had a direct effect on you when you were, say, twelve years old or perhaps younger. Science now says this is possible.

The upshot of this self-creation is that we also have the power within us to change the way we experience reality. In other words, we all have the ability to change our worlds and that is through the three-way interplay between spirit, human and the earth.

If we are as important to creation as we seem to be, the ability to focus our thoughts in the right way is absolutely essential to the future of our species. Both authors feel this is the way global society is going. We are being led, with some urgency now, towards a greater understanding of our true role in the process of co-creation.

We all have a responsibility to consider the role of humanity globally and to perceive and understand our individual reality that can affect others in so many different ways. When we understand our role as co-creators, we can start to make choices about how to live our lives and choose which decisions we consider most important.

As we have shown earlier, mindfulness is a step towards meditation and dedicated meditation is the most powerful tool available to us with which to affect our personal realities. Such meditation puts a person in a specific mindset that we believe enables better communication with the dimensions from which creation is born. That is a quantum process, and science agrees that this dimension of the physical is created from the one adjacent to ours, in other words, the subtle realms.

Spirit & Earth

'The body is of the Earth and the mind is a doorway to spirit.'

Chapter Five

Dowsing

What is dowsing?

The opening scenes of the DVD production, *Diverse Dowsing*, made by Tim, features his mentor, Hamish Miller, walking amongst the ruins of tin mine buildings on the wild Cornish coast. These deserted and derelict buildings stand like tombstones to an industrial age long since dead. As Hamish walks, he talks about how the men who used to work so hard underground extracting tin from the Earth were often doing so on information gained from dowsers. When seams of tin were buried hundreds of yards out beyond the shoreline, the mine owners had to be sure of their potential rewards in order to risk such costly excavation.

Dowsing has been recorded through the centuries as being used for many different mining applications and even today the modern oil exploration industry employs professional dowsers to help locate new deposits. Although dowsing is often dismissed by sceptics, such professional organisations wouldn't invest in processes that simply didn't work.

Dowsing was for a long time described in the Oxford English Dictionary as 'the art of finding hidden things'. It has been with humanity for aeons and while there still seems to be a lack of empirical evidence from the scientific community that it works, dowsers all over the world know that it does and continue to use it as a way of finding any information or object that is not immediately obvious or perhaps not even in the physical dimension.

Both authors work extensively with dowsing in their healing practices, working remotely to improve a person's wellbeing by influencing the energies of place in which their clients live or work. It is a very tangible link between the physical environment, i.e. the body, and the non-physical, the mind. The body is of the earth and the mind is a doorway to spirit. Seen in this way, human beings are a link between both spirit and Earth. And dowsing can be seen as a way to link spirit and Earth by using metal, wood or crystal to connect to unseen energies.

Dowsing has existed for thousands of years. Ancient cave paintings in Africa are thought to show the earliest humans using dowsing to find water. There are also hieroglyphs possibly showing some form of divining or dowsing carved into Egyptian sacred sites. The way in which people dowse has altered very little over the centuries, but the applications have changed considerably. Those who are unfamiliar with dowsing may mainly associate it with finding water.

The uninitiated are most likely to picture somebody wandering through fields being led by a forked hazel twig held expectantly in front of them, until it suddenly judders and points downward with a movement independent of the operator. There, beneath the feet, at a depth that the dowser can ascertain, will be a source of water. To most people, dowsing can seem completely inexplicable but, despite its bizarre appearance and public perception, it is a practice that works.

When a dowser/diviner searches for potable water beneath the ground, he or she will walk in a set pattern and wait for a response from their dowsing instrument. When they feel it twitch or move, that will indicate a good place to drill a borehole.

These days, the traditional forked twig is often put to one side in favour of a pendulum or a pair of metal L-rods bent at 90 degrees to sit comfortably in the hand, but what hasn't changed is the basic practice of asking questions that will result in a 'yes' or 'no' response. Both authors work with students to bring this wonderful ancient art up to date and by doing so, illustrate how it can be a useful part of modern daily life.

We find that people are attracted to the world of dowsing for a huge variety of reasons. Learning to dowse is incredibly simple and the rudimentary skills are usually easily picked up, but it is also something that requires patience and definitely demands practice. Many novice dowsers can become very disillusioned with dowsing, because after their initial success, they sometimes go through a period when their dowsing produces nonsense results.

Think of it like learning to write. When you were young, it was easy to pick up a pencil and hold it between your fingers, but it was slightly trickier to get the pencil to do what you wanted. After several years' practice, sentences would have begun to flow and the process becomes easier. If you extrapolate still further, it may have been decades before you were good or proficient enough with your native language to be able to write a novel or perhaps to earn a living from it.

The same rule applies to dowsing. It is easy to pick up the rods and/or pendulum to get a basic 'yes' or 'no' response, but to consistently get accurate results over a wide range of subject areas – well, that's going to take some time and practice.

The tools of dowsing

As we moved into the 21st century, the energy patterns around us changed, meaning that we had to start looking at the spiritual world, including dowsing, in new ways. There are still many people teaching outmoded methods, these are not harmful, just a bit old fashioned.

To begin your dowsing exploration, we recommend reading *The Wee Book of Dowsing* by Hamish Miller, and watching *Intuition - Your Hidden Treasure,* a DVD presented by Adrian and filmed/directed by Tim (see rear of the book for purchase details).

There are many different tools available for the dowser, including:

- L rods (brass, copper, stainless steel etc.)

- Pendulums (crystal, brass, wood)

- Aurameter

- The hazel Y Rod or 'Forked Stick'

- Dallys (see rear of book for details)

- The Bobber or Wand.

Then there are the dowsing variations possible using your own body:

- Whole Body Dowsing (involuntary movement forwards, backwards or sideways)

- Skin temperature or resistance (Galvanic Response)

- Movement of your eyes

- Interlocking your fingers

- Muscle response or Kinesiology

- Emotional feelings

- Hot or cold feet

- Hot or cold hands

- Tingling sensations

- Arm movements

No matter what you use to dowse, the most important thing is the process of asking the right question in order to get the right response.

How to Dowse

Dowsing is generally thought of as a journey beyond our five senses (touch, taste, sight, sound and smell), connecting us with the spiritual aspect of our lives and by using external devices (such as L rods and pendulums) it can help us gain answers to questions that we should naturally and psychically know – but that we are unable to tap into without help. Everyone can dowse, because it is something that is inherent to us all, but of course not everyone wants to.

There is a more natural way of finding out the answers without using rods or pendulums and that is by observing your body's responses. Body dowsing, using our body as a human pendulum, is almost as natural as breathing, but most of us won't notice this inner reaction to external or internal stimuli until it is pointed out to us. During our courses, we show how our body can react to other people's emotions, food intolerances etc.,

First of all, you need to find out your body's reaction to something that is positive or good for it and then its opposite reaction, to something detrimental or bad. We are born with this sixth sense, and it can help keep us safe, but in today's busy world much of this natural ability has taken a backseat to science and can go largely unobserved.

So, how do we tap into this largely unknown and unfelt ability? When teaching the following technique, we always advise people to have a chair in front of them that they can grab hold off as sometimes the body's reaction can be very pronounced.

To begin, relax by taking a few deep breaths, spending a little time in the 'now'. As with anything new, try to clear your mind of superfluous clutter, this will give you the best opportunity to experience the body's natural reaction to a question or outside stimulus. Don't rush, take your time, and if not successful the first time, take a few more deep breaths and try again. Practice *will* make perfect.

Stand upright, lightly balanced on your feet, with your eyes open, but ideally slightly unfocussed or hooded, then ask your body for its 'yes' response and see if you get a reaction. It might be an internal movement or a physical one, either swaying forward, backward or sideways. If nothing happens, try again.

Then ask for your body's 'no' response and see if you experience a different reaction or movement. Nothing happening for a 'yes' response could be the body's way of saying 'yes' and a different or sudden movement could be the 'no'.

It can take time for you to redevelop this natural ability, so don't fret if it doesn't happen straightaway and you may find that to start dowsing with rods or pendulums is more appropriate for you.

Using dowsing rods or a pendulum externalises what you already know, the message has been received psychically and the movement of the instrument is the body's way of giving you the answer.

Picking up a pair of dowsing rods for the first time, asking for a 'yes' response and then watching them move, is something that you will never forget.

The first thing to do is make a pair of L rods, unless you already have bought some. It doesn't matter what material they are made from, whether copper, brass or stainless steel – they all work the same way. The weight of the rods is down to personal choice, Tim, for instance, loves working with his beloved heavy forged steel rods made by Hamish Miller, but Adrian prefers much lighter extendable rods.

If you want to make your own to start with, acquire two metal coat hangers and also a pair of pliers. Cut off the twisted parts of the hook and straighten the wire. You now need to bend the wire into an L shape (90° angle) with approximately 3½ to 4 inches on the shorter side and 7 inches on the longer side.

Get two plastic Biro pens (they work the best), strip out the innards and take off the tops. Insert a single L rod into each sleeve, which will then allow them to swing easily. You now have a pair of rods – and you can start dowsing.

Holding the rods

Hold them, one in each hand, comfortably in front of you, with the rods parallel to each other, tipped down slightly from the horizontal with your elbows held loosely by your side, and then start to walk. This forward motion is important as it helps the rods move, and it relaxes both your body and mind, allowing the dowsing process to take place.

Many dowsing problems will come from either gripping the rods too tightly, hence the plastic sleeves, or because you are holding your arms too rigidly against your body. Don't forget that it is you moving the rods, via a muscle response, not telekinesis, so if the arms are not free to move then the response will be limited, or no movement will be seen or felt.

If seated, then we would suggest that as you ask the question you move your arms slowly in a forward motion to allow the muscles to do what they need to do, to show you a yes or no response.

To practice, try stretching a rope (the target) across your lawn and ask your rods to move, or cross, as you walk over the target. This technique will help you in several ways: it gives the brain something to concentrate on, and it gives the eyes something to fix on. The brain, as usual, will operate on logic – the left part of it, anyway – and is inclined to dismiss anything that it cannot see. However, the intuitive part, knows that there is something there and it will react accordingly, the rods will move through unconscious muscle action.

As always, it is about practise, so if the rods don't cross first time, try again. Ideally, you need to be relaxed and in a calm state as you are learning a new skill and it does take time for the brain to be trained. In basic terms, dowsing uses the masculine, logical left brain to form the questions and the feminine, intuitive right brain to provide the answers.

If you still haven't got a reaction, don't panic. Sit quietly, take a deep breath (or two) and try the following:

Dowsing Exercise

Place both feet firmly on the ground and relax your body. Imagine both feet sinking into Mother Earth: that you are part of her and everyone else living on the planet, and that a beautiful white light is gradually moving up your legs, through your body and your head, eventually covering you fully; this will help you be grounded.

To dowse, we need to connect to the Universe, and allow our brain waves to change, so be calm and still for a few minutes: give yourself time, then try again. Don't force the situation: just relax and see what happens as you walk towards the rope. Once the movement of the rods has become natural, the next step is to ascertain your 'yes' and 'no' responses. This is done, as before, by moving forward with the rods parallel and asking them to show you your 'yes' response and note what they do. In most cases they will cross in front of you and the 'no' response, therefore, is usually an outward movement of the rods. These actions are not the same for everyone, Adrian's 'no' response, for instance, is no movement of the rods.

When you have seen the rods cross when you step over the rope, it is time to hone your skills further. For example, you can dowse to see what time the post will arrive, or when an expected visitor may turn up, or if a certain food is good for you and so on. The list is endless. If you can ask the question, you should be able to get the answer, the only limit is how vivid your imagination is to come up with the question in the first place.

Pendulum Dowsing

Pendulum's are smaller and easier to carry in your pocket or purse than a pair of rods. Any weight tied onto the end of a piece of string can be used for this purpose which can make them more convenient to use than rods. Wedding rings, for instance, tied to a piece of cotton and held over a pregnant woman's stomach have been used over the years to tell the sex of an unborn baby. Car keys can be used and on one course he was teaching, Adrian saw an attendee using her mobile phone as a pendulum, by holding the cord and watching which way it swung.

Using a pendulum is a very convenient way to dowse, and they can be made of anything, brass, copper, wood or crystal.

Ideally, the weight at the end should be symmetrical to the central cord, and the string, cord or chain somewhere around six inches in length. There are many different pendulums on the market, and it is very much down to personal choice as to which one will work best for you. No one pendulum works any better than another, but do try a few different types before buying, the balance and feel is very important.

Hold the pendulum, so that approximately three inches of cord shows, this enables the weight on the end to give a quick and smooth response; the longer the cord, the longer the response time will be. Set the pendulum in motion, swinging gently backwards and forwards (the neutral or search position), then ask it to show you a 'yes' response and note the movement. Keep the swinging motion going, don't stop as this helps the speed of the response.

Follow this by asking for your 'no' response, it should be different. As with the rods, do take your time and allow movement in your arm. Resting your elbow on a table can alter the response times and in some cases actually stop any response from happening, better to have your arm by your side, free of any obstructions. Your technique may change over the years and responses can also change, so it is good practice, certainly in the early days, to ask three verifiable questions as you start dowsing, for instance the colour of your shirt or blouse you are wearing, did I have toast/cereal/eggs for breakfast? and finally is today Monday/Tuesday?

Practical applications

There are many practical applications for dowsing, not just finding water or underground pipes. Possible topics include:

General state of health

Allergies

Food intolerances

Vitamins and minerals

Location of bombs and mines

Earth energies including Geopathic Stress

Ghosts and spirits

Detrimental values of deodorants, shampoos, etc.

Technopathic Stress (Wi-Fi, mobile masts, microwave ovens, low energy light bulbs)

Archaeology

Oil and minerals

All hidden or lost objects including lost humans and animals

Underground utilities

Most suitable bottle of wine/beer

Most suitable local restaurants

Weather forecast

Auras and chakras

Best hotel to stay in when choosing a holiday

As you can see, there are so many practical aspects to dowsing, these are just a few. Often, although they won't usually admit it, utility company employees will use dowsing to find underground pipes or water leaks when their modern machines fail.

The police force has also been known to employ dowsers to find missing people and track down criminals. The Army has also used it to find enemy mines and tunnels. In the Vietnam War for instance, Louis Mattacia taught US Marines how to master the rods. And last, but not least, as we said earlier, dowsing is also used in oil and mineral exploration.

Dowsing can be used for healing people and/or places too. Dowsing a site like Stonehenge can bring some amazing results and help answer questions on who built the site, when and why. Though many of the more scientifically inclined archaeologists prefer to rely on geophysical instruments, and tend to dismiss dowsing as mumbo jumbo.

As well as the very practical method of dowsing for missing or hidden physical objects, there is a form of dowsing that is more akin to remote viewing, where a map or floorplan of a house or office can be used by a dowser to access information, even though they may be many hundreds or thousands of miles from the actual location.

In summary, dowsing can be used to ask a question when the answer is not obvious and is a skill that is encapsulated in the phrase, 'the art of finding hidden things'. But it is so much more than that. Despite all these very practical and acceptable applications, no one really, yet, fully understands how dowsing actually works.

The variable nature of its results, especially amongst novices, inevitably leads to mistrust, hence why dowsing is side-lined by so many. Even among the established dowsing community nobody can fully agree on how it works. Some dowsers suggest they find the object they seek due to a form of radiation emanating from whatever it is they are looking for; whether that be an underground stream, a buried artefact, a lost ring, an animal or indeed a person. This theory of radiation, however, doesn't explain how remote or distance dowsing works, when the dowser is nowhere near their target.

It is quite common for experienced specialist dowsers to find minerals from thousands of miles away simply by using a map or diagram to pinpoint an exact location. Missing people can be located in the same way. Even the plotting of detrimental earth-energy lines in a stranger's house can be achieved by using a simple floorplan as the 'link' to what the dowser is looking for. So there has to be more to it than just radiation.

Tim and Adrian both feel that you can't successfully dowse without there being some form of spiritual link to the Universe, even if you are unaware of this subconscious connection. However, having said that, it seems that the most likely candidate for the dowsing response utilises exactly the process that sceptics label it with to deny its plausibility. Dowsing seems to function based upon the 'ideomotor effect'. That is a reflexive response from a person's unconscious muscular movement of the body reacting to an outside stimulus. The authors suggest that the dowser is unaware of these minute muscular movements so, this is the reason why, when the rods or pendulum respond to a question, it feels as though the answers are coming from an external force and not connected to the dowser. But we suggest that the unconscious movements of the body seem to be stimulated by information being picked up from the quantum dimension of existence and so the ideomotor effect, far from denying dowsing's efficacy actually could be the reason it works. There is, however, no scientific empirical evidence for this, so dowsing remains an unexplained, hotly contested, fascinating practice.

Whether you believe it, or are totally sceptical, dowsing actually works and we have not yet met anyone that could not dowse to some degree.

In their professional work, both authors will dowse a series of questions to ascertain their client's emotional wellbeing and identify the energetic detrimental emotional energy in their home; this is mostly done from a distance. This information can be very detailed, even citing specific actions that have affected a client and the approximate age they were when these (usually traumatic) events happened.

To gain this type of information, there has to be some form of energetic or psychic connection and communication happening, and dowsing is simply the physical action required to consciously reveal the results.

It is likely that we are tuning into our clients and psychically accessing their emotional energy field. The dowsing response is our own physical body interpreting these results, allowing us to download the information we are receiving in a logical and structured fashion. It is suggested that information from the quantum field of existence can travel faster than the speed of light across very large distances. If this is so, then it explains how we as dowsers can download and interpret the data instantly.

Another statement that you will often hear mentioned when dowsing, is that we are communicating and working with our Higher Self. We have discussed the Higher Self in the spirit part of this book, and this is a possibility for how the psychic connection aspect of dowsing works.

The authors thought it might be helpful to describe how one of us works so the following is a description of how Tim dowses. As with any work in the subtle realms, it will be individual to each of us, but the basic steps will remain the same.

This is Tim's dowsing process when working on a client's house:

The correct frame of mind is important because it will help to attain a higher percentage of accurate responses. The correct frame of mind is one that is still and focused inward, with external distractions minimised (i.e. switch off your mobile phone).

The way information is gained and observed, regarding the inner world, will depend on you as an individual. Some people are better at visualising objects, some will feel sensations, whilst others will hear messages and so on.

Tim then asks the dowsing question and waits for the 'yes' or 'no' response. He focuses on the question and the likelihood of an answer as though in conversation. The attention is *not* on the rods or pendulum, it is focussed on the inner world where information may be received as an image, a knowing or a voice.

As that information is received, (from the Higher Self), the rods or pendulum will respond and move. Often the information starts to flow very quickly and it can be tricky to keep up with the 'download'. This is a learned process for each person. The key is to maintain the connection in the meditative state of mind but also jump back and forth to note down the results on paper or floorplan. In other words, to allow the information to flow from the subconscious to the conscious mind.

As with any dowsing, once the answers are received, further questions are likely to be necessary, as Tim has learned, if you ask the first thing that comes to mind, you will find you are often guided to ask the right questions to get to the answer you seek more quickly.

When starting as a novice dowser, people sometimes get stuck on what questions to ask, but this is also an aspect of dowsing that gets easier with practice. To help, we have provided examples of question strings in the next section.

Asking the right questions and repeatability

As we have described above, dowsing relies upon you receiving a 'yes' or 'no' answer in response to a question. Practice is essential to build confidence in getting good, reliable dowsing results. In the early days of their dowsing journey, many people find asking the right questions difficult. More often than not it is simply a matter of realising that one needs to ask a series of closed questions to deduce information accurately.

The scientific community relies upon its 'Scientific Method' in order to evaluate provability and give empirical results. As we have seen, dowsing is not empirical and never can be. So, the much-loved aspect of repeatability that science seeks cannot be achieved by numerous dowsers dowsing the same information, as they will get slightly different results. Often, the degree of difference among a group of dowsers is very small, but the results have so far never been consistent enough for science to accept. But subjective non-empirical *experience* in real life tells a different story.

For example, it is common that a water dowser when searching for a good place to drill a borehole will indicate that the best potable water can be found at an exact depth, say exactly 133.197 metres beneath his feet. So that's where the drill team, with their tens of thousands of pounds worth of equipment, will start drilling. And after cutting through hundreds of feet of solid bedrock to exactly that depth, water will, 99 times out of 100, be seen to gush to the surface. That is experiential evidence that once witnessed is much harder to dismiss.

The late Don Wilkins a reputable Cornish water dowser had close to a 100% success rate in locating positions to drill for water. The late George Applegate had a similar record and we would say this easily counters the sceptics arguments. However, it is also true that most dowsers admit to not finding the same specific things when they search, for example, for water or earth energies in groups with other dowsers. This could be because everyone is an individual and therefore will have their own unique thought patterns and ways of visualising what they are looking for. For instance, if we asked two people to dowse and locate an underground stream, one person would imagine a stream ten-feet wide and forty-feet deep, another person would imagine one that is thirty-feet wide and eighty-feet deep. The two people would be unlikely to find the same stream, ever.

However, if you can dowse with a clear open mind the results can begin to coincide. It is when you start to *think* that everything begins to go awry.

The parameters need to be set to achieve repeatability. Adrian explains: "As a beginner dowser, you need to be very specific in what you are looking for and be mindful of the way you ask the questions to access the information. The best way to do this is to ask a very wide and all-encompassing question and then begin to refine the search and get to the finite point as quickly as you can, by asking more and more specific questions."

With practice, the questions will begin to flow more easily and one answer will lead you naturally to the next question and so on. Before you know it, you will be dowsing for specific targets, asking unambiguous, precise questions and getting very positive results.

Effective dowsing relies upon practice. Start by dowsing something that you can easily verify, like the time your post will arrive, and progress from there. It is worth putting in the time and effort early on, to develop a feel for your dowsing device and the way it works with you and to understand the importance of asking the right questions.

As you gain more experience, you will start to look at other ways of testing your dowsing skills. Ask a friend or member of your family to hide something, say a set of car keys, inside the house and then go and find them using dowsing.

Question strings are similar to flow diagrams:

Are the car keys on the ground floor?

Yes/No.

If no - are the car keys on the first floor?

If yes - are the car keys in one of the bedrooms?

No.

In the bathroom?

No.

In the airing cupboard?

Yes.

Which shelf are they on? Top?

No.

Middle?

Yes

Another great exercise is to try finding someone who has hidden themselves from you during hide and seek; simply ask the rods to show you the direction the person walked and follow the moving rods until they lead you to them.

Another exercise for practice is to ask the rods to point north or south. You will soon find they can be an excellent compass. They can also act as a SatNav, guiding you to your destination when walking if you are lost. We don't recommend driving with one hand and trying this. Ask a passenger to do the dowsing while you concentrate on driving.

Once you feel confident in your responses, you could ask the rods to show you where the nearest earth energy line is and see which way they point. Follow them until they cross, then mark that point with a flag or something similar. Then ask for the far edge of the line and again mark that when the rods cross again. It doesn't matter if you don't know what an earth energy line actually is at this stage, the rods will guide or show you anyway – just have faith.

You can trace an earth energy line running through your garden, either by following the edges or by walking in a criss-cross manner, marking the edges of the line as the rods cross, until you gain the full picture.

You can do the same with a soak-away pipe, drain or electrical cable. Perhaps then move on to locating an underground stream or a water vein. Mark what you have found with flags so you can stand back to see where you have been and what you have found. The next thing to discover is the depth of the underground stream. You might also want to find which direction it runs in, or whether it is good for you to stand or sit above.

Counting with dowsing rods or a pendulum will allow you to do many things such as date a particular artefact, work out how deep an underground stream is, decide how detrimental an area is for you, or pinpoint when a particular event might have happened in the past.

To do this, simply hold the dowsing rod or pendulum in your hand and then start counting slowly, if you go too quickly you may find that you are well past the date before the rod has a chance to move, so go slowly.

Adrian describes how he would find when the Great Fire of London started, and his line of questioning is as follows:

"I would start by finding out which century it occurred in, by counting backwards from the 21st century and wait for an indication from the rods

21st century – *no movement*

20th century – *no movement*

19th century – *no movement*

18th century – *no movement*

17th century – *rod moves to indicate a yes response.*

Therefore, it will have occurred between 1600 and 1699.

Now we need to ascertain what year, but rather than count all the way from 1600 to 1699 I would try and narrow the search down quickly by asking was it between 1600 and 1650?

No response from the rods (or a no response swing), indicates it must be between 1651 and 1699.

I would then say between 1651 and 1661 – *no response*

1661 and 1671 – *yes response*

Then start counting upwards from 1661 then, as you get to 1666, the rods will indicate a yes response.

Then we need to ascertain which month, again the questions can be shortened by asking: 'Was it during the first half of the year'? No movement.

So, you then know that it started somewhere between July and December 1666.

Was it July – *no movement*

August – *no movement*

September – *rods indicate yes*

Then we need to work out what day

Follow the same procedure as above, by asking 'Was it between 1st and 10th of September? – *the rods indicate a yes response.*

1st September – *no movement*

2nd September – *yes response*

There you have it, the Great Fire of London started on September 2nd 1666."

Most people find it relatively easy once they get the hang of it. Remember, ask the wide question first and then narrow down the answer as quickly as possible.

What to do with the answers

What you need to do with the answers really depends on what you were asking in the first place. If it was something practical, such as dowsing to find out the most suitable vitamin or mineral supplement to take, then you would obviously act upon the answer by going out and buying it. If you were dowsing the best place to drill a bore hole, then you know where to start digging.

Dowsing can be done remotely, what you are dowsing for could be in the same town or in a different country. For instance, you might want to do some research before driving to a sacred site, to establish before you got there, where to go for you to gain maximum insight, the best stone to stand against or the best place to stand for healing on that day.

It is a good way to gather information before you start your journey. You could also ascertain the best time to leave and the best route to follow, avoiding any traffic jams.

Dowsing can also have great health benefits. You can dowse to find out what is good or bad for you to eat, drink, do, etc. It will give you a greater understanding of your body and your health.

Hydration is a major part of your wellness. Dowse to see how much water you need to consume on any one day (don't forget that each day is different), when you need to drink it and, of course, how beneficial the water is that you are drinking (e.g. is it filtered etc.). Score the beneficial results between 0 and +10, then the detrimental between -10 and 0.

The basic information given here is to help get you started, as this is not a book solely about dowsing. But we hope it helps you gain greater knowledge, not just of yourself, but of the seen and unseen world around you. It is a very grounded way of accessing the spiritual world, without you necessarily having any mediumistic skills, although quite often these will come to you over time.

Remote or map dowsing

Normally, one of the first questions asked when we mention remote dowsing during a workshop is, *'How can you dowse a problem in a house or locate an object when it is on the other side of the Earth?'*

The answer is quite simple: everything is connected. Everything has an auric field surrounding it, whether it be a human, an animal, a tea cup, a tree, a chair, a crystal and so on. It is perhaps by linking (faster than the speed of light) via this unseen energy network that the necessary information is gleaned.

Both authors use remote dowsing when working on their clients and client families and/or houses. It forms a very important part of gathering the information needed before carrying out a healing.

Proof of the efficiency of remote dowsing is the fact that there are many dowsers who locate lost objects, people, minerals and oil anywhere in the world by working over a map.

Try it yourself by dowsing the weather in Tucson, Arizona, or perhaps more challenging would be that in Dublin, and then logging onto a local website to see if you were right. It does take practice but, once mastered, the technique can be very useful. Remotely dowsing a sacred site before you visit, as we did with Coldstones Cut in the example below, can give you some excellent insights into what you will find there. Just pick up a map and start asking questions.

When we hold our Spiritual Earth Courses we like to visit local sacred sites so that the attendees can learn directly from the landscape. During a workshop in 2015, we went to a site in the Yorkshire Dales known as Coldstones Cut.

Coldstones Cut is a modern land sculpture completed in 2009, designed by Andrew Sabin. Standing at approximately 1,375ft above sea level, it provides some superb views (on a clear day) overlooking Pateley Bridge and the surrounding countryside.

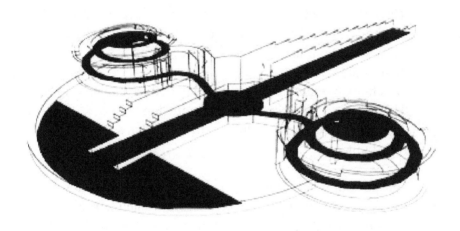

Designer's Schematic of Coldstones Cut, N Yorks
© Andrew Sabin and Hanson Group
■ = Public access/walkway

Coldstones Cut was built with money donated by the Hanson Quarry, which it overlooks. Many felt it was built purely as a local attraction, but the idea behind the design was to make people think and to stimulate their imagination as they walked up the hill.

The whole sculpture has been designed to draw the visitor in, to encourage them to explore the hidden nooks and crannies of the site, to walk the spirals and marvel at the views from the top platform overlooking the quarry and Nidderdale. It certainly does all that and more, as our dowsers discovered. The reason for our visit, when running the course, was to see how the construction of Coldstones Cut had affected the land since its completion. We wanted to find out whether it had a beneficial or detrimental effect on the area, especially the adjacent large quarry. Before we visited the site, we dowsed remotely using a plan to establish the following information:

1. Was the reason for construction beneficial to the land?
2. Has it helped the land since it was built?
3. Are there any earth energy lines that may affect the site? Where are they?
4. Have any lines been attracted to the site since it was built?
5. Is it, or will it ever be, considered a holy site or sacred space?
6. How would our ancient ancestors react if they saw it for the first time?
7. Has human intent played any part in it since construction?
8. Has it had an unexpected effect on the land?
9. Have any ceremonial or holy pathways been set up since it was built?

We had purposefully not informed the course attendees what Coldstones Cut was and what it overlooked, as we wanted to see what conclusions they would come to during their dowsing, both on site and remotely.

Overall the answers were as follows:
1. Was the reason for construction beneficial to the land?
Yes, mainly because it has focussed people's attention on man's desecration of the Earth. The quarry has been managed well by The Hanson Group, but it is still a large hole in the ground and that has led to a lot of land disturbance in the local area.
2. and 3. Combined: Has it helped the land since it was built and are there any earth energy lines that may affect the site?
Again, yes it has, but this time it is mainly earth energy related. We

have mentioned several times that humanity can influence energy lines and so can the Earth. Before Coldstones Cut was built there were no major lines influencing the site. However, now it is positively buzzing due to the attraction of two earth energy lines that run through each of the two spirals as shown below.

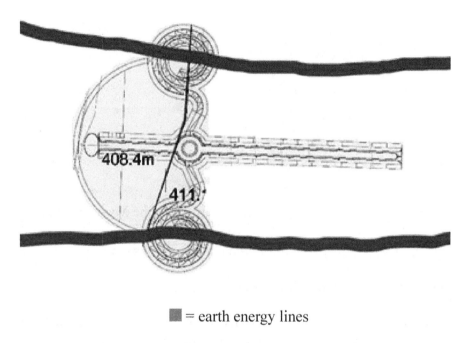

■ = earth energy lines

4. Have any lines been attracted to the site since it was built?

Since its construction an energy channel has been attracted to the site. This is very similar to the Michael line worked on and written about by Hamish Miller and Paul Broadhurst in their book, *The Sun and Serpent.*

Adrian has been plotting the male and female energy channels that run across the North Yorkshire countryside. Locally the male runs through Ripon Cathedral, skirts Brimham Rocks, runs through Coldstones and then Stump Cross Caverns as it travels in a westerly direction. See illustration below.

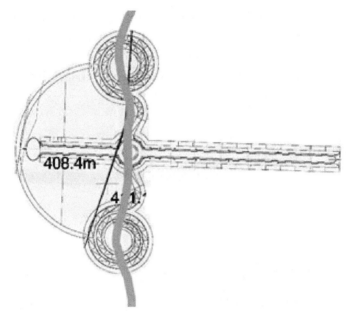

■ = Male energy channel (similar to the Michael Line)

5. Is it, or will it ever be, considered a holy site or sacred space?

The overall answer, from the group, was yes.

Even today, the site is being venerated, perhaps not by every member of the public who visits it, but certainly by anyone who may be considered sensitive, interested in old monuments, such as long barrows and stone circles, and, of course, earth energies. You also need to add people who love architecture to the list as well as those who are awed by the magnificence of cathedrals and churches, in fact any site that stretches the imagination and makes you think.

As soon as you enter the sculpture you become aware of the silence. The wind suddenly disappears (It always seems to be windy up there as it is so exposed) and the walls begin to tower above you as you walk towards the centre. The slightly raised centre is very womb-like. Straight ahead, the path takes you to the breath-taking viewing gallery above the quarry and to either side, the openings lead to the spiralling pathways.

As you walk into the spirals you can only see a few feet in front of you which adds to the mystique; you don't know what is around the corner and the walls take on a much greater height. You feel as though you are on a ceremonial pathway that could, in imagination, lead to the heavens. You are drawn ever upwards until, upon reaching the centre, slightly out of breath, you can again take in the far distant views. Buddhist monasteries often work on a similar principle to their approach paths, as in 'no pain, no gain'.

Although Coldstones Cut was not built as a sacred site, it is a most intriguing and thought provoking place. It is perhaps the unknown or the expectation that has enhanced the site. It is difficult not to get pulled into the spiralling walls that seem to close around and above you, giving the sculpture a cathedral-like feel. It has a sacred feel to it already and this can only build over the forthcoming years.

6. How would our ancient ancestors react if they saw it for the first time?

From Tim and Adrian's observation of how the course attendees reacted, our ancestors would have been intrigued, probably in awe and also suspicious of what they saw. Perhaps they would feel the sacredness as they trod upon the ground. Each turn would bring something new into their vision and, as the view opened up, they would perhaps begin to wonder further why it was built there, on top of the hill; perhaps to honour the Earth, maybe to worship the sunrise or sunset, to track the movements of the moon and so on. All in all, we believe they would be attracted to the site and would in time start to use it for their own ceremonial purposes, maybe even forming their own religion around it.

We know that spirals have been carved into rock for millennia. They may have been energy giving to those who created the patterns and those who used them in healing. For our ancient ancestors, had they experienced such a place, we feel that Coldstones Cut would have become a centre of healing, using the energies created by the spirals as places to heal the mind, body and possibly spirit.

7. Has human intent played any part in it since construction?

We would automatically say yes and the group agreed. Wherever a human being walks, they will leave an energy pattern behind them and an expert dowser should be able to track this, even many years later. So, each person visiting the site will add to this energy trail deepening the emotion held within it leaving an indelible imprint.

This is very similar to a Monk's Path, Funeral Path, Bridleway etc. All will contain small amounts of energy that will have been left by all the individuals who have trodden that ground. Pilgrimage routes, covered later in the book, are also a prime example of what would have started out as a simple path that now has thousands of people a year using it for many different reasons, including religious purposes.

8. Has it had an unexpected effect on the land?

We both felt that it had, and during the discussions with the group after our visit they all seemed to concur with our findings. The quarry had an unexpectedly peaceful feel to it. We all thought that the methods used in extracting the rock would create a lot of stress lines in the surrounding countryside and cause areas of detrimental energy. Our dowsing showed that this had been the case but, with the creation of the sculpture, much of that damage had disappeared. It would appear that Coldstones Cut is healing the land.

9. Have any ceremonial or holy pathways been set up since it was built?

The answer? A definite yes. As more people use the pathway it will attract others to do the same. It is not just a tourist spot, but a ceremonial location. People will start to feel compelled to walk the path, and as they do they will add further to the energies that are building up within the structure so that it acts rather like a beacon in the dark.

Now this may sound overly dramatic, but this might just be how Stonehenge and Avebury started. As newly built sites, the energies would have been raw and unsteady, but as time went by they would have settled and become sacred holy places. Let us see how Coldstones Cut feels in 50 years' time.

We wanted to know more about the thought processes behind the creation of the site, so Adrian approached Andrew Sabin, the designer. We were particularly interested in how he decided upon the overall shape of the sculpture. In his reply, he admitted to being 'a soft arch-sceptic' and not at all sure of the Earth healing energies created by the structure. We will leave you to draw your own conclusions from his intriguing reply:

"Regarding the spiral paths, well, that's complicated - I had a lot of ways of thinking about them - they are essentially a passage from the dark to the light, from not seeing to seeing (from no view to a view)."

He continues, "The whole work was a meditation on the big questions and in particular 'Where are we?', it makes some attempt at 'What are we?' and just about no attempt at 'Why?'

"At the time of designing the spiral ramps, I was thinking about the shapes and patterns of the very large scale, the shapes and patterns of the very small scale and also the shapes and patterns of our emotions and experiences. I know that I have designed something that has a mystical atmosphere and in a classically mystical way I might say that that was how it had to be (it couldn't be any other way) but on the other hand I also have a fairly rational set of excuses for all the decisions I made.

"In the end, the answers to the big questions are mysteries and when we make a stab at addressing them it's not surprising that we end up making something that provokes mystical thinking."

What is spiritual dowsing?

Spiritual dowsing is looking for information specifically from the spiritual realms. There is no difference in the practical method of dowsing, it is *who* or *what* we are seeking, such as Earth-bound ghosts or spirits of the deceased, which defines the difference. Two common phrases often heard in spiritual and self-development circles are that 'we are all connected' and 'all is one'. These are not simply spiritual platitudes, but beliefs that help us to realise we are not alone.

In Buddhism, for example, it is said that we all have the divine within us. It is the way we connect with all things and all things connect with us. We are energy and energy is all around us but we need to take time to feel these patterns, to know the microcosm of ourselves.

When dowsing for spiritual subjects, the dowser may prefer to focus their intent away from the Higher Self and towards a specific entity or being. For example, if one has encountered a deceased soul, then one can have a direct conversation with that soul using dowsing to get the 'yes' and 'no' responses from them. Alternatively, you may wish to connect to Source, the Divine or the Highest of the High to establish your answers.

Earth

"Empathising with someone is one thing, taking on board their pain and fear is another."

Chapter Six

Body & Home

Why do we need to be psychically protected?

At its most basic, psychic protection is all about keeping your body and mind healthy. You wouldn't go out in the rain without wearing a coat, the same applies to this form of protection. People with a robust constitution are much less likely to pick up detrimental energies and, if the aura (the energy-field surrounding you) is kept strong and clear, any detrimental thoughts from other human beings will bounce off. It will therefore be much harder to be psychically attacked.

We humans are very complex beings and whenever we start to use a dowsing instrument, or start meditating or healing, our energy state changes. Effectively, by asking a question or connecting to the higher realms, we open up our energy centres (chakras) to explore the Universal Library and then wait to receive the necessary response. By opening ourselves up we are, in effect, asking for guidance and help from any number of spiritual beings, both good and not so good. We would also be allowing other people's daily thought patterns, worries and concerns to penetrate our protective shield.

Therefore, the daily practice of putting psychic protection around yourself should become a natural part of life and just like the proverbial rain coat, if you are going out, put it on.

We are often asked if doing this lessens your sensitivity, empathy or connectedness and the answer is, 'no'. It allows to you to function as *you*, unaffected by other people's thoughts, whoever those people may be: family, friends or work colleagues.

Empathising with someone is one thing, taking on board their pain and fear is another and not recommended, especially if you are carrying out several healing sessions each day or working close to their body i.e. as a masseur, dentist, hairdresser, reiki healer, osteopath etc.

A good dowsing friend of ours recently announced that he doesn't protect himself whilst working with earth energies or at a sacred site. He said he prefers to experience everything that is going on around him and believes that psychic protection lessens what he feels. That way of thinking is all well and good until something detrimental becomes attached or a spirit wants to be playful.

We can of course clear ourselves of these detrimental energies, but only if we become aware of them. A sudden headache or an unexpected irritable feeling is a sure sign of a spirit attachment, but you may not realise it, and instead accept the pain as your own. It is possible that purely believing that psychic protection will block your awareness, means that it will. Therefore, we suggest you use the protection with the focused strict intention that protecting yourself psychically *doesn't* mean a loss of sensitivity, but that it is simply a way of making sure your thoughts and feelings are your own, and not someone else's.

We firmly believe that protecting yourself psychically is one of the most important things you can do for yourself on your spiritual path. The Management will always be there to help should you need extra defence, however, as previously stated, they do appreciate it when we make the effort to help ourselves first.

Sacred symbols and sacred geometry have also been used as security from evil spirits since time immemorial. The Egyptians wore amulets and invoked the protection of animals by placing statues in their houses and temples as a matter of course. They too sought protection from other people's thoughts and actions. We feel that much of their geometrically shaped jewellery was worn as a guard against these external detrimental energy patterns.

One of the most common forms of modern symbolic protection, here in the UK, has been the St. Christopher medallion, the patron saint of travel. Although it is not seen as often now as it was in the mid- to late 20th century.

Using sacred symbols in conjunction with psychic protection is the safest way forward, especially when walking the spiritual path. This protection will help you in the physical world, to fend off other people's emotions, worries, stresses and hurt and, in the unseen realms, (spirit world), to ward off ghosts, attachments and other detrimental energy patterns you might encounter. As your spiritual light begins to grow brighter you can easily become a target for some of the darker aspects of life.

Keeping your home clear of muddled emotions

A healthy outlook on life is important, as is an uncluttered mind to create that outlook. The less stress, anxiety and turmoil we put ourselves through the easier and better our life becomes. As electromagnetic beings, we are constantly giving off energy. This is not always healthy for us or others, as we have seen. The energy patterns of others can be detrimental to us, clouding our thoughts and, if we are sensitive, can cause major disruption in our lives.

Clearing or healing your home each day should become a natural part of your life. It doesn't matter if you have just had a visit from your family, closest friend, a carer, or similar professional social worker; their energy patterns belong to them and you don't want them or need them in your home once they have gone. Your home needs to be all about *you* and your family. You don't need to be influenced by other unwanted energy.

It is well-known that a house is sold (or not) within five seconds of the potential buyer walking into the building. In that time, they can, often subconsciously, decide whether they either like or dislike the atmosphere or 'feel' of the place. What they experience is all to do with the emotional patterns set out and laid down by all previous and current owners of the property. Home should be where we unwind, de-stress, let go of the rigours of our day and relax. So where does all of that pent-up emotion gathered during the day go?

Day after day, week after week, your poor home is bombarded with detrimental thoughts, stress from work, commuting, teenagers arguing, worries about money – the house sees it all. All of this emotion has to go somewhere, and so it soaks into the walls, ceilings, floors, furniture, paintings and ornaments. It is this that you will feel when you visit someone else's home and they will probably feel it when they visit yours too.

For detailed information on how to clear your home of detrimental energies, using dowsing and energy healing, we recommend you get a copy of Adrian's book, *Heal Your Home*. It goes into great detail on all the things to look for, how to diagnose them, and then how to heal them. Then it's just a case of doing a spring clean every now and then.

How you can be affected by attachments

A healthy diet combined with enough rest and relaxation will help to keep you well at every level: physically, mentally and spiritually. Cigarettes are known to clog your upper chakras, making it difficult for you to connect with the spiritual world, and recreational drugs tend to instil paranoia rather than help your tuning in process. Though a glass of wine or the occasional pint of ale doesn't hurt, everything in moderation and balance.

If you are involved in activities like healing, dowsing, counselling, life coaching, teaching, selling, or in fact anything that involves interaction with the public, then there are other things you need to consider in your efforts to maintain a healthy lifestyle. The issue is just how easy it is to pick up other people's detrimental thought patterns that we mentioned earlier. Once these are embedded within our energy field they can take on a more defined form and then they are referred to as 'attachments'.

Creating attachments is a natural part of being human, we can't help it. As we have seen, arguments, heated discussions, worry, stress, unkind words or actions can lead to emotional energy fields being created and these can form 'black blobs' of energy that are then free to attach themselves to people and, depending on their strength, start to push the new host's emotional buttons. Depending on how powerful the attachment is or how robust the person is onto which it attaches, it can lead to irritability, mood swings or instant and unexplainable headaches. It can make a person feel 'not themselves', act out of character, or feel depressed. In short, a person affected badly by an attachment or attachments can experience something of an emotional rollercoaster ride.

In the same way as our emotional energy can affect a building, it can also seep into those we spend time with, or conversely, we can be affected by those around us. So be careful what you say, think or do. It can have major ramifications on someone else's life.

From the day we are born and even in utero, we are being affected both mentally and physically by other people's comments, thoughts, actions, beliefs, egos and energy patterns. It can make it very difficult to love others or ourselves unconditionally, with this programming in place. Unconditional love is a facet demonstrated by the subtle spiritual realms and we as humans long to achieve a similar feeling within our emotional state.

If we consider that we are just a vibrational frequency, we can see that we are being bombarded by external forces that actually lower our frequency. It is rather like using a dimmer switch to turn down the lights in a room. The stronger those external energies are, the weaker (or darker) we become in mind, body and spirit. We are so battered and bruised that it becomes impossible to imagine or realise that we are all very special and unique. Our journey through life adds to our character which can only enhance our uniqueness further. We are all magnificent beings, beings of the (holy) light. We are the sum of all that has gone before us, our living and learning now and in the future.

There is no doubt that we are ALL very special people. Once we realise this (and have therefore gained enlightenment or liberation) we can begin to work on raising our vibrations further, restoring them and us to our rightful place. We can then use this newfound power to look at our lives anew. As we become more inwardly and outwardly aware, our frequencies will begin to change, and we will begin to live at an increasingly perfect pitch. As we start to connect with a higher energy force we will be more able to leave the earthly worries and stresses behind us and literally begin to channel the light.

Buddhists say that God is inside us all. We are all made from the 'God Spark' or perhaps the God Particle is a better way of explaining it. We are all sacred. We are our own holy or sacred site.

There is no one else like you anywhere and that makes you God-like indeed. Both the Buddha and Jesus spoke of 'the Kingdom of God' as being within. The Dalai Lama in 'The Good Heart' says,

'The Kingdom, or reign, of God translates from the Greek word 'basileia'. Its roots lie in the Jewish concept of the power of God in 'Heaven' which is not always visible on Earth. Jesus modified the idea and stressed the inner life that is required in order to 'enter the Kingdom.' The Kingdom is, therefore, both within us and among us.'

Most Buddhists don't believe in a god, but believe in the goodness of humanity. They believe that each human being is precious and important and that we all have the potential to develop into a Buddha – a perfected human being.

We are taught that we must be true to ourselves, that we should not do anything that does not resonate. We must always come from the heart and see goodness in everything around us. All hardships that we experience in life are there purely to add to the richness of self and add to our knowledge.

Chapter Seven

Crystals & Symbols

What do crystals do and how can you use them?

Crystals would appear to have the ability to cure almost anything. But we believe, that to get a crystal to work for you, it has to be connected to a power source. Think of quartz used in watches; there also has to be a battery to supply the energy in order to move the hands of the watch.

Do crystals, therefore, really work when they are just sitting on your desk, in your pocket, resting on a client's body or used at the end of a wand? Crystals are like any other object. They have an aura that can be dowsed and this can expand or collapse as you direct your thoughts towards them. It is known that they all vibrate at different frequencies, but just like dowsing, it hasn't been scientifically proven that they can heal or affect our bodies.

It's a symbiotic relationship

Let's start at the beginning: a crystal's journey to your home is rarely a happy one. More often than not they have been taken from the Earth, broken up, tumbled for hours to create a smooth surface and sometimes even dipped in acid. So, when you buy a crystal, we would recommend carrying out a healing by cupping the crystal in both hands asking that it be flooded with white light from Mother Earth and spirit and that any and all detrimental energies be taken away and dispersed into the Universe leaving the crystal in peace, balance and harmony. Then programme it using the following exercise:

Firstly, introduce yourself to the crystal, it is important that they know who you are. Ask that any old programmes that might be stored within them are cleared away and they now only work with you. If you wish for them to work on healing a particular aliment, then tell them so. However, that could be limiting what they can do for you. Better to ask that they work for your overall wellbeing.

You become the energy source that activates the healing energy within a crystal. It is your intent that lights up, or powers, the crystal, once the crystal is cleared and activated. It can become your healer and protector. It can, of course, be used in various rituals too.

Are some crystals better than others?

It really does depend on what you have programmed them to do. If you believe that a certain crystal is good for grounding, then that crystal will only be good for grounding. Try not to be too specific or limiting when programming them. It is your *intent* that is important to perfect here, not necessarily which crystal you decide to use.

You can always dowse your crystals to see if they have been programmed to perform only one task and if they have you can re-programme them as explained above, and then hold one in your hand and see what happens. Rose quartz is known for promoting self-love, for example, but is that really all it does? Try meditating with a piece in your hand and asking it what it can do for you. See what message comes back and programme it accordingly.

How to use crystals for healing the mind, body and spirit

Crystals can be used in many different ways, a small piece can be kept in your pocket or purse for protection or healing during the day or hung around the neck to ward off other people's emotional energies (if that is what you have programmed it to do). Here is another example of how you can bring the healing power of crystals into your daily life: using dowsing, find out which is the best crystal to use to energise your drinking water, for example, and how long you would need to keep it in before the healing has worked. Place the crystal in a glass of water and wait for the necessary time to pass then start to drink. See if the water tastes any different.

NB. Please don't forget to take the crystal out before drinking and double check that the crystal you choose doesn't become adversely affected by being immersed in water as one can dissolve, or like raw malachite, give off toxic gasses.

If you don't want to get your favourite crystal wet then you can use an 'Energy Teleporter' card, such as the one pictured on the next page (we would suggest that you scan it and print multiple copies off, to save spoiling the book).

Simply place a glass of water on the 'Absorbing' end of the card and a crystal on the 'Project' circle, then either wait for your intuition to tell you, or dowse for, the time it needs to energise or heal the water.

You can try this if you have run out of headache pills. Write the brand name of the tablet you usually use on a slip of paper and place it on the project circle, put a glass of water on absorb, then wait for the required time (dowse it) before drinking it. The water will hold the energy vibration of the tablets, and hopefully have the same effect as taking them.

If you have an intolerance or allergy towards this type of medicine, please do not try this.

This method can also be used for the projection and absorbing of flower remedies into the water. This negates any intolerance that you may have towards the small amount of alcoholic content in the remedies themselves. Use the above method, placing the bottle or name of the remedy on the project area and a glass of water on the absorb area, with the intent of transferring just the flower essence. Again, dowse the time needed and then sip it slowly over the next hour or so.

PROJECT

©2018 Spirit & Earth

ABSORB

Crystals can be placed on your body at specific locations to allow healing to happen. We suggest that you dowse which crystals you need to carry out a specific healing, whether on yourself, a friend, a family member or client. Each of their needs will be different and the crystals will vary. If you wish to take this aspect of healing further, then we would recommend you attend a local crystal healing course.

When it comes to placing the crystals, you can dowse where they need to go. You will find that it is not always necessary to place them directly over the chakra points or on the part of the body in distress. Experiment with the stones and see what they say. They will direct your intuition if you let them.

Adrian recounts that, during a healing, he dowsed for and then placed a small fire agate crystal on a client's third eye. During the session, he noticed that it had begun to fizz like an effervescent tablet. His first thought was to remove it, but intuition told him to leave it there. When the client came round, she said that that was one of the best healings that she had ever had. "It felt like all the rubbish and pent up emotions in my head and body were being released," she said. The crystal got a good wash with full cleansing intent after that.

You can use a crystal pendulum to take away detrimental energy patterns, by asking it to spin one way to remove the noxious energies and the other to give healing. Once it has stopped, the work is done, but don't forget to ask that whatever had been removed be dispersed appropriately into the Universe and then fill the room with light and love.

You can wear crystals around your neck or wrist and also place them as a grid in your home to help to disperse any detrimental emotions that may be found there. This can be particularly useful when building a new house, placing the crystals in the foundations as they are being laid. Again, dowsing comes into its own when laying out this form of grid, pick up a crystal or crystals and ask where the best place to put them is for protection against psychic attack, for example, or in your healing/ meditation room to promote your spiritual connection.

Crystals can also be programmed to help with psychic protection, but they should be used in conjunction with a daily exercise or mantra and not as the only source. They may not be powerful enough on their own to fully protect you.

There are many ways of keeping your crystals clear of detrimental energy, you can leave them in the light of a full moon, bury them in the garden, wash them under spring water, or leave them in sunlight. Do what feels right for you, and best for the crystals. The most powerful way that we have found is flooding them with light and love asking that all the detrimental energy attached to the crystal or crystals (you can carry out a mass healing on your crystal collection) is taken away and disposed of into the Universe leaving the crystal(s) in peace, balance and harmony.

Crystals need looking after and just like us, they respond well to love and praise.

Will crystals work all the time?

Dowse to check the crystal is the best for the job in hand; bear in mind they will have good days and bad days and be affected by humidity, the moon cycles, cold weather and so on. Perhaps they don't want to work with you on a particular day or you need to carry out a healing on yourself as you may have a number of attachments that will be very off-putting to the crystal.

How to use Crystals to link ancient sites

In the past, human intent was used to connect sacred sites. These early links can be described as human intent lines, leys or holy lines. They would be used to manipulate the energy patterns found at individual sites, transferring and enhancing them so that some became more energised during the summer months and other sites during the winter.

In recent times, much of that intent is no longer with us or has been diffused. Holy sites have been desecrated and in many cases the sacredness has gone and has been replaced with either sadness or melancholy.

At Avebury, many of the stones were either destroyed or buried by crowds spurred on by religious fervour, hoping to clear the site entirely. This started sometime in the 14th century when many of the stones were toppled into deep pits dug by local villagers, it was presumably to destroy any trace of past pagan worship and perhaps what they considered to be witchcraft. Further destruction of the circle was witnessed by noted historian William Stuckley in the early 18th century.

So many of these special places need to be re-energised or re-connected to help them return to their former glory, so they can once again do what they were designed for; to help harmonise the energies of the land and the beings that live on it.

Unless you are well-practiced or very single-minded, intent can easily become diluted, which then becomes less effective when trying to link these sites together. A more permanent solution is called for and that is where crystals come in.

We would always suggest connecting with the guardian of site or spirit of place before doing any work there. (We discuss this more in Chapter Nine) Some guardians will be happy for you to do so, others not. So please be aware and be careful. If you can't use your intuition, dowse to see if you are allowed to do any geomancy (Earth healing) or people healing whilst you are there. If not, then walk away.

Adrian feels that many of these sacred places need to be reconnected. He is keen on collecting small stones or pebbles from the sites that he visits but does, of course, always check that it is right to do so with the guardian before disturbing anything. If he is allowed to take something away, he will always leave an offering behind, whether it be a physical object, say a stone from another site, a crystal or something non-physical in the form of a healing.

When arriving at a site that needs healing, he will firstly ascertain that he is allowed to work there. If he gets confirmation that he can, he will dowse to see if it is a crystal or a stone from another sacred site that's most suitable to leave behind and where it needs to be placed. Some guardians will prefer a crystal whilst others will like a sacred stone. It is always polite to ask what is most pertinent.

Once the crystal or stone has been placed in the correct location, Adrian will dowse to see which stone or pebble he is allowed to take from the site for use at another sacred site. Doing this at each site he visits helps to restore the connection between all these wonderful ancient sacred sites. It is rather like reconnecting the neural pathways in the brain.

This method will help restore sites that have become very sad and neglected. For instance, there is an ancient standing stone in Harrogate which is much happier now that it has been reconnected to the network of holy sites in the North. It had long since been abandoned and forgotten about when Adrian found it and any sacredness that it might once have enjoyed in the past had gone.

This was illustrated by the fact that in more recent centuries, it had been adapted for use as a signpost with place names carved into it. Small stones from a holy site in Brittany have now been buried close by, as they have at the Thornborough Henges and a single standing stone near Summerbridge. This linking allows the sacred energies to travel between these sites and to rekindle the past intent patterns laid down by our ancestors.

Remember that any changes you make at a sacred site need to be agreed with either the guardian of the site or the Spirit of Place. The sanctity must be maintained at all costs as even the taking of a small pebble can have ramifications to both the site and you. Always tune in and/or dowse to see whether this reconnection is something that will benefit the site, before you do it.

Where to put the crystal at a sacred site?

Adrian prefers to hide the introduced crystal away from public gaze, usually by burying it. That way it will always remain there. Members of the public wouldn't know or understand that the crystal had been left as an offering to the guardian. They would see it sparkling in the sun, pick it up and take it away with them. If that does happen, it doesn't necessarily mean the connection you have set up or rekindled will be broken, as the intent will remain there long after the crystal has gone. In fact, at that point the network of holy sites will probably have strengthened and therefore be able to keep the link going all by itself.

NB. If you are going to carry out this type of work, please don't climb onto a dolmen or scale a standing stone; instead place the crystal in the ground or in a hollow. But please, above all be respectful of the site.

Sacred symbols and geometry enhance energy patterns

As our ancestors began to evolve, they started to use symbols as a means of communication. Cave paintings, for instance, have been discovered in many countries throughout the world. Some of them are incredibly complex and their meanings are yet to be deciphered, whilst others are very basic.

Were cave paintings done purely for decoration, or for some other purpose, such as communicating with the Gods or enhancing the Shaman's connection with a higher power? Or was it both?

In the early part of the 21st century, a new theory has been put forward regarding cave paintings, suggesting that they are actually maps of the stars, but stylised as groups of animals, thereby hiding the information from the uninitiated.

Cup and ring marks on rocks and stones are also found worldwide and again, in most circumstances, their use has not yet been interpreted. Some say, like cave paintings, they are maps of the stars or possibly mimic the surrounding countryside, but nobody has truly 'cracked their code' and the mystery remains. Perhaps they were shaped or carved to enhance the powers of a local sacred space or site.

In Ireland, the 'burial mound' of Newgrange has a beautifully and intricately carved stone at its entrance. It must have taken a stonemason many months to carve the amazing spirals. At the time of writing, neither Tim nor Adrian has had the opportunity to visit the site, but when dowsing a photograph of the stone, they can get an idea of the power behind the carvings.

If you dowse any ancient burial site you will find any number of earth energy patterns and energy vortices running through the entrance and spiralling into the side chambers. You will sometimes find that these energies have been manipulated by man's intent. They are literally channelled to run into and around the site, enhancing the special sacred feel or 'buzz'.

However, at other sites, the earth energy patterns would have occurred naturally, and our ancestors would recognise or 'feel' the power and then build an edifice (long barrow) over them to capture their energies.

Symbolism was important to our ancestors, whether it was used to pass on information, enhance the energies of a site or for personal power. Intricate medallions have been worn around the neck of shamans for centuries and the Egyptian Pharaohs were adorned with many different items of geometrically shaped jewellery too. Many symbols from different religions are now being used in Earth healing today.

We have heard people say that relating the Indian chakra system to our sacred sites here in the UK is wrong, as it is not part of our natural heritage. Frankly we say, 'if it works, use it!' But we would suggest that you check with spirit or your Higher Self to make sure it is appropriate, before you commence any healing. For instance, placing an OM symbol, a universal symbol of God, on a person or a site that needs healing can be just as powerful and effective as using the Awen symbol, associated with the Bards, Ovates and Druids here in the UK.

Experiment with symbols that you find, whether it be a Buddhist mandala, the Tree of Life, a Metatron's Cube or Antahkarana. Just dowse to see which one is the most appropriate for the healing that you wish to carry out.

Is the healing that can be achieved using a sacred symbol to do with the shape of the symbol or the intent instilled into the symbol over many years? Or is it due purely to the belief of the person using the symbol? This is something that we will be looking at later in regard to processional ways, pilgrimage and ceremony.

The Triple Spiral: A truly sacred symbol

This symbol has been used for many things over the years. It was originally called a Triskelion, or Triskel for short. It was adopted by the Breton Celts as a religious symbol and used by their National Party. This sort of ancient symbology surrounds us on a day to day basis, mostly unnoticed. For instance, it is interesting to note how, using the power of three, it is similar it is to the flag of the Isle of Man. The power of three: we are reminded of Father, Son, Holy Ghost, or past, present, future.

The Triskelion is also a very distinctive pattern that can be found by dowsing in earth energy and is a sure sign that a site has been intensively used for ceremony in the past. You will find that most, if not all, burial mounds are built around or over a triple spiral as they seem to increase the sacredness or potent energies found within the tumuli, a special and revered place. It now seems unlikely that whole bodies were placed in these long Barrows (for example at West Kennet in Wiltshire) due to the lack of space over time. Perhaps the ancients believed that, for example, thigh bones of Shamans or village elders would be sufficient to contain the necessary remnants of his or her spirit, which, with the help of the upward rotating energy spirals, allowed them to ascend to the heavens, joining their ancestors.

Near to West Kennet is The Sanctuary, where the Michael and Mary lines cross on their twisting journey across England. It is an exposed place and the energies there can feel quite uncomfortable at times. We believe that entire bodies of Shamans, were placed here to rot, the smaller bones would have been carried away by rodents and birds during this process, leaving the larger ones behind and it is those that were taken away and used in special ceremonies. The femur, or thigh bone, (the largest bone in the body) would have been then placed into a sacred site, in this case, West Kennet Long Barrow. These relics added to the energies and the mysticism of the site.

Anyone visiting a Temple or spiritual site in India, Tibet, Nepal and the far East will be very aware of Mandalas, a form of spiritual symbol used particularly by Hindus and Buddhists to represent the universe or cosmos, both on a metaphysical level as well as symbolic one. They adorn walls and ceilings as well as floors, as Adrian found out on one of his trips to India. He and his friend Subash Tamang were extremely lucky to be invited into a Buddhist Temple to watch monks construct a 'Sand Mandala'. Fine particles of coloured sand are painstakingly arranged into complex patterns and pictures over several days, before being used in a special ceremony. Once the ceremony is over, the mandala is swept up, placed into a silk bag and taken to a nearby stream or river to be returned to nature. This is symbolic of the transitory nature of our material life here on Earth.

The Tibetan 'Never Ending' knot pattern (below) is now commonly seen around the world but we would doubt that many people seeing it would actually recognise it as a sacred symbol pre-dating Christianity.

We can also create our own symbols. In fact, any pattern that has been drawn with good intent can be regarded as sacred and used in healing ceremonies and they do not have to be ancient or recognised patterns to work. As an example, there are many different types of colouring books available online and in high street stores that contain drawings for you to colour in (search for books on Mindfulness, Mandalas, Anti-Stress etc.). As you work in these books, keep a specific person in mind that you wish to send healing to and once finished write their name at the top (or place a photograph over the finished drawing). This helps to anchor your intent and we feel, this is the reason why our ancestors would have generally used symbols.

Don't be afraid to experiment.

EARTH

Chapter Eight

Elementals

It is easy to dismiss elementals because they are considered to be beings from a lower vibrational energy than the angels and archangels. We would advise, however, that it is perhaps better not to think of the vibrational scale as going up and down in layers because this can suggest a ranking of superior down to inferior. Rather, let us consider these different vibrational aspects of creation as an old-fashioned radio set where the tuner moves the indicator dial along a horizontal band to find the different wavelengths; which are all equal, just different.

In our geomancy work, archangels are called in to re-balance and clear. Elementals, however, are often encountered as being lost or trapped in houses where they can cause all sorts of problems. They then become labelled as 'detrimental' because they are causing difficulties for the home owner. However, in their own environment, most elementals are not detrimental.

Elementals are an ancient devic energy that is closely allied to the Earth and nature itself. If you ask for their help when starting practical work or an outdoor project, you can find things go a lot smoother than they otherwise might.

There have been stories of elementals helping people throughout the ages, right through to the present day. They will gladly assist us if called upon, probably more so in the garden, as that is very much their realm. Elemental activity outside in the garden is prodigious because their energies are magical; they help plant growth and ensure abundance. There is much joy and fun in the world of the elemental. Encouraging them into your garden or green space is a delight for both them and you.

Any promises made to elementals should be kept, as they have a strong sense of right and wrong. Never promise them something that you cannot deliver and make sure that any discussions you have with them (even if you can't hear their responses) are heartfelt and honest.

Dowsing can help you with this. Just imagine the rods or pendulum are the elementals that you want to speak with. Ask a question and see what happens. For instance, "Are you happy?" If the rods indicate a 'yes' response that is good. If you get a 'no' then you need to find out what their problem is. It could be an untidy garden, the lawn might want cutting, or that they are unhappy with the next-door neighbour's cat that comes into their space.

Be patient with them, remember to thank them often and be genuine in that thanks. A happy elemental will create a happy garden, which we feel is essential for balanced living.

Humanity's arrogance has largely separated us from these amazing beings. But it may not be entirely our fault. Rather, it may just be a cyclical process that plays out every few thousand years, which may depend, perhaps, on where the Earth is on its travels through the universe.

What are elementals?

In most countries throughout the world the 'little people' make their presence felt, and humanity in general has been aware of them and worked with them for thousands of years. Today, in some of the Nordic countries, the 'wee folk' are even consulted in the construction of roadways; if a Fairy Path or Troll Path is discovered, the road will be diverted or in some cases, not built at all. Such is the respect given to the little folk.

Elementals, also known as nature spirits, are very much aspects of the natural subtle energies of the physical world. Where we find any aspect of air, earth, fire or water, we will also find elementals associated with each. Like individual personalities of their element, it's almost like they were created as the detached personality aspects of consciousness of their associated element. Each element has its own elementals, namely:

Earth: Gnomes, Dwarves, Fairies and Elves.

Air: Sprites and Sylphs.

Water: Undines.

Fire: Salamanders.

There are many unseen aspects of the world around us that we can access. It just takes a little time, patience and practice. Some people are lucky or sensitive enough to automatically go into a mental state in which they can access these less obvious aspects of reality. For the rest of us, the easiest way to explore these realms of peace and harmony is by utilising the straightforward and grounded practice of dowsing.

As with all experiences, these creatures and nature beings come into our awareness through our inner experience, that is, our individual subjective perception. While they are not often evident to everyone in collective objective awareness, the results of their labours are very much in evidence all around us in the natural world. We just need to know what to look for. So, elementals sit firmly in the subjective sphere of our awareness; the area that can be accessed via dowsing, our intuition and, of course, the channels of our imagination. When we say imagination, please don't think we want to belittle these beautiful spirits or say they are purely 'made up'. Our imagination is a very powerful tool and one of the most underrated and dismissed aspects of human personality.

The more natural the location, the easier it will be to tune to in or have access to these wonderful beings, but we can, of course, tune into elementals anywhere. For instance, you can invite them into your life by inviting them into your garden, even though they will probably be there already. By setting the intention to make contact, you can start to experience their magic in the privacy of your own space.

By working with them or inviting elementals to share your life, you not only bring the enchantment of their presence to all living things around you, but also enable them to influence the way that your life flows.

The Collins Dictionary definition of 'elemental' is:

Fundamental; basic; primal - the elemental needs of man

Motivated by or symbolic of primitive and powerful natural forces or passions

Relating to earth, air, water, and fire considered as elements

Relating to atmospheric forces, especially wind, rain, and cold

Relating to, or denoting a chemical element

Historically, in ancient times, it seems likely that as man became more self-aware, the chakra system started to advance, and the four elements of earth, wind, fire and water were called upon to help develop and sustain the planet along with their spiritual elemental aspects. Ether was, perhaps, not assigned to the planet at that time and only in more recent years has it become relevant to us.

Originally, our ancestors worshipped the Earth, stars, Sun and Moon, perhaps a connection to the angelic realms wasn't pertinent to us at that time. However, now that humanity's third eye and crown chakras have developed, (with more to come we believe), our connection to the angels is paramount for the species' future spiritual progress.

We believe we are starting to see the three worlds of humanity, elementals and angels converging into one.

The Buddhists actually refer to a fifth element, ether, which to us is the spiritual element and our connection to the Creator. Everything on this planet has an aura, a surrounding electric field, which connects it to all animate and inanimate objects. This electromagnetic field vibrates at different frequencies and this, we believe, attracts or repels people and animals. Vibrating at a lower frequency can attract a different type of person to you compared to someone vibrating at a higher (spiritual) level. Because they exist at a different vibrational level they are not always seen by people but your pets will be very aware of them and actively avoid the grumpy ones. However, there are people who can tune in to this secret world and will not only see them but, in some cases, actually converse with them.

We are all connected via the Earth; we are of the Earth and therefore need to re-establish our place on the planet, to learn how to re-root ourselves and start working again with all the elements.

The term elemental was first used by Paracelsus (1493 to 1541), a Swiss physician and alchemist; someone who worked on the principle that metals were the key elements of the universe. Alchemists are commonly, and mistakenly, referred to as those trying to turn base metals into gold.

Paracelsus travelled all over Europe, mixing with many different people from many diverse cultures, gaining much eclectic knowledge from which he began to look at the body as a chemical system. He regarded it as having to be in balance, not only internally but also in balance or in harmony with its surroundings. These days, we know that most eco-systems in the natural world need to be in harmony and that if one aspect of their biodiversity is out of balance it affects all the others. Elementals are a part of the inter-dimensional biodiversity of our planet. It was Paracelsus who first started to consider the effect that changes wrought by humans might have upon them and he started by categorising the little people, as though they were a species of plant or breed of animal.

From Wikipedia:

The concept of elementals seems to have been conceived by Paracelsus in the 16th century, though he did not in fact use the term "Elemental" or a German equivalent. He regarded them not so much as spirits but as beings between creatures and spirits, generally being invisible to mankind but having physical and commonly humanoid bodies, as well as eating, sleeping, and wearing clothes like humans. Paracelsus gave common names for the Elemental types, as well as correct names, which he seems to have considered somewhat more proper, "recht namen". He also referred to them by purely German terms which are roughly equivalent to "water people," "mountain people," and so on, using all the different forms interchangeably. His fundamental classification scheme on the first page of Tractatus II of the Liber de Nymphis is based on where the Elementals live, and he gives the following names:

Of the names he used, gnomus, undina, and sylph are all thought to have appeared first in Paracelsus' works, though undina is a fairly obvious Latin derivative from the word unda meaning 'wave.'

He noted that undines were similar to humans in size, while sylphs are rougher, coarser, longer and stronger. Gnomes are short, while salamanders are long, narrow and lean.

The Elementals are said to be able to move through their own elements as human beings move through air. Gnomes, for example, can move through rocks, walls and soil. Sylphs are the closest to humans in his perception because they move through air like us, while in fire they burn, in water they drown and in earth they get stuck.

Correct Name (translated)	Alternative Name (Latin)	Element in which they live
Nymph	Undina (undine)	Water
Sylph	Sylvestris (wild man)	Air
Pygmy	Gnomus (gnome)	Earth
Salamander	Vulcanus	Fire

We believe there is something very deep within people that recognises that we have an affinity with elementals and we instinctively understand their significance for our species. Many people, however, believe them to be unpleasant and ugly beings. Although neither of us has seen elementals clearly, we just get an impression or outline of them, we gather from others who have seen them, that they are not necessarily the beautiful beings seen in picture books.

We fail to see how they can all be ugly and/or unpleasant. Perhaps people have encountered these nature spirits when they were having an off-day, and found a disgruntled elemental. But, just because we may meet one grumpy elemental, it doesn't mean we should assume they are all that way. As with humans, they will have different appearances, personalities and attitudes.

Tim spent several years co-ordinating a healing group that worked with elementals and the devic kingdom to assist endangered animals and plants in the natural world. It became very clear, through doing that work that at one time, we humans and the elementals were very much in harmony and had great respect for each other.

Gradually, humans lost their insights and connection with this ephemeral aspect of creation. We started to develop our selfish ways of exploiting the Earth and all she offered in an unforgiving way. It seems it may be difficult for the folks of the elemental kingdom to accept that we aren't all like that all the time. There is hope for change, as more and more people come to recognise the power of working with these beings to create wellness for the natural world once again.

An example of this occurred when Adrian carried out a house healing and clearing on Tim's property in the Forest of Dean, soon after they first met. As any of you who have read Adrian's book, *Heal Your Home,* will know, a house healing involves clearing out detrimental energies and that includes grumpy, misplaced and frequently lost elementals.

Tim explains: "Adrian didn't tell me what he had found during the initial healing, but a few weeks later when I was going to the outhouse in order to carry out a mundane chore, I felt a strange presence.

"It wasn't an energy pattern that I immediately recognised and I asked of this presence what it was and what the problem was. In my mind's eye, I saw a very short, frustrated little person step forward and exclaim that he had been ousted from the house and decided to take up residence in the outhouse instead. He was none too pleased about it either. This was a gnome whom I later learned liked to be called Benjamin.

"I apologised to the little fella and explained to him that he had obviously been caught in Adrian's healing net as he must, at that time, have been identified as being detrimental to us and the dogs, perhaps because he was in such a foul mood.

"From what I remember, after a short exchange about who was living here first and the rights and wrongs of moving him outside, we decided that he could take up residence in the house again by living within a moderately sized lump of stone that he had originally arrived in as we now kept that stone inside the house."

Tim continues. "That cheered him up no end and for years we lived side by side mutually ignoring each other but each aware of the neighbourly presence. When we decided to move to North Yorkshire, the stone and Benjamin came with us and since then, Benjamin has become an integral part of the healing team that goes into action when working on a client's house. He now works with a young dragon and helps to clear up the energies after the archangels have done their bit in re-balancing the spaces."

Such is life with an elemental. Benjamin is a very happy gnome these days. Gnomes are just one of the nature elementals and there are many and varied beings assigned to each elemental category, as the following list illustrates:

Spirits of the earth:

Gnome: a small, humanoid creature that lives underground.

Dwarf: a being that dwells in mountains and the earth, associated with wisdom, mining, and crafting.

Pixie: slim, fay-like humanoid, light-weight with a flitting, dancing movement, believed to inhabit ancient underground ancestral sites such as stone circles, barrows, dolmens, ringforts or menhirs. Often considered mischievous in folklore. In Ireland, they are called leprechauns.

Troll: massive, stompy, they can be miserable beings, often accompanied by a large club, dwell in isolated rocks, mountains, or caves, usually considered dangerous to human beings.

Elf: similar to pixie and fairy, a being with magical powers and supernatural beauty, ambivalent towards people.

Fairy: generally described as a winged humanoid with seemingly magical powers. Can be aggravated by human interaction, often prefers company of children to adults.

Imp: often shown as small, sometimes misshapen and not very attractive creatures; pranksters and mischievous.

Goblin: usually small, from a few inches high to the size of a dwarf. They have magical abilities and usually are greedy, especially for gold and jewellery.

Spirits of the wind:

Sylph: invisible beings of the air.

Will o' the Wisp: Jack o' lantern etc., atmospheric ghost lights often over swamps or peat bogs, thought to be gas igniting.

Fairy: Associated with the wind as well as the earth.

Spirit of the fire:

Salamander: a fantastic, sometimes magical, beast having an affinity with fire. They are thought to live or dwell within volcanoes, feeding off the toxic smoke and chemicals, possibly the cause of new eruptions.

Spirits of the water:

Undine: invariably depicted as being female and usually very beautiful. Found in forest pools and waterfalls. Sometimes shown with tails, hence in this respect similar to merpeople.

Sprite: these beings are said to be able to breathe water or air and sometimes fly, when they can be perceived as being similar to sylphs.

What do they do?

Each branch of the elemental kingdom is distinctive from the others. They all tend to have separate roles, but come together as one force to work with and for Mother Nature. They are tireless in their work, defend their territory resolutely and help to keep the world going.

The list below is by no means exhaustive, but it provides you with a general idea of what each of the five elements is responsible for. Some people reading this will view these beings as purely energetic patterns and others as ethereal creatures, i.e. not taking solid form. We also know people that regularly see them clearly, especially the earth elementals. Many people will just have an awareness of 'something' close by, maybe when working in their gardens or perhaps visiting a sacred site.

Spirits of the earth:

These delightful creatures tend the flora and fauna; they are there to encourage plant growth, to help the birds and insects and to safeguard our gardens, land, trees and more. They are also linked to physical manifestation; they can help turn your thoughts into reality. These 'little people', as they have become known, come in many different shapes and sizes. Some are not so small. Trolls tend to be large and quite fearsome looking.

Spirits of the wind:

Anyone that has stood on top of a mountain could be familiar with sylphs and this family of creatures. There is, of course, the joy of reaching the summit, but hearing their squeals of delight as you do is just breath-taking. Their voices, the noise of the wind whistling, can be hypnotic and sometimes a little disturbing. If you sit and listen, you can sometimes hear them calling you. They control the world's weather patterns and this in turn helps to transmit messages around the globe. They are ultimately responsible for the quality of space too. These delicate wispy creatures can, if called upon, rearrange the weather for you, if you need a sunny day, but only for a special purpose.

Spirits of the fire:

This part of the elemental family are extremely powerful beings for they are responsible for creating fire, arguably the greatest asset to mankind. It keeps us warm, allows us to cook food, wards off dangerous animals and so on. These elementals control volcanoes which link to the tectonic plates of the planet, the building blocks of our world. Fire elementals are also associated with transformation, just like the Phoenix rising from the ashes, changing the face of the planet at a whim. They can also bring changes into your life but beware when you contact them as you will literally be playing with fire.

Spirits of the water:

Rather like the fire elementals, this side of the family is to be considered extremely potent. The power of water is constantly in the news. Flooding is devastating to millions of people every year, worldwide. It brings life with the monsoons irrigating otherwise arid land, but with the rains can also come misery and tragedy. The water elementals combine with the energy of the moon to create the tides and waves and this in turn helps to oxygenate the oceans water. Water is needed to sustain life on Earth, as it is vital to our health and wellbeing. The water elementals control the rain, give us the early morning dew on grass and snow which in turn solidifies giving us the climate controlling polar ice caps.

Spirits of the ether:

If we consider how long the Earth has been in existence, then we believe these elementals have only comparatively recently been assigned to our planet. They are helping with our spiritual connection, lifting the veil between worlds to allow us glimpses of a life beyond ours. Their life-promoting and thought-provoking powers help them move freely between the different realms. They are bringing new energy patterns to our world, giving us greater insights into the meaning of life. Sensitive people are becoming more sensitive, vibrations are being raised, allowing greater inventiveness and understanding. There is more to come, the 21st century is the time of the ether elementals.

Although we can list typical visual characteristics of all these elemental energy beings, each person's awareness of them will be slightly different and of course completely unique. This is one of the differences of this subjective awareness compared to the everyday normal objective information of the physical realm. Ether elementals seem to be even more faint and elusive, sometimes being detectable as wispy and vague smoke-like forms.

It would be very beneficial to us individually, and collectively, to become more aware of the influence that elementals have on our lives and become more observant of them, as their signs are everywhere. During a visit to Brimham Rocks for a *Nature Spirits* workshop, the weather was inclement. It had been a cold and windy morning, the outlook didn't look like the weather would improve and so we set off all wearing our warm coats. Then as we were conducting a ceremony at one of the rock formations, the sun suddenly appeared. The transformation was sudden and dramatic, the rain stopped, leaving drops sparkling like Christmas tree lights on the heather. The sky was an amazing deep blue. The sun only appeared for the length of the ceremony, but it was a heart and body-warming 'thank you' from above, made possible via the elementals. Once the ceremony was over, it disappeared as quickly as it had arrived and the rain returned.

What do elementals want from us?

Though elementals don't technically need anything from us, they do appreciate our interaction, our connection, and our help in taking care of the natural world around us. It is important for us to keep our connection with Mother Earth, both physically and mentally, near the top of our priority list. By doing so, we join all the other beings, including elementals, who are helping to keep the planet, the flora and fauna in good working order.

For thousands of years humanity mainly lived in harmony with nature. We most likely would have had close links with all these wonderful beings, but as the Industrial Revolution came about, bringing with it machines for ploughing, sowing, reaping and harvesting, we have moved away from this symbiotic relationship with everything in the natural world around us. This is of course a generalisation as there are many people who spend a great deal of their individual time connecting very deeply to the Natural world and there are a great many more actively fighting for its survival.

Despite the growth of the New Age movement, our being connected to the Earth is still low on a list of most people's daily priorities. Technology has become many people's main concern and is a double-edged sword as it both connects them to people all around the world, but at the same time disconnects them from their immediate surroundings, the here and now. This digital age has taken many of us further away from our natural connection with the planet and the elementals. Many of us spend hours each day sitting in front of a computer instead of being in the garden. Mobile phones mean that we are contactable at any time of the day or night. Being this preoccupied with technology means that we are in danger of missing out on the natural beauty that surrounds us. Working with the elementals helps to raise the vibration of our gardens, holy sites and/or sacred spaces.

The following exercise should help you to connect with the elementals. Don't forget that forging this connection takes patience, practice and a certain amount of belief:

Sit in your garden, in the countryside or in a nearby park. Be quiet and still, slow your breathing and gradually become aware of what is happening around you. There may be a sudden gust of wind. The sun might appear from behind a cloud for an instant. You may become aware of rustling noises nearby or an odd noise in the distance. These can all be messages or affirmations that you are at one or connecting with your surroundings. Signs will come in many different guises. Accept them all and listen for any messages or thoughts or ideas that arise. When you feel you want to finish, pause a moment longer, then simply thank the elementals for connecting with you and move away.

When doing any work outside, you can ask the elementals for help, whether you're planting, weeding, pruning or just mowing the lawn. The more respectful you are, the more help you will receive. Before working in the garden, it is a good idea to inform the elementals what you are about to do. Don't just charge in and start pruning or cutting down trees, ask for their blessing to begin, so that they are prepared for what is about to happen.

Simply acknowledging that elementals exist, helps to strengthen their presence and energy levels. It seems to encourage them and gives more purpose to their existence. Placing fairy doors on trees and walls of houses and putting plastic gnomes and wells in your gardens are all ways to acknowledge that the little folk exist. No matter how trite or insignificant these acknowledgments seem, it all helps the elemental kingdom. Perhaps by stirring public imagination we will begin to see a return to some of the old ways. We believe that talking to nature spirits should be as natural as talking to a neighbour.

Elementals and animals

Adrian and his partner Allyson have a pet called Annie, a nine-year-old Springer Spaniel. Although Allyson's mother Janita is her registered owner, Annie has two homes, one in Worcestershire and the other with Adrian in The Yorkshire Dales. In Adrian and Allyson's garden is a sheltered location beneath a fir tree and several large bushes, a quiet dark place with a secretive feel to it. Adrian and Allyson know that this is a no-go zone for humans. It is clearly a meeting place of the elementals and therefore sacrosanct. The only thing that they have done, after checking to see if it was allowed, was to put a fairy door in place as an acknowledgment of the elemental presence.

Annie, unfortunately, takes no notice of this. Even though she has been warned by Adrian many times, she seems to make a beeline for the elementals' home. When this happens, Adrian sees a mental picture of miniature tables, chairs, cups and saucers flying in all directions, total chaos, as this giant hellhound charges through the elementals' previously private hidey-hole.

The elementals do fight back though. They sit and wait in the bushes for Annie to appear and when she does they attach themselves to her auric field from where they exact their retribution. She comes back into the house, looking very down in the mouth, takes to her bed and lies there shivering, often taking very furtive glances around the room as more elementals mass for their next wave of attack.

"I do get a little fed up of having to clear Annie of these disgruntled elementals," says Adrian, "Though I rather empathise with them as I would feel very much the same way!"

Once she has been cleared by Adrian and the little folk have been gently relocated back to their camp, Annie returns to normal... until the next time!

The elemental connection

Adrian says, "I had spent twenty-something years owning and running a busy estate agency practice in South-West Surrey. At the time, I would have described myself as sceptical but open-minded. I had been working with the renowned palmist, John Benedict, for several years and was beginning to look closely at spirituality and all its implications. I had come across the term 'elementals' several times over the years but, like Tim, I did not have a great understanding of who they were and what they did until I was introduced to magic mushrooms."

N.B. This was a one-off and never again repeated experience, please do not think that Tim or Adrian advocate taking any form of hallucinogenic drugs: they categorically do not.

"This experience took place in a cottage in a remote glen in Scotland and was one of the most profound experiences of my life at that time.

After imbibing the mushroom tea, which tasted awful, I sat and waited to see what would happen. At first, I was aware of a growing warmth all over my body, then of feeling a little spacy. The effects gradually increased, raising my awareness of previously unseen objects and creatures all around me," explains Adrian.

"A picture in the room came alive, the trees seemed to grow out of the frame and into the room, vines wrapped around my feet as I became an integral part of the expanding scene. As I started to re-focus my attention, the room cleared. Then, as I began to relax and look out of the window, I saw thousands of elementals walking, jumping, climbing and working on the steep hill opposite the cottage. The whole of the countryside was alive with these busy creatures. The colours were so vivid, I had never seen a sky so blue or grass so green. It was magical, a kaleidoscope of colours so mixed that I felt I was part of a Disney cartoon.

"I had never felt so connected before. As I went outside, elementals played at my feet. Some jumped up onto my lap as I sat down. I admit to feeling a little like Gulliver at first until I was put at my ease by the beauty and serenity of my surroundings. I sat there spellbound by what was happening all around me. Never in my life had I felt so connected to nature, a part of the whole and at one with the elementals.

"Since that day, I have rarely seen the solid forms of elementals, but now have a distinct awareness of them around me. I often glance at a tree and see a hazy or shadowy outline of the spirit there. I talk with them and will always ask their permission before doing any work in the garden or at sacred sites.

"Elementals can pop up when least expected. Recently I was throwing a ball for Annie on the playing fields in Kirkby Malzeard, a small pretty village near Masham, when Annie became a little fretful and kept glancing to her right as she ran back towards me with the ball in her mouth. I suddenly became aware of a large figure looming in my peripheral vision. I turned to look and there was a troll, about 15ft in height, standing watching us. I am not sure who was more surprised, him for being spotted or me for actually seeing him.

"I introduced myself and asked him his name, he replied that it was Norse and he was guardian of the playing field. He was about 30 years old, as far as he could make out, and his job was to safeguard the people and animals that used the field. He admitted that he didn't like dog owners who didn't clean up after their animals had left a mess or people who littered. Apart from that, he seemed very happy and we parted company leaving him to enjoy the sunshine."

Both authors agree there are many other ways of tuning in to the natural world without taking magic mushrooms. But the point of this story is to illustrate how abundant elementals can be in our direct environment. Meditation, mindfulness and gentle observation will also, with practice, enable us to be receptive enough to subtle energies to start to experience similar impressions through a gentle shift of awareness within.

At the point in his life that Adrian took the mushrooms he felt he needed an experience of total immersion in nature, to be completely enveloped by the elementals, so that he could fully appreciate who and what they are.

Praising elementals

Sending your approval or thanks to the elementals not only revitalises them, but also gives them the verification and affirmation that we not only care about our planet, but also the nature spirits themselves that help to keep it going. We all like praise, we all like to be told that we have worked hard and that we have made a difference. Praise a child and watch them grow taller with pride. Nature spirits enjoy praise in exactly the same way.

There's nothing that demonstrates this fondness for praise more than asking one or more nature spirits to dedicate themselves to the wellbeing of a particular plant or tree. When you do, just sit back and watch as it grows quickly into a beautiful thriving healthy shrub but remember to thank the elementals for being so wonderful in helping that plant so well.

The elementals will help you too, if you ask. During your working day, it is good to have the four elements around you. Open a window to let the sylphs in to play. A watered plant takes care of the earth and water aspects. For the Salamander, the fire elemental, just light a candle. Notice what a difference it makes to your day. Give them your thanks and praise but make sure, when leaving your working environment at the end of the day, that you have blown out the candle, and that the elementals have all left the building. Otherwise who knows what mischief they might get up to at night?

Why are elementals significant to us and Mother Earth?

Everything is connected. We cannot adjust or affect one thing without it having a knock-on effect on others. When we interact with elementals, though we are seeking their help, our attention towards them adds to their energy. Therefore, any interaction we have with them has benefits for both sides.

The natural world is built on finely tuned mathematics. 'Chaos Theory' is just one example found in nature. Its significance grew in importance as computers became more powerful. The bigger processors and larger memory could process the masses of numbers and fractals needed to reveal what lay at the heart of all natural processes.

Other areas of science such as the study of statistics, has produced formulas that show how the rise and fall of different species can be predicted. These numbers illustrate how growth and collapse in animal populations are numerically dependent, just as so many other processes are throughout the natural world.

The mathematics has also been able to highlight how, as a species of animal declines, it will reach a critical point at which there will either be a sudden expansion of numbers or the population will be annihilated and disappear. This is known as the 'Hydra Effect', named after the Greek myth about the many headed snake monster. As one head of the monstrous snake-like creature was chopped off, two would grow again in its place.

The Hydra Effect is the difference between a reduction in numbers of a species either leading to a massive and rapid repopulation, or if the reduction has gone slightly too far, to its complete collapse and total extinction.

The difference in determining the fate of animals at the critical point between the two scenarios is minute. Unfortunately, at the current time in human history, many species are facing sudden extinction due to humanity's interference. We have upset the delicate equilibrium just at the wrong time. The natural world is now desperately out of balance.

Rediscovering a connection with the elementals is, therefore vitally important, to regain the trust of the devas and enlist them to help all endangered species. It is critical that we begin to do this as soon as possible. In order to do this, ironically, it helps if we remember our origins as spiritual beings. We were incarnate on the Earth in human form for a reason, but a part of being human is also our spiritual potential. We never lose our spiritual connection to the other dimensions, to all that is and to that 'place' we came from and go back to when we 'die'.

Therefore, if we consider the world and our environment from a spiritual point of view by looking at ourselves as spirit beings and not, as we commonly do, as just human physical beings, then we can, once again, be part an integral part of nature in all its facets, as that includes the elemental and other spiritual dimensions. The spiritual dimensions create this physical one and so being able to integrate with both dimensions, a foot in *both* camps as it were, we can achieve a connection with other spiritual beings and with the physical world around us too.

The world is in the unfortunate state we currently perceive it to be partly because (at the time of writing) the 7.5 billion souls on this planet unintentionally contribute energy to keeping it like this, through their distribution of inappropriate thought and emotional energy. We have been given the chance to live this experience, at this time in this physical environment, for a reason. The big question is why? It seems likely that discovering compassion and a state of living that is as close to unconditional love as we can get, is a part of the answer to that question.

Striving for and then realising how unconditional love positively affects other beings (people, animals, plants, places, spiritual beings i.e. the entire conscious environment of our reality) would mean when we reach the end of our life here on the Earth, we will do so with a much greater understanding of how we can help, when in the higher realms, in an altruistic manner. Such altruism is based on love and enables the growth of the universe on all levels.

Connecting with elementals

To connect with elementals, first, you need to set your intention. Second, you need to be in a receptive mood, ideally in a calm, grateful and respectful state of mind. Then it is up to you to interpret the interaction in whatever way makes sense to you and the change in feeling, or visual input, should tell you whether you are making an elemental connection or not. Those impressions should be similar to the ones you had when you first started to receive psychic feelings, when you began to explore your spirituality. The chances are that you will either sense their presence, feel a change in energy or hear them speak.

If, at any time, you start to feel uncomfortable or hear something that you are not happy with, simply stop what you are doing. The most important thing is not to encourage the feeling, but don't be scared of it either.

As far as we know, elementals will never suggest or say things that are nasty or unpleasant. They may be a little mischievous, but certainly not in a harmful way. If you feel unhappy, simply tell whatever it might be to go away, and ask the archangels for assistance or close yourself down. When we include elementals in our lives they will assist us, sometimes in ways that are perhaps not expected.

The Church traditionally used to regard elementals as being detrimental to us. However, there have been many stories passed down through history about the little folk helping individuals with their chores and/ or their animals. This includes the well-known story about the tailor who comes down in the morning and, upon entering his workshop, discovers a special suit made for him overnight by the fairies, as a thank you. We both feel that these 'fairy' or 'folk' stories have their origins in 'real life' and believe that elementals are on our side. Should you ask for their help with a project then the work should start to flow much easier.

All those 'little DIY jobs' that start well, like putting up shelves, can suddenly turn into major projects, with everything going wrong. The simple answer is to stop and ask for the help and assistance of an elemental. An industrious and hardworking gnome or dwarf will then be on hand to ensure the job goes as smoothly as it can. This may sound bizarre, but try it and see what happens.

Tim will normally ask for elemental assistance, especially when tackling odd jobs around the house, but like all of us, he does forget at times, only remembering when things start to go horribly wrong.

There was, undoubtedly, a time when humans worked with and lived with elementals. It would have been commonplace, a natural and expected part of our life. Here in the North of England, in the days before machinery took hold, as miners went underground they would sometimes leave an offering to the elementals, normally in the earth, as a way of saying thank you and ensuring a safe return to the surface.

Equilibrium was maintained in the ancient days of humanity, as people only took what they needed from the land and repaid their debt to the elementals with small gifts or offerings. As with so many things, there was a balance.

Death

When Tim was a child he would often wonder what it was like to be dead. As he explains, "I would spend hours thinking about death, trying to work out what it meant and how it would feel to die. These thoughts came predominantly from my church upbringing, from seeing images of Jesus hanging on the cross week in and week out."

In the early stages of writing this book, Tim asked spirit the question, "What is it like to be dead?" He received the following simple and logical answer:

"You will never know."

What did they mean by that? We believe it means that we are living, breathing souls experiencing a physical life, right now. When our brain and body stops functioning, we cease to exist in this physical world and are pronounced dead.

But as spiritual people we must believe in life after leaving this physical realm. We accept that we continue to be alive in some form. Words like 'dead', 'deceased' and 'death' are all inappropriate, as they do not describe the circumstances of what we become in the next life.

But what if we are wrong? What if this life really is all there is? What if our existence and experiences down here on the Earth are all there actually is and, when our bodies stop functioning, we really do die, and we cease to exist? If that is the case, we won't know, will we? Because to be dead in those circumstances means no awareness whatsoever.

So, 'dead' means dead: lifeless, not alive, no consciousness, no further observation of the moment, nothing. No awareness equals no pain, no worries, no stress, no trauma. All the bad stuff just goes away as we close our eyes for the final time. Perhaps that thought should comfort us?

But, to reiterate our earlier statement, all spiritual thinkers have a belief that something does actually exist beyond the veil of death. 'Death' being a state that means we cease to take such an active part in the physical world. This, of course, is what spirituality is all about.

If you try to keep hold of that perspective and start to look at the world from the viewpoint of us all being collectively spirit, then you will begin to see that the global chaos you feel so close to you is nothing more than a background, an illusion, created by us as a situation and backdrop in which we play out our lives. All of our individual lives are being played out with negative themes of stress, fear, anxiety, loss etc being echoed on a global scale. All thoughts of worry, strife, turmoil and confusion that we experience in our daily personal lives are magnified a thousand million times and played out by the population, across the world. There are of course also positive themes like love and joy being played out too, but it is the negative ones we are so often fixated upon and which lead to a negative view of the world.

We don't know if these same themes are played out in the wider cosmos, but the picture increasingly given by those who channel information from their spirit guides, is that the universe is a changing place. It certainly isn't a quiet, calm procession through space, but rather a volatile and chaotic place in which worlds bounce off each other like billiard balls. Galaxies exert extreme gravitational forces on other galaxies pulling them apart, akin to the images of hell created by the old masters in their visionary paintings. It is a place of chaos, just like our lives often seem to be too.

Elemental chaos

So how does that chaos apply to our view of elementals and nature?

It means that we can consider elementals as an aspect of our inner worlds. They are aspects of consciousness that appear separate from us who we can either work with and nurture or continue to neglect. The power to nourish and create connections with elementals is up to us and there is no doubting the joint relationship between us, them and Mother Nature. We cannot perceive them as being separate from us and the universe as they are our subjective personality-based connection with nature.

Elementals are the Universe's way of reflecting what is inside us, something that can be used to protect and cherish our outer world in a very direct and meaningful way. The energy that elementals comprise, whatever aspect of the creative force they spring from, has character and personality just like us.

We are perhaps here to help the Universe understand and recognise its origins. The elementals play a similar role for us; they are here to show us that we are an integral part of nature.

We probably antagonise the Universe with our repeated mistakes, but it exhibits ultimate compassion in continuing to love us all, unconditionally. Elementals can have a similar effect on us – sometimes they can be irritable, bad tempered and downright stubborn, but, as a species we love them and need them.

We *are* an integral part of nature and, therefore, have a duty of care to help to restore the balance that has been lost over the years. Just as the elementals care for us, we must, in turn, care for them, to respect the world they and we live in. We cannot go on thinking that, just because we are human beings, nature is entirely separate from us - it isn't.

Is our connection to elementals greater at sacred sites?

The Earth is sacred and therefore everyone, everything and every location in our world must be considered to be the same.

But, if we use the term, *sacred* in the more traditional manner, to describe the constructions and places that were created for the purpose of veneration, like stone circles, henges etc., then we would say that our connection to elementals will indeed, be very much stronger at sacred sites.

The veil between the dimensions of reality is at its thinnest at sacred sites. These are places where we are more likely to experience spiritual visions or have a spiritual encounter through one of our five earthly senses, leading into our sixth sense. This is partly because of our physiological reaction to the focused and concentrated energies at these holy places. We must remember that elementals are keen to connect with us, as they enjoy our company. They do feel that humans are very naïve and susceptible to their childish pranks, such as hiding the lens cap of your camera or untying your shoelace.

When we visit sacred sites, it is often easier for us to connect with these beings. Perhaps it is because we are in a more receptive state of mind, ready for and expecting new revelations. It is likely that our brainwaves move closer to that significant meditative frequency pattern, increasing the chance of experiencing a connection with these wonderful beings.

From the elementals' point of view, they see us as being more receptive to them at these sites also.

We can assume that all elementals will wish to make contact with us, but when we make contact we should remain passive, unobtrusive and respectful whilst in their territory. If you do identify them, but they don't seem happy to interact, it is probably a good idea to walk away and leave them in peace. Most importantly, when visiting a sacred site, you must set your intent that you really want to communicate with them.

We have looked at the power of intention before and once again it is not *what* you do that is most important, but the way that you do it. You need to ask the question, 'What is my purpose and intention for wanting to do this?' or 'Why do I want to communicate with elementals?' Curiosity is fine, no one (except you) is sitting in judgement on this. Just being curious works. After all, if we weren't curious, we wouldn't want to connect with them and learn how they can help us.

Tree spirits

Most trees have a spirit or guardian. In their younger years this is not always the case, so when planting a sapling, it is always a good idea to invoke the help of a misplaced tree spirit, as this will help to ensure its safety and future good growth. As trees mature, elemental spirits will attach themselves. They tend to be tree specific, so for example, an oak tree will have an oak tree spirit linked to it. These entities are recognised in countries across the globe and worshipped in many different ways.

Offerings are often left, at various times of the year, to both the tree and the attached spirit. It is said that the Bodhi tree at Bodh Gaya where Gautama Buddha attained enlightenment, is constantly moving, its leaves rustling continuously even when there is no wind blowing. Sceptics say that it is due to the structure of the leaves. However, believers attribute the movement to the resident deva and this is written about in the Bhagavad Gita, *'O Ashvattha, I honour you whose leaves are always moving'.*

Tree spirits and their tree hosts should be viewed as helping the connection between Heaven and the Earth, being anchored to the ground via their root system then rising majestically into the sky touching the gods/spirit.

Tree Healing

The healing attributes of trees are well known to many. Even just sitting under a tree's branches can bring relief from the stresses and strains of daily life. Before approaching a tree of any size, it is always best to ask their permission before you get too close. We suggest that you either dowse or, if clairaudient, ask the question and wait for the answer. Most trees will be happy to connect with you, but a request is always gratefully received. Once there, ask which is the best side to sit to receive the healing you require from both the tree and its attached spirit.

Tree hugging is also a lovely thing to do. It is great to feel the tree's vibration and vitality, but please make sure the tree wants to be hugged. They have a personality and feelings too. How would you feel if a complete stranger walked up to you and threw their arms around you? Treat the tree in the same way you would like to be treated. With respect and courtesy.

When you are with a tree and working with it for healing, be calm, relaxed and grounded (take your shoes and socks off), acknowledge the flora and fauna around you, introduce yourself to the tree and its guardian and then sit quietly in their presence.

Become aware of the changing sounds around you, expand your aura to encompass the tree's aura and begin to feel at one with your surroundings. As you merge and be as one with the tree, you will find that the tree spirit will communicate with you. This can take time. Patience is needed here as well as the correct intent and a good heart to help the connection process.

Once you have connected with the tree and its spirit you can ask questions such as:

1.　Is the tree happy? (If not find out why and how you can help them)

2.　Can you send healing to the tree? (Do you need to be in situ? Does it need to be at a certain time: hour, day, week etc.)

3.　Does the tree have a guardian spirit? (If not, can you help to find one?)

4.　If it is in your garden, does the tree need pruning?

5.　Does the tree need protecting?

6.　Does the ground around the tree need healing? (e.g. earth energy lines, energy spiral, water etc.)

7.　Does the tree need to be grounded?

8.　Does the tree and its spirit need to be connected to other trees?

How to see tree spirits

Tree spirits are probably the easiest of the elementals to see. Although they are a part of the natural world, they do differ from the other elementals as they only tend to inhabit trees rather than shrubs or bushes. The larger the tree, the more chance you have of seeing its spirit.

Stand a little way back from the tree and look up to the top of its trunk. Ignore the leafy canopy. Slowly let your gaze drop down the trunk of the tree until your eyes naturally want to stop. Consciously you may not be aware of anything, but your subconscious will have noticed something. Soften your eyes and continue to look. You might glimpse the outline of a figure or perhaps see a hazy outline or shadow of the tree guardian.

If you see nothing at first, persist. Be in a relaxed state, take a deep breath and look again. The softening of your vision can take time to perfect but when you do, the world will take on a totally different appearance.

How to help release elementals from vows or traps

During remote healing work on houses, gardens, lands and businesses, both Tim and Adrian have come across elemental beings that have been trapped or are unhappy for many different reasons. They may have wandered into a home by accident and then become bewildered, angry and scared. Sometimes they have been forced into a situation not of their own making and they want out. They may also have been trapped by other elemental spirits, shamans, magicians and/or witches that placed them in jeopardy.

By dowsing, you can find out if the elementals need help or if they need to be rescued from their plight. You will probably know instinctively if it is safe for you to do so. Sometimes it is better to do this remotely but, if you are fully protected psychically, it should be safe to carry out a rescue or help to release them while you are in the same space as them.

Should you find an elemental or elementals that need your help, we suggest the following exercise to help them:

Grounding yourself to Mother Earth.

Visualise roots growing from the soles of your feet, going through the Earth down to the centre of the planet, where you will find a 24-carat bar of gold with your name and date of birth inscribed upon it. See the roots wrap around it keeping you fully anchored to the ground.

Feel the healing energy of Mother Earth enter via your feet, move up your legs and continue through your base and sacral chakras, coming to rest within your solar plexus.

Tim normally visualises a huge crystal belonging to Archangel Raphael at the centre of the Earth and he prefers to connect with that, but the choice is entirely yours about which image you use to ground yourself.

Once fully grounded, bring your focus back to your body.

The next step is to complete the link between the Earth and Heaven with you at the centre as the bridge.

To achieve this, you send a beam of white light from the top of your head, via the crown chakra, high into the sky, connecting you to the Universe, the higher realms. Feel the healing energy coming back, entering your crown, third eye, throat and heart chakras, then connecting to the earth energy held within your solar plexus. They merge together at cellular level and then expand, a beautiful white light moving through your body to the outer edge of your aura where it remains as a protective bubble.

Should you wish to take this protection and healing two steps further, you can connect with the Sun via the front and back of your solar plexus chakra and the Moon through your skin. Bring them both into the central point merging with the Earth and higher realm healing light, then expand them through your body and aura as outlined above.

This has done two things. It has cleansed your body, chakras and aura of any undesirables. It has also helped to protect you whilst you carry out any healing work.

What you do next depends on how you encountered or became aware of the troubled elemental. You can either send out a beam of white light to find them (that white light is your consciousness), from which they will perceive you as being utterly safe for them to connect and communicate with. Or, if you have already made contact with them, begin to visualise their plight or start to think about how you might carry out the necessary healing on them. Dowsing can help with this.

Alternatively, you can call on your spirit guides to help you. You could connect with the guardian of the site or, if needs be, go higher with your request and let one of the archangels carry out the work whilst you sit back and watch.

If you carry on with this rescue work, you will, one day, become aware that, instead of having to concentrate and focus your intention to rescue a trapped creature, the healing will 'just happen'. You will become an external witness, an observer of the true realms, the ones beyond your five senses. This is magic. And it will occur when you have truly connected and mixed with the world of the elementals.

In the early days though, you might find it easier to connect with these unseen realms through dowsing. Dowsing, as you have hopefully realised, is a grounded, physical way of working with, or tapping into, the spiritual world. You begin with baby steps and gradually work your way to full-blown psychic abilities. This can take many years to achieve, but don't be put off. The 21st century energies are helping us to connect with the divine much quicker and easier than in the past.

Here are some questions that you could ask to ascertain why these elementals might be in trouble. They are your starter questions, you may need to expand on them as the answers come through:

Why are they trapped?

Did they become disorientated?

Were they scared or fearful of other elementals, people, animals, etc.?

Did they need shelter or seek comfort?

Are they being punished by someone because of their behaviour, e.g. mischief at work?

Was it bad human interaction?

Had they neglected their duty?

It doesn't matter how we connect with these other realms. Some people will have stronger pictorial representations than others. Some will just have an awareness or a feeling and there are others who 'just know things'. When working with spirit, it is recommended that you search for and nurture the awareness of feeling things, but with elementals you may find your awareness of them is different and as you are not likely to be so intimately involved with them as spirit that is OK.

The difference? When we converse with elementals we are not trying to elicit information from them (but you can if you wish) or to conduct a heavyweight conversation. We are simply trying to connect in a loving and accepting way, to achieve a harmonious balance for all parties concerned.

"Don't be concerned about HOW you do it, just work on your connection with the elementals in whichever way you wish," says Tim.

He explains, "I'm a very visually orientated person and most of my sensory input comes through as visual information. This came in very handy when making video programmes and documentaries. In my mind's eye, I would see the shots that were required and, when writing scripts, I could visualise the actual film's scenes, shot for shot, playing out in my head.

"All those years of writing professionally has helped to improve my visual perception," he continues. "When in the right frame of mind, I see a lot of the 'unseen realms' with my inner eye. The interaction with these unseen realms, for me, is a mixture of seeing the images in my head accompanied by a feeling that helps to reinforce this inner vision. This creates a sensation as though it was an 'outer' real-world image. I can illustrate better what I mean by recounting an experience I had some time ago. This may help you when you are working with elementals.

"About a year after we moved to North Yorkshire, I went with some highly spiritually attuned friends to a part of the Dales known as Yockenthwaite. It is a lovely timeless area, untouched by mankind's intrusions for hundreds of years. Of course, nowhere in the Yorkshire Dales is truly untouched, but parts of it are less travelled than others, Yockenthwaite being such a place. It's a beautiful area of rolling high hills crossed with dry stone walls and isolated barns standing weather worn against the sky.

"We set off on a short walk along the riverbank in the delicate Yorkshire sunshine, crossing over a Victorian stone bridge that seemed to echo the clattering hooves of horses pulling carts in days gone by. We passed an old farmhouse accompanied by the barking of a tethered sheepdog, ambled by a disused limekiln and continued up the valley until we found our destination. We found ourselves beside a rather modest stone circle, perhaps fifteen feet across, laid out on a flat area of grass just a matter of yards from the river's edge.

"As is customary when visiting sacred sites with a group, there was a period of exclamations and pronouncements on how each of us initially felt before we went into our individual inner worlds to experience the atmosphere more deeply.

"I asked the guardian of the site to allow me to tune in and was happily granted permission. I sat outside the circle, level with its centre about ten feet away, and slipped into a meditative state. I immediately had a feeling of squirming, heard chattering and saw movement within the circle. It was undoubtedly the little people or nature spirits. At this stage in my life, I had very little contact with elementals, but I was sure it was them that I was feeling.

"I had a feeling of movement that I had never experienced before and, to me, it could only be fairies or pixies. They were just a few feet tall but, collectively, they seemed to rise up as I focused on them, as if they were responding to my thoughts. They were delighted in one sense but also seemed a little uneasy and to me this didn't feel quite right, it wasn't what I expected of such folk.

"Those within the circle felt very sad and, although they had a 'quirky energy' about them, there was also a weariness and despondency mixed in with their excitement. I sensed all of this in a matter of seconds. (Often these impressions are described as 'downloads' as it is as though the information arrives as a large clump of data).

"There was no clarity in what I was seeing through my mind's eye, but I had the feeling that the ground was alive with movement. There were arms waving and heads bobbing up and down as they moved as a collective group. They were certainly happy to see us at their stone circle.

"I just sat there quietly and casually wondered why they didn't leave the confines of the stone circle. Then it hit me - they couldn't.

"Another download of information arrived, and it suddenly became clear that they were trapped within the circle and couldn't leave. They had been this way for several hundred years, cursed or imprisoned by a magician.

"I asked if I could help and was told that they could only be released if I was able to lift the spell that contained them. I set my intention and asked my guides to help. Suddenly the elementals began to move out of the circle. They poured out and they ran, leapt and jostled each other with delight. After all those years, they were finally free, and their joy brought a lump to my throat. They were just like young children, running and leaping with their new-found joyous freedom. They surrounded me, thanked me and then ran up into the hills and across the valley.

"They were just like a swarm of bees and kept pouring out of the earth for several minutes until the last one appeared. The sight of them will stay with me forever."

When you look for elementals, expect to use all your inner senses. Set your intention and allow whatever you are hoping for to come to you. What you are doing is accessing your subconscious mind, allowing it to flow into your conscious awareness. When it happens you will know. Once it has occurred, it is a matter of practicing and enjoying repeated experiences, remapping your neural pathways so that the feeling becomes recognised and strengthened.

How to work with elementals and nature spirits

The first step is to talk to them. With elementals, it is all about communication. The more you talk to the little people and associated nature spirits, the better and easier it will be to connect with and work with them.

It is the job of elementals to look after the flora and fauna of the planet and they are closely associated with all that we call Mother Nature. It has been proven by scientists that plants have feelings and can, in fact, sense what we are thinking. Cleeve Backster, in the 1960s, conducted various experiments using house plants. He connected them to a galvanometer (also known as a lie detector), a machine that measures electric currents, and he began to note how the plants responded to various human activities. For example, when one plant was watered the indicators moved in a gentle motion but when Backster thought about harming the plant the gauges started to react moderately. It was only when he, reluctantly burned a leaf, that the indicators went wild.

Backster was intrigued by the recording of the moderate movement seemingly in response to his thoughts, and conducted various thought-based experiments from a distance. His findings showed that the plant had the same reaction whether he was in a different room or several hundred miles away from it.

If you are interested in further research on this fascinating subject we can recommend *The Secret Life of Plants* by Peter Tomkins and Christopher Bird.

When you first start talking to elementals it is a good idea to be in a meditative or relaxed state. It helps the communication process and shows respect. As you gain in confidence it will be sufficient for you simply to think about what you want to say to them, and they will hear you and understand your intentions.

Emotions and our connection

As we have seen, elementals are linked to us in ways that many of us wouldn't expect. Therefore, if we continue to see them as being completely separate to us, we will miss out on what is considered to be their true purpose and value, which is the symbiosis of our joint existence. Connecting with them appears to adjust our own energy pattern as well as theirs, and this happens on an emotional level. If we consider that everything is connected (a key tenet of spirituality in general) then nothing will ever happen purely by chance. As we have seen earlier, our connection to the subtle realms is, at least partly, regulated by our emotional state of mind, hence our brainwave frequency. We don't need to be plugged in to brainwave monitoring equipment to know whether we are in a suitably receptive and beneficial state of mind. Our emotions indicate that every moment of the day. If we are feeling low or sad, we will be less able to connect to our intuitive side. If we are stressed and anxious, we will also be less able to connect to that aspect of self that enables a substantial spiritual connection. And the big barrier is anger.

If you are feeling angry or upset, please do not try to connect with the spirit realm or the elementals. In fact, in most cases it probably won't be possible, which is just as well. When working with any aspect of reality in the subtle realms, it is advisable to do everything with the highest possible level of intent, by that we mean with as much love as possible and therefore doing things for the 'greatest good'. Anger will often prevent us from being able to connect to the subtle realms, but sometimes it can be possible to connect, and while we are 'open' our emotions get fired up and this can have some rather 'interesting' results, as Tim found out.

This is what happened: "One day, whilst dowsing in the kitchen, I suddenly got really angry over something rather silly as I held the rods. I was in the middle of quite an extensive question string when my mind was suddenly distracted by my young son who, although not intending to be annoying, did something that irritated me and I reacted adversely with a flash of anger while I was still dowsing. In a way, I guess it was like lashing out energetically, it was only the briefest of angry thoughts, but I was shocked when that action appeared to blow a fuse on our electric cooker I was standing next to. The synchronicity of the thought and the small explosion behind me in the cooker was indisputable. Sealed with the loud click of the trip switch terminating the damaged circuit. It actually made me feel quite sick and I was certainly very ungrounded for a long time afterwards. And it has to be said, I was perturbed by the implication of the power of thought for some time afterwards too."

In many traditional esoteric schools of training, it is recognised that one doesn't use one's connection to do any act that is not for the greatest good. Acts of aggression, or those that are driven by personal gain, even if they are not fuelled by negative emotions, are recognised as being detrimental to the person controlling the thought. It is said that whatever one gives out when connected to the subtle realms will be delivered back several times over.

So, when working with any aspects of the subtle realms, it is important to be in the right frame of mind to get a connection in the first place, and then to be able to maximise the effectiveness of that connection and the manipulation of the energy for the best possible outcome. That includes liaison with elementals.

There are some very simple ways which, with practice will help you get in the right frame of mind. Cultivating a mindful way of being is integral to success, as is developing a sense of gratitude, which is one of the most effective keys to unlock the connection to the subtle realms. When in a state of gratitude, there is an acceptance and a peace with everything which creates a sense of inner calm. It is this inner state of being that opens the doorway to the power of one's intuition. It is often suggested that we cultivate an *'attitude of gratitude'*, and for good reason. This is one of the most important things to remember when working with the elementals and probably one of the easiest emotional states for us to overlook. The general default mode for human beings is certainly not gratitude, most of us are rarely thankful for the things we have. And most people want more than they currently have.

An attitude of gratitude will certainly help with your connection to the elemental realm. Your life may start to flow smoothly, projects will evolve and develop with little effort, good thoughts will arrive and you will simply feel in touch with everything. Maintaining that attitude of gratitude is so much easier if you can see or feel those nature spirits sitting by the back door ready to help you.

As you become tuned in to the world around you, and the subtle realms, look at the flowers in your garden, they will have taken on a different appearance. The colours of the petals will look brighter and deeper, the grass will look lusher and the shrubs will appear happier and healthier. It is so much easier to feel a connection when you can see evidence.

– 184 –

This is one example of how the elementals can help us in our emotional lives. To take down the barricades around us and allow us to stay in the flow of all that is. We are part of the manifesting process as well as part of creation.

Maintaining your Garden

There will always be two perfect places in your garden for your latest shrub to be planted: where you want it to go and where it wants to be. We would always suggest asking the plant for its preferred location within your garden. Dowsing will help you here but, be warned, it may not want to be put where you want to put it. If the plant or shrub tells you that it wants to be put in the middle of your lawn, then we would suggest asking it for its second best location.

You can then dowse for its ideal planting depth and which way the plant wants to face. Then ask for an elemental to dedicate itself to the plant's wellbeing, stand back and watch it grow into a fine healthy shrub.

A friend of Adrian's was having problems with a troublesome gnome in her garden. It would keep coming into the house and, once there, would give off terrible smells, make light bulbs blow and cause chaos with their ginger cat.

Adrian tuned in and gently removed the gnome from her home and encouraged him to stay outdoors. However, he wasn't totally set on the idea. "I found out that they had a large Yucca growing by the back door so tentatively asked the gnome if he would dedicate himself to the wellbeing of this magnificent plant," explains Adrian. "He was delighted to have been asked and jumped at the chance. From that day on he has never ventured into the house again and no longer torments the cat."

He was christened 'Gnorman' by the couple living there and every now and then they would leave him a little gift to say, 'thank you' for his work, which has resulted in a happy gnome, a happy house and a happy family.

Earth elementals are proud beings and they take great delight in having an attractive garden to live and work in. They can, however, be very territorial and get easily upset when someone spoils the ambiance, especially cats and dogs, who have little respect for where they do their business.

It is rather like someone continually dumping their rubbish on your driveway, or local children throwing rubbish over the fence into your garden. The elementals in our gardens can easily become upset with the resident pets and it is quite normal for them to hide in the bushes until the poor unsuspecting animal walks past then jump out and mug them.

As mentioned earlier, Annie (Adrian's mum-in-law's dog) has no respect for the elementals in Adrian and Allyson's garden. She gate-crashes their party and they retaliate, so clearing work is done on a regular basis both on the elementals and the dog.

Larry the ginger cat was often targeted by Gnorman the Gnome and the other nature spirits that lived in their garden. Larry's owners, Jools and Nathan, would often see him sitting at the bottom of the garden afraid to venture across it. Adrian would often receive a text asking for his help and as he explains, "One morning, Larry disappeared from the garden and hadn't come back by nightfall. The weather had turned nasty and the owners were worried. I just got the feeling that this wasn't a typical problem with the elementals and asked my friend Kate Salway, a very good animal communicator, to tune in and ask Larry what was going on."

In Kate's words "All I saw was this yucky green colour, something quite nasty, attached to Larry. He was very scared and disorientated."

As it turned out, Larry had a lawn elemental attached and a very unhappy one at that. Once Adrian knew what it was, he could do the healing work, appease the nature spirit and return it to its garden. A short time later, Larry returned home where he was fed and watered and settled down comfortably to sleep in his warm bed.

We would suggest dowsing your pets and other animals on a regular basis to make sure that nothing detrimental has become attached to them.

Equally, a lot of the problems that you face in your garden will be dependent on how beneficial or detrimental the energy patterns are that run through the plot. Underground water, earth energy lines and spirals will all give you specific problems to deal with. Some plants and trees are known to thrive in detrimental areas, whilst other species prefer 'lighter' zones, free from potentially heavy patterns.

Your lawns will face similar difficulties. If you are having constant problems with weeds or moss, get out the dowsing rods and start asking questions. First, check to see whether the energy patterns are the cause. It might also be due to a lack of certain nutrients (or too much), or potentially the energy arising from crossing points of underground water.

Try some Earth healing by calling in the nature spirits to help. If you are tackling grass problems, ask the lawn elementals, but be prepared as they may require an offering or gift to be fully appeased.

The same process will apply to an ornamental pond as there are many things that are detrimental to the fish and supported wildlife, anything from herons to earth energy lines and much in between. In an ideal world, it would be best practise to dowse for the correct location of a pond in the garden but in most circumstances they have been inherited and you have no choice.

You can check, using dowsing rods or a pendulum, to make sure that the fish, frogs, toads and newts etc. are happy in your pond. If they are not, it might be time to call in the undines and ask them to refresh the waters of the pond to benefit all the flora and fauna that surround and live in it. These beautiful creatures are always happy to help, but they do need to be asked. They will then start to oxygenate the water and work alongside the sylphs (elementals of the air), whilst the earth elementals bring nutrients to the pond.

It is all about thinking about the four elements as a team and asking the associated elementals to help with each part, consciously working with the symbiotic relationship between all things.

Light a fire

Is there anything more spellbinding and magical than sitting around a blazing bonfire or fire-pit? Especially at night, when you are surrounded by darkness and are cosseted by the warmth of the flames.

You can easily imagine an era when there were no street lights and perhaps no houses, memories of a primeval time, when dangerous animals roamed the countryside and the fire was, perhaps, your only protection from them.

We can often take so much for granted today and the flick of a thumb on a lighter or the striking of a match easily brings fire to life. Is it possible to imagine what it must have been like for our early ancestors to be able to create the life-giving flame by rubbing two sticks together or creating sparks by banging together two pieces of flint?

This is the realm of the fire elementals, the salamanders, thought by early man, to live in volcanoes and to be the creatures ultimately responsible for them erupting.

In order to connect with the fire elementals, one of our favourite things to do is to take photographs of fire. Simply take photographs of the flames, then when you have taken a good number of them look at each photograph. What shapes can you see?

In the evening, after a recent elementals course in Yorkshire, we gathered at Adrian's house in Darley for drinks and nibbles and to see if we could experience or capture images of any fire elementals.

Expectations were high, helped possibly, by the occasional glass of wine or beer. We all had our mobiles and iPads at the ready. The fire was lit and the clicking started.

"I think that most of us were disappointed to begin with," says Adrian, "but, as the evening went on and the fire became more established, the resulting photographs showed some amazing and startling beings coming from the fire-pit.

"One clearly showed a small dragon, almost as though it had just been born. Another was a clear outline of a griffin with wings outstretched ready to fly. We even had a Devil complete with his pitchfork!"

The experiment worked really well and the resulting photographs captured some wonderful beings that were only there for a moment and then scattered to the winds. Try it yourself, you never know what might appear on your screen.

Be open minded with a willingness to believe

Children are rarely closed-minded. And as such, are far more able to connect with Mother Nature and her workers. It is not just a purity of heart that we leave behind as we get older, it is a willingness to believe. We can become sceptical, blinkered and restricted in our thinking.

The saying 'seeing is believing' comes from the modern and logical scientific way of looking at life. The question it emphasises is, *'How can we believe something exists if we can't see it?'*

But in the spiritual world, it is well-known that actually, 'Believing is seeing'. That it is our belief that magic exists that allows us to see it. It's our belief that elementals exist that allow us to connect and work with them.

Scepticism is fine so long as it is a healthy scepticism. However, it can lead to a closed mind which means the magic in life dies.

Try to look at the world with new eyes and with open thoughts. Allow the beauty that surrounds you into your heart. As you do, you will find that it comes alive again in many different and amazing ways. The sky becomes a deeper blue, the flowers seem to glow and the breeze even carries a natural perfume. Rejoice and the world rejoices with you.

When you are able to achieve this mindset, you will hear the elementals cheer as you sit amongst them. You will commune with nature and connect with the miraculous planet that we live on, just like our ancient ancestors would have done.

Chapter Nine

Visiting Sacred Spaces

Guardians of sites & Spirit of Place

A guardian of site was the first being from a higher realm that Tim connected with. He encountered the personality and guardian of a couple of earth energy lines running through his home near the Forest of Dean. Once acquainted, the guardian became known simply as 'Jane' and it was Jane that started Tim on his spiritual path.

One of the main problems or issues that arises when connecting to a personality in spirit, is that they can be hard to identify, as, obviously, they do not actually have a physical body. You have to feel whether they have a feminine or masculine energy, for example. Dowsing is one way to access who and what the personality is that you are connecting with. The more you dowse, the greater your awareness and sensitivity at all levels will become. (Dowsing is covered at length in Chapter Eleven) You will, by asking questions and then verifying the answers through research, be far more certain of whom you are dealing with, whether it be a true guardian, an imposter or a mischievous spirit.

Until you become a proficient dowser, you can make sure that you are talking to the correct person or the 'being' that you wish to connect with, by using common-sense and gut feeling.

In our physical world, it is easier because you can see the person and hence see their body or facial language. Or you can hear their tone of voice or you trust and know them because you have been introduced to them via a friend or colleague. But consider how you would fare if talking to a stranger on the telephone and they pretended to be somebody else that you knew? Do you think you could spot the difference? Would you know if it wasn't your friend or someone you could trust?

The chances are that you would, and this is the same process you need to adopt when connecting with a spirit being. The example given here is, of course, a lot simpler as voice recognition helps us, but asking the right questions, using common sense and trusting your gut will help you in identifying who you are talking to.

If, for instance, you enter a sacred site of Neolithic standing stones and ask to communicate with the guardian, then you will be relying upon your intuition to detect whether the personality that answers you is, in fact, genuine, or whether it is a tricky spirit or imposter. In most cases, it would be the guardian, as they are the main custodians of the site. They are immensely powerful and keepers of all knowledge of the site.

A part of their role is to manage and control the mischievous spirits. However, sometimes a dowser, or question asker, may have a lesson to learn (the importance of psychic protection, for instance) and a prankster may be allowed through.

You need to listen to your sixth sense or intuition and be very aware of how you are feeling. If you feel uncomfortable, back away, take your time, ground yourself, increase your protection and then ask again to connect with the true guardian of the site. It is not just your intuition, but it is also in your heart or gut. You will know or feel deep inside that something isn't right, just as you do in the real (physical) world.

You will find that you come across a mischief maker every now and then but, in reality, that will be extremely rare. People who say they regularly encounter these detrimental beings are usually being over-dramatic, perhaps not in a good place themselves or simply shouldn't be accessing the subtle energies at that time as they are attracting these dark energies without knowing or protecting themselves against them. We suggest that you don't pay them too much attention, as unfortunately some people like to (or need to) find detrimental energy, negative beings or dark patterns everywhere they go.

If you find that you are connecting with these meddlesome spirits regularly yourself, you should start to question why. Perhaps put your dowsing on hold for a while and talk to someone with more experience in these matters who may be able to help you. Tim and Adrian are more than happy for you to contact them if you are having problems, their email addresses will be found at the end of the book. They also hold regular courses on how to access the unseen realms safely.

As long as you set the correct intention beforehand, put your psychic protection in place and call on Archangel Michael for his guidance and protection, you should be on the right track and ready to connect.

Setting your intention, being in the right frame of mind and in a good emotional state are all very important. If you are surrounded by emotional and mental turmoil, trouble, stress or strife then we would suggest you do not begin to explore these subtle realms until you have processed the problems, dealt with them and ejected the baggage that has caused the upset, so you are not in a state of being overwhelmed by them. We would also say that drinking alcohol whilst dowsing or connecting to spirit can be disrespectful and the energy 'vibration' of alcohol can attract unwanted mischievous beings.

These are words of caution as everybody has had, or currently has, a degree of angst and turmoil in their lives. If you feel that you have control over it and are mentally strong enough, then there is very little danger when you are accessing these subtle realms. And when you do, you will be met with love and gratitude and receive a very warm welcome.

Differences between guardians of site and Spirit of Place

Guardian of site: We believe that every sacred site has a guardian. They seem to be an integral part of the hidden structure of reality that is the subtle realms. Guardians of site can be found *everywhere*, even in places that are not typically recognised as or labelled as 'sacred sites' have guardian personalities that can be accessed. This information comes from the many conversations that Tim has enjoyed with Jane over the years, especially in the beginning, as at that time he knew very little about the energy patterns that surrounded him.

Guardians can be referred to as either male or female, despite not having a gender in the physical sense. When you tune into their energy, you are likely to feel more of a masculine or feminine presence. They won't be offended by being referred to as he or she, as they know that it makes it easier for us to relate to them. They are intimately connected to the earth energy system where they dwell. Their guardian role is really within their dimension. In our physical realm they are usually observers impinging upon our senses when invited or when they need help from the physical dimension to influence theirs. Within their own dimension, they have the ability to affect the energies of the place and control them. In our physical dimension we just experience the very faint results of their deeper influence in dimensions that originate outside the physical. We believe their presence greatly contributes to the feeling of a site; their energy is part of the life force which contributes to that special feeling.

The Spirit of Place is, more or less, the essence of the *physical* elements of a site or area, the spirit of nature that emanates from all places and which has its roots in the physical form. It's almost like an aura of nature, more often known as the Genius Loci. It is a presence that seems to spring from the earth and is often found across a wider area than guardians of Site.

The Spirit of Place usually has less contact and interaction with humanity than the guardian. They are, perhaps better thought of as, a stabilising pattern or influence within the subtle realms, holding the memory of place within its structure. As with all things, it can be communicated with using dowsing or similar mediumistic techniques.

When healing a house or business, we will sometimes find the Spirit of Place has been upset by human activity that has disturbed and distorted the natural pattern of the environment. Urban decay within major cities, for example, is very upsetting for the Spirit of Place as it takes a pride in its surroundings and likes order, not chaos.

The guardian of site and Spirit of Place seem to have similar powers, but they would each need to be consulted on differing aspects when you are working to heal a space. The guardian of the site does seem to have more influence and control when you want to adjust the earth energy flows, whereas the Spirit of Place is a larger, more widespread and less human-like personality that holds the space.

Both forms of these energetic beings can be found wherever there is human activity, but if you wish to specifically connect with either one of them, you are likely to find it easier at a place where there has been sacred ritual or spiritual ceremonies.

You can work with either of these energies at sacred sites. It is good manners to ask the guardian's permission before entering a ritual site, which will you get off to a good start with them, by showing respect.

You will need to be prepared for the possibility of unusual humour that can emanate from the guardians but be aware that some can be quite serious. On the whole, though, they do seem to be amused by our efforts to communicate with them.

Guardians of Site will usually answer any questions you ask about their site, but they will also rejoice and celebrate your presence, without the need for any questions. You can sit, share or purely connect with them, to simply 'be' in the space in which you find yourself, both as an observer and participant.

How to work with guardians of site or Spirit of Place

If you are a dowser, as you approach a sacred site, before you enter it, set your intention to connect with the guardian of Site. If it is your intention to do any healing work once you get to the site, we would suggest asking (by dowsing the question) whether it will be appropriate to do so before you leave home, especially if you live many hours/miles away. This sort of forward-planning can save a lot of disappointment and a long car journey.

Once on site, your opening question should be 'May I communicate with the guardian of the site?' As you ask, watch your rods or pendulum and see how they react. They should give you a 'yes' or 'no' response. If the answer is 'no', then it may be a good time to walk away. Although you can always ask if there is a better time, or what the reason might be. If you get a 'yes' then you are welcome to enter but do tread carefully as you are now on hallowed ground.

You may or may not hear or feel other energetic exchanges along with these dowsing responses. This will depend very much on how you receive information from the subtle realms, how confident you are with dowsing and, also how relaxed and open you are.

Everyone has mediumistic potential (that is the ability to talk to those who have passed over into the spirit realm) and conversational dowsing is most definitely an example of mediumship. You are, as the dowser, talking to, or communicating with, the divine or spirits from the higher realms. Some people will receive messages clairaudiently (hear them), some clairvoyantly (see them) or clairsentiently (by sensing them). There is no one way that is better than the others, they are just different forms of interaction with the energies.

It is up to you to find out the way that works best for you and this can change over the years as you become more comfortable with this interaction. You may find that your other senses will also begin to develop.

Asking questions of guardian energies

When dowsing, there is, perhaps, no such thing as the one *right* question to ask. It is more a series of guided questions that enable you to get the information you need to progress to the next level. By using each answer as it comes in, you can very quickly drill down through the question-string far enough for you to be happy with what you have found. But, as we mentioned before, when you make contact with the guardian of

Site, listen carefully to what they say as they will soon tell you if they are not happy with the line of questioning you are pursuing.

In order to connect with the Spirit of Place, simply meditate in the space, and allow thoughts and impressions to come to you, but make sure you are fully protected psychically before you do so.

Once you have done that, set your intention to make contact with, or to converse with, the deity or spiritual being you want to connect with. Often a good way to start, assuming that you have already asked permission, is simply to ask of your Higher Self to be shown, with the aid of dowsing rods, the best place to sit within the sacred site in order to liaise with the spiritual being.

Ask the question *'Show me the most appropriate stone to sit on or beside within this stone circle'*, or *'Guide me to the most appropriate place to sit so that I may tune in to the guardian of the site/Spirit of Place most effectively'*. After asking the question, follow the direction indicated by the rods/pendulum, wait until they have crossed or have indicated a specific stone, then sit, meditate and tune in to the energies.

Incidentally, when you ask for permission to enter a sacred site, you might not get an immediate response. Please don't assume that it will be okay to enter. If you are going there purely as an observer, not wishing to carry out any work, then generally permission is rarely needed. However, if you are there to commune with the guardian or to do other 'work' be aware that you are on their patch; manners are expected.

There is no point in assuming that you will *not* be welcome though and, if you do receive a *'No'*, then ask the questions to find out why. It may be that you have attachments that need clearing, or you are bringing something detrimental to the site. Go outside of the site and do some healing on yourself then ask again.

If you are not wanted it may be made very clear to you in the physical realm. The weather may suddenly change for the worse, a stranger might engage you in conversation outside the site or a herd of cows might suddenly appear to chase you off. You will find that distractions are suddenly all around you, pulling you away from what you were wanting to do.

So, the assumption is that you are allowed inside their sacred space, but always show respect, be humble and act with humility.

Just what is, or makes, a holy site?

Clearly the spiritual nature of a site counts for everything in the context of answering this question: *'Can a site only be considered holy if it is associated with a formalised religion such as Christianity?'* This question was one of the first things we asked ourselves when compiling the Spiritual Earth series of courses that we teach here in the UK. At that time, we were not looking any further afield or at any other religions, hence the focus on Christianity.

We know that it is a bizarre question and potentially a dangerous one too as you might find that your long-held beliefs are suddenly challenged, but it did make us take a closer look at what the word 'HOLY' means to us personally:

Do we consider angels to be 'HOLY'? Yes.

Do we consider elementals to be HOLY? No.

Do we consider us to be HOLY? Yes and No.

Do we consider humans to be sacred? Yes.

So, after much pondering, discussion and thought we came to this conclusion:

Sacred implies a sanctity, a treatment of respect, an attitude of care, of looking after the valuable.

Holy is more about GOD: the ultimate creator, as in HOLY relics, items used in the adoration of the gods or goddesses, the veneration or worship of a higher being or figure.

Perhaps that is where the difference lies: HOLY is connected to the deity of creation, whereas SACRED is a less definite link to creation. For example, we, as humans, can create sacred sites that are devoted to social harmony, but are not necessarily linked to the creator or GOD and are not necessarily connected to the manifesting process.

This is what an online dictionary says about the word HOLY:

'Dedicated or consecrated to God or a religious purpose; sacred: for example: *the Holy Bible, the holy month of Ramadan*'.

And this is what the same dictionary says about SACRED:

'Connected with God or gods, dedicated to a religious purpose and so deserving veneration: *sacred rites; the site at Eleusis is sacred to Demeter*'.

Cathedrals and churches are inevitably thought of as holy but pagan sites such as dolmens and stone circles are not, although they are still sacred. They are as worthy of respect as a church and they should also be treated with sanctity and awe.

Generally, the overall definition of a holy site and a sacred space is that they are both places at which we can worship something outside ourselves.

What is a sacred space?

We have established some parameters for what exactly a sacred space is compared with a holy site, in the section above. We believe it is possible that *human* intent plays a greater part in creating a sacred space than it does a holy site.

For example, if Tim was sitting at his desk replying to his emails, he would not consider that he was sitting within a sacred space. However, when he begins his remote healing and energy work with clients, he is. So how does this change occur?

The first thing that he does is to spiritually clear the space, clearing away any detrimental or unnecessary energy patterns that have built up in the room whilst he has been involved in more earthly matters. He lights a candle, recites a short prayer and then sets out a row of haematite crystals to define the sacred space at his desk which he wants to create.

In other spiritual practices, like Druidry and Wicca, this could be carried out by making the shape of a circle with a wand, sword or staff. It could equally be any magical tool or even the wave of a hand, as intention is the important thing to bear in mind here. It is also very important to reverse the process once the work or session has finished, by closing all 'doorways' that have been opened intentionally or unexpectedly during the healing and then ending with a prayer to finally close down. The same applies with the closing or uncasting of a created circle.

When Tim carries out this process, he doesn't feel there has been a measurable change in the space around him, but what has changed is his attitude towards it. To him, the space has a tangible boundary, in this instance, he uses crystals to form the edge. He could place objects outside that border, but if he wanted to use them as part of his healing work, Tim would prefer to have them within the perimeter as they would then be fully protected from outside influences.

As humans, we do like rituals and the above is Tim's preferred way of working. It is his subjective world, it helps him to relax and focus on the task at hand. Beliefs are an important part of spiritual healing, therefore knowing and trusting that you are safe within your own sacred space is essential.

James, a friend of Tim's, used to experience a lot of unexplained disturbance at his house. Admittedly he and his wife were very sensitive people and may well have attracted this unwanted activity. All this was happening before Tim had become aware of the intricacies of the spirit world, as he was still fully involved in running his filming company. James, in order to protect himself and to reduce the disturbances at his home, had started to carry a black obsidian crystal with him because a wise woman had advised him to do so. Black obsidian is a beautiful stone and mystical powers were attributed to it by the Incas, however, the wise woman could just as easily have given James a piece of white linen instead, telling him to wash it daily as a protection method. It would have done exactly the same job. It isn't the object that is important, it is the belief that goes with it. So, when we talk about a sacred space, we need to be aware of our *intent* and, of course, therefore, our belief systems.

If we view all of life as sacred, the Earth must be thought of in the same terms. However, because the planet is so huge we, perhaps, find it difficult to think of it as a sacred being and we can only really interact with the small part that we see on a daily basis. We suggest that part of our sacred routine and belief system should be to remember to give thanks and honour to the Sun, the Moon and the Earth each day, as they give us life. The positive, life-affirming aspects of nature are far more important than all the negative aspects of our so called normal life.

We should also honour and give thanks for our lives too, remembering daily that we are here to enjoy our time on the Earth, to be fully in this reality however hard it may feel at times. We can make life work *for* us more easily if we can remain in a positive frame of mind or in a life-affirming mode. This would involve working on keeping ourselves clear of all unwanted emotional energies as it is all too easy to be pulled into negativity.

But it's not *just* about thinking either negatively or positively. Positive thinking on its own doesn't work in terms of us being able to consciously manifest our reality in the way a book like, *The Secret* suggests, as positive thinking alone, doesn't fully address the subconscious levels of our existence.

The more we deliberately focus on the positives (beneficial energy) and honour the fact that we are alive, the more we begin to create and progress in our reality. To begin to adjust our subconscious and let go of the negativity held within us, we need to learn about ourselves and deal with the baggage that we carry with us. Using mindfulness is the key to observing the habits of our subconscious and once identified, then the issues can be cleared or healed in whatever way is appropriate for you at that point in your life.

It is a process of looking at and accepting what makes us, us. Acceptance is a huge part of knowing who we are and we need to come to terms with our discoveries. Acceptance marks the beginning of finding peace in balance.

No problems exist separately from us. When we identify an external problem, it's sometimes most effective to address it by taking a good long look inside ourselves, to consider how this issue reflects a concern that sits somewhere deep in us and then decide how best to move on from the issue by using whatever healing is appropriate. Sometimes that healing can be achieved by mindfully interacting with a sacred space.

Sanctity of self

A sacred site can, in fact, be anything that is treated with respect and sanctified. Each human being is, for example, an individual sacred space, but we rarely view ourselves that way. Rarely do we appreciate how special we actually are and even less often do we give ourselves the inner attention and credit we deserve.

Try this: for the next few minutes, just sit quietly and think about the way you treat yourself. Focus on who you are in a positive way and think about all the good things that you do. Think about how much you enjoy some of the things that you do and consider the people who give you pleasure in your life.

It is easy to enter a sacred place like Avebury henge, for instance, and express our reaction to it in words of awe as it is a stunning masterpiece. It not only looks spectacular, but also feels very special. We must treat ourselves with the same reverence and look after our physical body as it is the one thing that is with us all the time while we are here on Earth. But we often do exactly the opposite. We ignore or mistreat our body and soul when we should be cherishing or worshipping them.

A visual fascination with a place

We all know what the Earth looks like. We have seen images of the planet taken from space and these pictures are indelibly set within our minds: a beautiful blue marble spinning in space with billions of people on board, the third rock from the sun. How can that not be seen as sacred?

Many of the ancients knew the planet was vast, but we feel they would have worshipped the life-giving qualities of the physical form that was directly in front of them, with which they lived with on a daily basis, rather than having been concerned about the planet as a whole. It would have been through these places they knew intimately that they would have venerated Mother Earth, rather than being concerned with the whole huge Earth as a concept.

We will never truly know what our ancestors really thought or felt thousands of years ago, especially when they were visiting a sacred site. But, given that archaeologists believe that basic human emotions haven't changed very much over several thousand years, it is safe to assume our ancestors reacted like we do today, with wonder, awe and reverence.

When visiting a sacred site, we need to sit quietly and tune in, to begin the connection process. What is your immediate reaction to the location: how do you instantly feel as you enter and what do you see? We must be very aware of our 'gut reaction' just as our ancestors would have been.

Consider Brimham Rocks in North Yorkshire as an example. Our ancestors would have seen both human and animal faces and shapes in the rocks. Sadly, we are now so used to seeing images on television that the natural sights and shapes around us can easily be taken for granted or missed completely. Our ancestors did not have the same distractions. They would surely have been acutely aware of all the sights, sounds and smells of the land around them. For the ancients, visiting Brimham Rocks or Avebury for the first time must have given them a sensory overload. They probably had a sense of wonderment and been in total awe as they entered the site.

Today our reactions are probably somewhat muted due to our knowledge of how the strange shapes are caused by erosion: the effects of ice, water and wind over thousands of years. It is doubtful if our ancestors had this awareness and therefore the place would have been seen as magical.

Brimham Rocks is an example of a sacred space that has been created naturally without any interference or construction work by humans. It proves that a natural site can, and will, create a sense of wonderment, and reverence even if it is not what we would regard as a 'typical' human-made sacred space.

Many such sites should be viewed at differing times of the day, month or year to be fully appreciated. The light and shadows cast by the rocks play a great part in the overall atmosphere of a place. The rising sun creates a totally different feeling from the setting sun, for example. Likewise, clouds passing overhead on a sunny day will highlight certain areas which will suddenly, in isolation, become very significant to the observer. Light and colour adds to the wonderment of any sacred place. Veneration then becomes a natural part of the interaction process.

Natural springs, unusual rock formations, folds in the hills, unnatural looking hill tops can all become part of a sacred landscape and combine to form a sacred space.

The Marlborough Downs (particularly around Fyfield) are a good example of this. These hills were the birth place of the sarsen stones at Avebury. Even today, as you walk along the footpath above the village, you can see stones that were being worked on, perhaps to be included within the circles.

The village of Cherhill, in Wiltshire, is also worthy of a visit, and not just to see the white horse. The folds in the hills are magical, so much so that a very large hill temple was constructed at the top with the most amazing views towards Avebury, West Kennet Long Barrow and Silbury Hill.

Active observation, that is, the ability to stop, look and listen with focussed attention, adds to the appreciation of the theatre or spectacle displayed at these sites, especially on days when the mysterious shapes loom out of fog or mist. It is easy to see how the Druidic priests might have used these forms of dramatic scenery to enhance their teachings and ceremonies. Modern religions have also used that same wonderment and reverence in their places of worship. Just look at some of the magnificent churches, cathedrals, mosques and temples that have been built in the name of God. The size, shape, height, statues, stained glass windows are all there to give that 'wow' factor as you walk in, perhaps also to make you feel slightly insignificant and suitably humbled.

Can holy sites exist without human interaction?

To answer this, we need to quote that well known and possibly infuriating philosophical question, *'If a tree falls in a forest and there is no one to hear it, does it make a sound?'* Most people's immediate answer would probably be, 'Of course it does!' But you need to ask yourself why should it make a sound? Is a noise necessary if there is no one there to hear it?

Perhaps we need to start with an even bigger question first. *'If humanity is formed in the image of God, can anything happen without human thought or interaction?'* And if the answer is no, how does it apply to the energy of holy sites and sacred places?

We have seen that it is common for many earth energy lines to merge or cross at sacred or holy places. There are also the holy lines that cross beneath the altar of most churches and where underground water is often present to give the 'buzz' that many people feel when they either enter a church or stand close to the altar. Many of these lines will be influenced by man or created by intent, but not all of them.

To illustrate this, consider Tyne Cot cemetery near Ypres in Belgium where the graveyard (for allied troops from World War I) is laid out in the shape of a church when seen from the air and the altar is formed by a large white marble cross positioned on top of a ruined German gun emplacement. When visiting there, Adrian dowsed to see whether there were holy lines running up to and crossing beneath the altar. He got a 'Yes' response. When he asked the follow up question, 'Were these lines formed by human intent or action?' he received the answer, 'No.'

It seems they were formed naturally and this is very similar to the process of erecting a large standing stone or building a stone circle. They automatically become attractor points, drawing the necessary energy lines and water to them, perhaps to create and maintain the sanctity of the site. Is this Mother Earth at work or, maybe, an even higher force?

It would appear that sites can become holy sites, without human thought, intent, action or interaction.

What was the first ever holy site?

As far as our ancient ancestors were concerned, water was probably one of their most precious commodities. This leads us naturally to believe that the first holy site must have been a natural spring. It would have been seen as a life-giving gift from the gods. The spring might disappear for a few weeks during the warm summer months, then miraculously reappear weeks later as sweet and pure as it had been before. It would begin to be treated with the utmost reverence and gifts would be left for the gods or deities.

The spring would naturally attract visitors to the site and, after drinking the water, one person's troublesome illness might suddenly disappear. In their eyes, a miracle would have occurred. Word would quickly spread and a certain mystique would build up around the spring. In time, it would have become a holy site, revered by many.

Lourdes in France may have started that way, but let us take The Malverns, as a more local example, here in England. The Malvern Hills contain many natural springs and over the generations, some have been hollowed out (to allow easy filling of buckets etc.) and now go under the generic name of Wells.

There is an abundance of wells with curious names. For example, the Eye Well and The Dripping Well, both of which were apparently used for general cures. Then there's Walm's Well for skin diseases, Chalybeate

Well for nervous complaints, worms and melancholia, the Holy Well which was used to treat not only leprosy, but also eye disorders and ulcers and there is even The Devil's Well which was supposed to help cure spells from malevolent Fairies and Hobgoblins. These all appear on maps of the area. Even today, people hold them in such high esteem that a Well Dressing event happens each year.

In the past, doctors and physicians were few and far between, and only afforded by the rich. Superstitions abounded, curses and spells were perhaps seen as everyday occurrences. Therefore, any hope of a cure must have been seized upon. Holy springs and wells must have been a source of great comfort and hope to these people and this 'taking of the waters' continued into the 20th century at places like Harrogate, Bath, Royal Leamington Spa, Cheltenham, Ilkley and so on.

There are, of course, the two famous springs at Glastonbury in Somerset, the Red Spring (chalybeate water) found within The Chalice Well Gardens and the White Spring (calcite) opposite. Their healing properties have been well-documented and have been known for centuries. They are now highly venerated, although both did fall into disrepair over the years, and the White Spring was incorporated into a Victorian reservoir.

Water is the lifeblood of the planet and we humans cannot live long without it. So it would make sense that the first holy site would spring from our necessity to survive.

Holy wells, springs and connected deities

All holy wells and springs have their own guardian spirit, many in the form of a 'White Lady'. They are normally very elemental places and perfect for communing with the local deity. Depending on the age of the well or spring and whether it is still venerated, the White Lady (the Maiden) could have moved on through her life stages and now appear in her second stage as the Mother or the third stage as the Hag or Crone (the Wise Woman).

Sadly, many of these beautiful guardians have gone altogether. This can happen for many reasons. The spring or well may have simply dried up, and the deity moved on to another one, but so often it is because they have lost their significance. Their true meaning has been lost to most humans living close by and they are no longer revered or respected. You sometimes find that the guardian has gone because of pollution and sometimes due to vandalism.

Often, springs and wells simply need to be revitalised and 'spring cleaning' is a perfect way to bring life back to the site, to energise it. Thank and encourage the guardian. Do your best to get the water flowing again as that gives life to the land and hope for future generations who visit the site. Springs and wells are as special now as they ever have been, perhaps even more so, as they are the sacred spaces of nature.

If you would like to connect fully with nature, we would recommend you look at Druidry and the Ogham. This practice should give you the opportunity to commune with the Earth in an organised, worshipful framework. Both authors admit to knowing more about Buddhism than Druidry, however, there is a link between the two philosophies, not just in their love of nature but of trees in particular. For example, the Druid Tree of Life is very similar to the Hindu/Buddhist Ashvattha and the biblical Tree of Knowledge. The saying 'As above, so below' encompasses much of the link between this Celtic religion and that of India, Nepal and Tibet. Earth worship is as important as spiritual practice. Chanting or incantation, for instance, sends out a vibration that resonates and connects with both aspects.

What questions to ask when at a sacred or holy site?

Before Adrian sets foot out of the door to visit either a holy site or sacred space he usually asks the following question: 'Is it a good time for me to visit?'

If the answer is 'no', then he would choose another site and dowse the question again. There will be good days and not so good days to visit these sites. It really does depend on what you want to do there. If it is purely to have a walk around then the answer to your question will mostly be 'yes', but if you want to dowse, do any healing (Earth or human) or start to dig any deeper into the past then just be aware of the site's moods.

Once at the site, it is good to sit and take stock of what you are wanting to achieve during your visit. A good friend of Adrian's, Tom Graves, is adamant that you should sit and take in the energies and atmosphere of the sacred site before doing anything else. By observing and listening to what is going on around you, you can become aware of what the site is trying to communicate to you.

When a group of dowsers gets to a sacred site they, more often than not, are off like greyhounds, with their rods stuck out in front of them, trying to get as much information as they can within minutes of being there. But charging in like this means the subtleties of the site can easily be missed. It might be patterns in the grass concealing a fallen stone, alignments with the hills surrounding the site or other indications of how or why the site was built where it was.

Preparation is the key to a successful site visit. The questions below will help you to focus and come away from a holy or sacred site with the information you were seeking.

Try to look at the site in a different way from others, use fresh eyes, as much of our history is muddled and may come from a historian's fanciful mind. For example, who actually built the stone circles at Avebury and Stonehenge and when?

On a motorbike trip to Brittany in 2013, Adrian was amused to see a sign at La Roche aux Fees (The Rock of the Fairies), a huge 'alle couverte' (Passage Grave) or Dolmen that is some 19 miles southeast of Rennes, saying, *'No Celts took part in the building of this site or any of the other Dolmens, Stone Circles or Menhirs across Europe!'*

So, who was responsible? Time to start dowsing the questions:

1.   Are the stones here for a religious/ceremonial purpose?

2.   When were they erected?

3.   How many people transported the stone or stones?

4.   Was the site in daily/weekly/monthly/yearly use?

5.   Who built the site (mankind, aliens/shining ones)?

6.   When was the busiest time for the site (Winter/Summer etc.)

7.   Were the solstices or cross quarter days special times (Winter/ Summer)?

8.   Did the Moon play a part in any of the ceremonies?

9.   How many stone circles were here originally?

10.   Did man add to these over the years?

11.   Are the stones producing an electrical/magnetic field?

12.   Are they communicating with each other?

13.   Does the energy field fluctuate during the day/night?

14.   How heavy is the stone?

15.   Is there anyone or anything buried beneath it?

16.   Does water play a part in energising the circle/standing stone?

17.   Are there energy lines running through the circle?

18.   Is there a special stone to stand beside/hug today?

19.   Can I do any healing on the site or space today?

20.   Was the circle built for Earth healing purposes?

21.   Was the circle built for any other healing purpose?

22.   Are there different energy bands running up the stones?

23.   Is there anything interesting for me to find today?

24.   Is there a male or female aspect to the site?

25.   If so, show me where.

26.   Did sacrifice play a part here?

27.   If so, was this part of the original purpose?

28.   How many different uses has the circle had?

29.   Are there any pictograms/manifestations here for me to find?

30.   If so, please show me where.

Obviously, all the above questions can be used for different purposes. The word 'stone' or 'stone circles' can be replaced by 'church', 'spring', 'hill' (like Silbury), 'crop circles' and so on. Don't be afraid to experiment but, as you do, try to dig down as far as you can to find the answer that is pertinent to the time of your visit and make notes.

As far as question 23 is concerned, don't be afraid or embarrassed to go where the rods guide you, but do please respect private land. Adrian and Allyson have been known to stand in the middle of a ploughed field before now, once for fifteen minutes, just because the question had been asked. They never did find out exactly why they had to be there, but it had to do with an energy transference from above to Mother Earth. Ask this question and follow where the rods take you, you will get some strange looks, but that makes it more fun.

The question list is not exhaustive. Please add to it as you see fit. As you ask questions, others will come to you. It is often interesting to see ultimately where such questions lead you.

What's in it for me and why should I bother?

There is no reason for anyone to bother about the past, but understanding more about our ancestors can, hopefully, give us greater understanding of both the present and the future, especially when it comes to sacred sites, holy places and Earth worship.

Our forefathers had a great connection with the Earth as well as working with spirit. Combining the two brought greater insights and helped them in many different ways. By using the same energies, we can help not just ourselves, but others too. Whether that is with newfound insights or increased healing abilities. The question remains, though, does working with the Earth and spirit have any relevance in modern society?

In answer to that, we feel you only need to look at how many people are still visiting Avebury, Stonehenge, Glastonbury Tor or any sacred site on a daily basis. They are not all there purely to take photographs. Some want to experience the buzz that an ancient site holds; the energies that can, in some cases, be tangible. Some who visit these sacred places may get flashes or insights into the past that can have meaning for their life today, or they may receive a message that helps them to answer a question or questions they may have had in their head for a long time.

Whether any of this information is useful in your daily life really depends on what you have asked for, how you want to use the insights given to you and your willingness to start on the next leg of your spiritual journey, as that is generally where it will lead.

Much of what you can learn at sacred sites about your intuition, understanding, perception and intelligence comes under the heading of 'wisdom'. Sometimes it can take days, weeks, months and even years for the relevance of what you have discovered to become clear to you. Time is a human construct, it doesn't exist in the heavenly realms, so try to be patient.

Taking time out at a sacred site, such as a stone circle or holy well can help you exit the physical world for a period of time and help you to release the stresses and strains of your daily life. You can, in effect, leave much of your so called emotional junk or baggage behind in the minutes or hours you spend within the confines of the stones or henge. It could be the start of a healing process that will bring greater clarity into your life or purely help you relax, unwind and escape reality.

Modern day spirituality is much softer, and more transparent than many of the current and past religions. Many of the concepts of those religions are now outdated. We therefore need to look at what modern spirituality actually means. We believe spirituality is a non-religious term and involves acceptance, helping others, unconditional love, caring for the planet, charity, healing, personal transformation and psychological growth.

It could also be described as a personal journey inside yourself to understand who and what you are, something that gives you the ability to change what you don't like and liberate yourself, which in turn can lead to enlightenment. Energy patterns are changing all the time, nothing ever stands still, so we need to be aware of these variations and combine them with the wisdom of our ancestors, that is contained within our DNA.

Living a spiritual life in the 21st century is not easy. Don't be fooled by people who say that since they have discovered spirituality their lives have been wonderful, it is not that way for everyone. Learning about yourself is not easy; to come to terms with who you are is difficult. To bring changes into your life is harder still. It can be a long and twisting road, rocky with loads of forks and crossroads.

But as you walk your path, you will meet some wonderful people who will help you. The lessons can sometimes be unbearably hard, but once over each hurdle there is often a rainbow waiting. No matter what happens along the way, never lose faith. There are a number of basic tools and practices that can help to keep you on track and if you set your intention for change then they will come to you as you find you need them.

Travel – a road to enlightenment?

We all learn and gather information in many different ways, some from books and television and others from travel, taking in the sights, sounds and smells of foreign countries. Whichever way you choose to experience life, it will bring changes to the inner you. They may be very subtle to begin with, but if you continue with your adventure they will become more profound and deep-seated. Eventually, a new you will emerge. You only need to look back over, say ten years, to see what you have learned and how you have put those new lessons into practice.

Travel is significant as it can take us out of our comfort zone. By travel we don't mean a typical package deal to Benidorm, although that could be eye-opening, but more like a trek to the Himalayas, to see how others live. Placing yourself in new or strange environment can be quite daunting to begin with, but seeing life through other people's eyes and observing their customs is important and humbling. You may begin to see that life as we lead it here in the Western World is quite demanding: physically, mentally and spiritually.

Many of us are not connected to the Earth, we live in our heads. We get used to living a certain lifestyle and become very unhappy if anything fundamentally changes this. We want to live in the style to which we have become accustomed. Or is it a style that we have been led to believe will make us happy?

When the Dalai Lama visited Nottingham in 2008, Adrian was lucky enough to attend all five days of his teachings. One of the most important things that he learned was the Dalai Lama's understanding of *enlightenment*. He said it was one of the most misunderstood words of the 20th century and that he preferred the word *liberation*. His advice was to look at the life you are currently leading, become aware of who and what you truly are and then begin to change the aspects of yourself that you are not happy with.

This self-examination and realisation will allow you to transform your life. Adopting this inner knowledge into your life and adapting to the changes will be liberating and allow you to become a new you. Liberation is, therefore, 21st century enlightenment and that realisation enables you to change the world around you.

The Impact of our Emotions

Human beings are energy-beings and emotional-beings. We leave patterns of our energy everywhere we go, whether sitting in a chair, lying in bed, walking to work, driving a car, it doesn't matter where, we all naturally leave energy traces of ourselves.

When walking to a holy site or sacred space, we become more sensitive and our emotions become heightened by the expectation, the exertion, the possibility of being healed and the prospect of connecting to a higher realm.

As we mentioned earlier, Adrian often wondered why so many Buddhist Monasteries were difficult to reach or were perched on top of a steep hill or clinging to a mountain. Years later, the steep walk up to Coldstones Cut, in North Yorkshire brought back the memories of the 'No pain, no gain' thoughts that were constantly niggling in his mind during one of his trips to the Himalayas. But he slowly began to realise there was more to it than that. Perhaps the placement of the Monasteries is meant to echo our lives, if, like goals, they are too easy to reach, then nothing is learned.

As you begin your walk to the Monastery you are excited, not sure what the journey will bring, what you will find along the way and who you will meet. You start to tire as the long ceremonial climb upwards continues. Doubts about reaching your goal begin to set in as you start to dig deeper physically and mentally. You are out of breath often due to the altitude and the slope seems to get steeper and steeper. Are you going to make it? Are you worthy of reaching your goal? Suddenly, as you turn a corner, in front of you stand numerous stupas (spiritual monuments) that you then walk between to gain access to the temple. Relieved, in wonderment, emotional, dehydrated, tired, possibly hallucinating and certainly elated, are all ways to could describe how you feel. But you made the journey. You got there, however hard it was for you to do so. You were worthy and you joined with the energy patterns left by thousands of pilgrims who have made the same journey over the years and gone through the same process as you.

Because of this tendency to leave both our emotional patterns and an energy imprint behind us, anybody can trace or track human ramblings over the planet, and dowsing makes this possible. The stronger or deeper the emotions have been, the easier it is to track the journey, to uncover where people have been, how long they stayed and why.

Some years ago, on a trip to Bruges in Belgium, Adrian visited several of the churches to view the magnificent architecture. As he entered one, all that he could see was a thick mist in front of him and it wasn't from the incense that had been burning earlier. It was almost cloying, thick with deep human emotion that seemed to hang in the air. It had been left behind by the hundreds of people who had visited the church over the years. He admits that he walked straight out, the atmosphere was so uncomfortable that he couldn't stay. He did carry out an appropriate healing later, with permission of the church's guardian.

Buildings such as churches need regular clearing of human emotional patterns. They are places to confess your sins, seek redemption, grieve at funerals and celebrate wildly at weddings. They are places that can provide hope and salvation to many. Because of this, some very deep emotions can be left behind and these will often have a detrimental effect on other visitors in the future.

Many of the footpaths that we use daily today can be traced back hundreds of years; some will have been used by drovers, some as funeral paths and others simply for the requirement of walking between villages. As time went on, some would have been enlarged, tarmacked and then incorporated into part of the modern road network.

Although many of the routes that pilgrims used on their journeys between holy sites have been adopted as public footpaths and bridleways, they still contain the emotions, the hopes and desires, of those that have walked them in the past.

Our countryside is covered with these pathways. Some now form part of long distance footpath systems like the Ridgeway, the Pennine Way and the Pilgrims Way (which runs from Winchester to Canterbury). Before the car and our public transport system was formed they were probably in continuous use and for many different reasons.

They would have carried the rich and poor, the sick and healthy, pilgrims and other devotees, farmers with their herds of sheep or cattle going to market and, of course those that preyed on these folk... thieves, robbers, bandits, highwaymen and so on.

Strong or deep emotions can leave imprints that can remain for hundreds of years, affecting future generations in many different ways. Depending on their sensitivity, some people will see visions of this past human traffic, whilst others will feel what has gone before. Spirits can be found using these pathways, living purely on instinct, trudging along the same route that they used whilst alive, especially if there was a pub at the end. Pubs are always a good draw.

All sacred or hallowed sites will have pathways leading to them. Some could be described as ceremonial but, we would suggest that, these are mainly created by the holy men and women who would be leading the ritual. We would refer to the others as ancestral pathways and suggest they came into being purely with the amount of human traffic using them. Perhaps they should be called 'emotional pathways'.

Try dowsing the energies whilst you are out walking on any path. Find out when they were first trodden and by whom. Ask about their usage, whether they formed part of a holy walkway, bridle path etc. Are there any spirits still walking their traditional route and so on? This can bring much enjoyment to your walk as well as increasing your knowledge of the lives our ancestors lived.

This can also apply to your walking of a labyrinth, itself similar to an ancestral pathway. It has a beginning section, followed by a long walk (depending on the size of the labyrinth) along a twisting and turning route that weaves in and out, eventually leading to your destination, the centre.

We suggest that walking a maze is similar to walking a labyrinth, but the Victorians turned them into more of a novelty or the curiosity that we associate with them today.

We do not have to walk a labyrinth to connect or journey into ourselves. Just being in the great outdoors should help. Clear your mind, feel the breeze through your hair, the ground beneath your feet and the fresh air entering your lungs. Let yourself go, enjoy the freedom, the release of all pent-up emotions. And maybe reflect upon the fact that you, like those who walked that path before, will be leaving your unique energy patterns behind for others to follow.

Processional ways and ceremony

We believe that processional ways should be regarded as sacred sites just as much as solid constructions like long barrows, henges, stone circles and churches. In an earlier chapter, we mentioned the power of intent and the power of integrating it with the movement of your body. Walking, therefore, is a perfect example of mixing intent with physical movement. Additionally, a procession is usually a group activity, so it combines intent and the physical energy of the collective (or tribe) working together, all with the same focus of attention.

As you are probably already aware, people working together with a common goal will always exponentially magnify the intended effect and a ceremonial gathering can be a powerful thing. But is there even more to ceremony than that? Back in the 1980s, researcher Rupert Sheldrake termed what he called, the Morphic Resonance Theory:

'Morphic resonance is a process whereby self-organising systems inherit a memory from previous similar systems. In its most general formulation, morphic resonance means the so-called laws of nature are more like habits. The hypothesis of morphic resonance also leads to a radically new interpretation of memory storage in the brain and of biological inheritance.

'Memory need not be stored in material traces inside brains, which are more like TV receivers than video recorders, tuning in to influences from the past... each individual inherits a collective memory from past members of the species, and also contributes to the collective memory, affecting other members of the species in the future.'

His theory is very similar to the thoughts of psychotherapist Carl Gustav Jung with his notion of the 'Collective Unconscious'. He suggests that the human species has collective archetypal symbols within its psyche, i.e. within the group subconscious, and that these symbols and their symbolic meanings drive the species. He also suggested that they could appear in an individual's dreams.

Sheldrake posits that the laws of nature, to which man's behaviour also applies, (although many generally tend to exclude Mankind from being a part of nature) are collective memories passed through the ages of time from generation to generation. We suspect that Sheldrake associates these morphic fields with the ether, with the etheric mind or states of consciousness that are primarily associated with these other dimensions.

We believe that what Sheldrake is suggesting can be applied to ceremonies also, in that when people gather together to perform a ceremony they are subconsciously tapping into the past generations of people that have conducted the exact same ceremony at exactly the same place.

By repeating the patterns of past ceremony as closely as we can, it is possible that we can cause the modern ceremony to gain greater power: this is the legacy left to us by our ancestors. It gives us the ability to tap directly into the intent (sacredness) that was built up by all the previous generations who used the site for that same purpose.

Many rituals have been passed down through the years by word of mouth or storytelling and in some cultures passed from generation to generation by song. Eventually, they are often written down and saved for future generations to use.

The history of many tribes and societies has been vocally recorded in this way with information being passed from person to person, probably from Shaman to Shaman, through the centuries and learned by rote.

It is fair to say that the most important aspect of any ceremony taking place at a sacred site is, once again, intent. It is the intent of the practitioner or those responsible for leading the ceremony that will tap into, or draw upon, the energy of any similar historical activity that has taken place at the site.

Direction of walk

It is clear from many of the ceremonial pathways in the world that they were mostly walked in a clockwise direction. This follows the way of the sun as it travels its path, from rising in the east to setting in the west.

For many of the eastern religions and philosophies, Mount Kailash in Tibet is considered to be the Holiest of the Holies and the kora (peregrination) or ceremonial route around the mountain, is walked in the time honoured clockwise direction by Buddhists and Hindus. However, this is not the case for the Bonpo (possibly from Bond-Pa meaning 'to invoke the gods') or Jains, as they both walk around the mountain in an anti-clockwise direction, against the sun. There are various stories about why they do this, some quite amusing, but it is certainly the harder of the two journeys. The climb from the northern valley to Dromla Pass (18,200ft) is steep, slippery and arduous, the southern approach isn't a great deal easier, but is more manageable, as Adrian can testify.

Walking anti-clockwise is referred to as widdershins (possibly from the German widersinnen: to go against), viewed as a contrary direction and often considered unlucky. Most labyrinths are walked in a clockwise direction, so we suggest that, when entering a holy site or sacred space, you turn to the left unless you have dowsed beforehand and been told that it is acceptable to turn right.

Pilgrimage routes

Whereas processional ways are found at individual sites, pilgrimage routes connect many sacred sites within the landscape. The Camino de Compostela, for example, is a pathway linking numerous churches and holy sites along its almost 500-mile length.

If you decide that you would like to go on a pilgrimage, you will need to give some thought to what you want to achieve by walking it and look at possible countries. Routes in the UK and Europe are well-travelled and are, perhaps, more comfortable than some you will find in Asia. Visiting India will assault every one of your senses, but you will see some amazing sites and sights, and perhaps experience a special kinship with those you meet.

A key part of going on a pilgrimage is not just getting from A to B but those you meet along the path. Connecting with others and learning from them eventually helps you to learn about yourself, to begin to liberate yourself from past rigid patterns.

Pilgrimage routes are very similar to what we refer to as ley or holy lines that link various sites here in the UK. The Michael Ley, running from Cornwall to Norfolk, is considered to be a prime example.

There is a well-worn Monk's path forming part of the North Downs Way and another in Wales that ends at St David's, the site of a magnificent Cathedral. Many of these pilgrimage routes would have led to or connected with various abbeys, churches, holy wells or springs and ancient sites, like Thornborough Henges, along their length.

Before Henry VIII's dissolution of the monasteries, they must have been very busy places, especially those that housed the relics of saints and earlier martyrs. Glastonbury Abbey, for instance, was the supposed resting place of King Arthur. No doubt the Abbot made no secret of this and might have charged the visiting pilgrims to view the bones.

There would have been a huge impact not just on the land, but also on the people living close by these holy routes. A whole new infrastructure to make money from those travelling these pilgrimage routes would have developed.

People's homes would have become resting places for the weary traveller, somewhere safe and warm to sleep. Hospitality would have been given, in exchange for gold or other coinage, to these pilgrims, many of whom would be in various states of dilapidation. Many would have been performing a penance, perhaps fasting, possibly in bare feet, but probably wearing the obligatory hair shirt. Whatever their state, they would undoubtedly have been in dire need of sustenance.

These hostelries were very similar to today's service stations found on our motorways. They were there to provide food, water and shelter for the people and their animals on their long journey and, of course, to offer a safe haven. As these holy routes became more popular, the impact on the land and local people grew. Bigger hostels were needed to house the increasing numbers of pilgrims travelling these sacred pathways.

What was originally a small hamlet would have suddenly expanded to become a village. More and more people would have tried to make more money from the travellers. For those following their path, emotions and passion would have been running high and religious fervour would have been the driving force. Nothing else would have mattered but getting safely to their ultimate holy destination.

These people would have been preyed upon by the more unscrupulous. They would have been robbed, beaten and sometimes murdered for what they carried with them. The rich probably travelled side by side with the poor and none were safe. You can see why many pilgrimage routes still hold a lot of detrimental emotions along their path. This emotional charge would have had an effect on both the land and people. Therefore, Earth healing is very necessary as, of course, is the healing of the people who live on these ancient pathways, dealing with unknown and detrimental energies.

Knowlton Henge – ceremony caught in time

Knowlton Henge is one of the most holy sites to be found in Dorset. It ranks alongside the Thornborough Henges in terms of archaeological importance. Today it consists of a large henge (i.e. a bank and ditch) with a Christian church built in the centre.

Interestingly, when we get a very hot, dry summer, a good number of other henges can be seen from the air in the surrounding fields. Sadly though, they have all been put to the plough over the years and have virtually disappeared. Certainly, nothing can be seen from ground level.

The site must have been magnificent when in full use, the ceremonies must have gone on for days, maybe using different henges for different purposes: one purely for the priests to conduct their mystical practices, another for the young initiates, and so on.

In May 2013, Adrian organised for the British Society of Dowser's Earth Energies Group to visit the site. When there, they not only looked at the energies affecting the site, but also dowsed for the different ceremonial pathways and processional routes leading into and around the remaining henge, many from a pre-Christian era.

There was a difference between the later Christian pathway to the church and the earlier pagan/druidic ceremonial way, which, instead of aiming directly at its destination, flowed around the circumference of the henge finally to arrive at the meeting place, just off the centre.

Adrian's group dowsed that the Druid priests would split as they entered the henge, males going to the left and females to the right. They would then walk around the inner circumference to the opposite side, meet and leave the henge. They would then re-enter the site through two mature yews (only small yews are there today) often with linked hands or arms, then perform a ceremony standing slightly off the centre of the henge.

Adrian picks up the story:

"We marked out the route with coloured flags, took photographs and made notes before we took the flags away. Then, to our surprise, (we shouldn't have been surprised as it was Beltane, after all) a party of local Druids appeared and began to conduct their ceremony. We watched as they entered the henge, men to the left and women to the right. In fact they walked the exact route that we had dowsed some hours before.

"They were delighted when we told them what we had found and what they had done instinctively. They had not been taught, they had just done what they felt was right. This was definitely a case of shadows of the past affecting the present."

Chapter Ten

Building Sacred Spaces

Why build or construct a sacred space?

As we have mentioned before, it is not the destination that is important, but the journey getting to your final goal. The same could be said for building a sacred space. When building a sacred space, planning is everything. You need to decide what you want and why you want to create it, in other words, what you want from the final construction. It could be said that the time spent in working this out will be very similar to meditating. It is taking you away from your normal life and allowing you to become introspective, to look within yourself for the answer.

Creating a sacred space is a great way to improve or help your connection with the Creator, Mother Earth etc; that helps your spiritual advancement and meditation is a good way to help plan your sacred space. When doing so, images can often appear, seemingly out of nowhere. These pictures in your 'mind's eye' can point you in the right direction, to help you decide what form your sacred space will take, what materials you will use to construct it and where in your house, garden or land it needs to be built.

Another reason for building a sacred space is perhaps you want somewhere that anchors your focus and underpins your intent, rather like an altar in a church, a power centre whose energies will become more and more enhanced each time you enter the space to carry out healing or just to connect to the powers that be.

The space can be used for healing purposes, whether mental, physical or spiritual. It can be a place where you go to leave the 'real' world behind, to clear your mind of the day to day stresses and strains, to let go and just be. If you build a small stone circle, for instance, the act of entering should, automatically, allow you to leave your cares and concerns outside so you can concentrate on enhancing your spiritual connection. The more the space is used, the better the energies will become. Group meditations and dedications will help this process too.

Manifesting your hopes and aspirations could also be a reason for constructing a sacred space, but a word of caution is necessary here. Be very careful what you wish for as your thoughts and dreams can come true, but not always in the way you want them to. Be clear in your intent and check that your reasons for your manifestation desires come from the heart and not from the ego.

Self-gain, for instance, can be interpreted as greed by the Management. It is not a very pleasant human vice. It is so much better to manifest help for others, to become selfless and not selfish. Selflessness however, doesn't mean always putting others before your own needs, health and wellness. It is a wise person who maintains their own mental and physical health in order to help others.

Sacred spaces can also be used to harmonise areas of geopathic stress in places that have seen human suffering or hardship such as battlefields and hospitals, as well as your own home, village or town. Once a sacred space has been built, the energies will start to grow and expand outwards. The more healing that takes place there, the further this beneficial area will spread.

It is believed that so called burial mounds were built purely for this purpose, namely Earth healing, which in turn brought massive benefits to the people. It is the same today. Building a sacred site with the right intention will have a massive beneficial impact on the local population.

However, one thing to watch out for is if the sacred site you have built is in an area where others can use it too. It might lead to them abusing it. Any action or ceremony that is not in line with your intent in building the site will be an act of abuse as it will disrupt the energy flows of the site. So, you need to be aware of how you and others will use the space.

This is one reason why it is advisable to cast a circle in which to do your sacred work and then to ask for it to be removed when you have finished. The physical structure of the sacred site will enhance the cast circle and contain it and the energy of creating the 'magic' circle enhances and contains the act of ceremony within that time and space.

Why build a stone circle?

Our ancestors had many different reasons for building a holy site or creating a sacred space. This includes people healing, Earth healing, a place to venerate the gods, a place of celebration, a place to meditate and so on. Many of these reasons have been explored earlier in the book.

You may like to explore these further, to find out at first-hand what our ancestors were trying to achieve by building or constructing a stone circle. You will then be able to experience the changing energy patterns of the site as it matures and witness changes during the year on notable dates, such as the Summer Solstice, as well as what happens during full and new moon phases.

The first thing you will have to decide is how big the circle is going to be, how large the stones will be and, of course, where it is to be built. Size does matter, or at least it did to our ancestors, otherwise Stonehenge would never have been constructed, neither would Avebury and Silbury Hill. But most of us don't have acres of land to play with so build your stone circle to a scale that is realistic and within your budget.

A circle can be of any size, but our ancestors, perhaps through experimentation, found that the bigger and more complex the circle the more powerful it became, but that could be put down to the strength of intent of the builders.

If you have a small garden you may choose to place stones around its perimeter. It doesn't have to be an exact circle, in fact most of them weren't – they were slightly oval in shape. Intent is probably the most important thing here; you will get out of the circle what you put in. So, as you build it, place each stone with a specific task in mind - for example – Earth healing, animal communication etc.

This is where dowsing can come in very useful. You can dowse to see how many stones are needed for an Earth healing circle (there may be more or less for a different-purposed circle, one for purely meditational use, for instance). Dowse to find the stones that you should use. Perhaps your local garden centre might have a selection to choose from.

When Adrian builds a temporary stone circle in a village hall, he utilises small granite blocks that are more commonly used to construct a driveway. Even pieces of crystals can be used, but they can be expensive, especially the larger crystals. You will want to see the circle, even when the grass has grown. Choose your material wisely as the circle could be there for some time.

You can dowse to find out when to start construction. The new moon period is often good for new projects. Dowse to find out where each stone wants to go, which direction it would like to face and how deep it would like to be buried. You might like to bury small offerings beneath each stone, like crystals. Again, dowse for what needs to be done for your specific circle to enhance its energies.

Some people have constructed a stone circle to match exactly with the cardinal points of the compass (north, south, east and west) then perhaps marked the two solstice sunrises and/or sunsets, plus the various cross quarter days. Others have dowsed for and put the stones over the crossing points of water beneath the ground. Have in mind what you want from the circle and you will be guided.

Whether the circle is 20ft to 30ft in diameter or just a few feet, it doesn't matter so long as you use it for the right purpose. You can meditate quite happily in a circle that is only 3ft across, but if you wanted to include other people in a ceremony it would need to be bigger.

Once the circle is complete, dowse to see if there are any energy lines running through it. You might not have any to begin with, but they will arrive. The more you use the circle for healing and ceremonies, the quicker it will start to attract an energy line or ley. You might suddenly find that two underground streams have diverted themselves and now cross under your circle, just as you find underneath an altar in a church. It will add to the potency of the circle and increase the healing that comes from within.

Why construct a Vesica Piscis?

A Vesica Piscis is a sacred and secret symbol that was known intimately by holy men in ancient times and then taught to their acolytes, but only after years of training.

In essence, it is the basic motif for the Flower of Life.

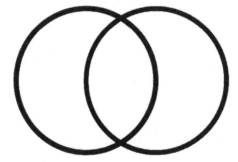

You might be more familiar with the symbol below, the shape forms a part of the whole and is similar to a fish, it is often used as a symbol of the Christian faith.

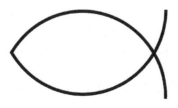

Many geometrical shapes can be formed within the two circles.

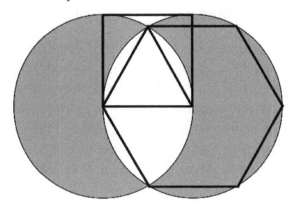

It was seen as holy and mystical, a symbol to be venerated and revered throughout history. Mathematical scholars and seers knew the power of the Vesica Piscis and kept it a closely guarded secret.

It has also been referred to as the Divine Feminine. The elliptical shape made by the interconnecting of the two circles resembles and is supposed to represent the entrance to a woman's womb, especially once the vertical line has been added.

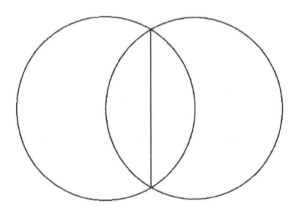

It can also be easily recognised as the Gothic archway that leads into many of the older churches here in the UK. Perhaps the builders deliberately echoed the shape of the Divine Feminine?

This is a life-changing shape and we can use it in so many different ways, to improve our food, water, sleep, environment and so on. To

start with, simply draw the Vesica Piscis on a piece of paper or card and place it under your plate of food before you start eating. You can stand a glass of water on top of the symbol for a few minutes and then see how it tastes. The molecular structure and energetic value of the liquid will have changed. Try dowsing the mineral content as the water comes out of the tap and then after it has stood on the symbol for a while. It should be much better for you.

The list is endless. Have one in your car, your pocket or wallet, tape one to your mobile phone and see if the detrimental effects are lessened. Put one under your pillow or mattress and dowse to see when it is most beneficial for you, it may not need to be there all the time.

You can use pebbles to lay the shape out on your lawn or patio then sit within the central oval and see what happens. Then get two friends to sit in the main circles and begin to meditate. The results can be quite surprising and profound.

Adrian and Allyson spent several hours at a friend's yoga studio in Devises, Wiltshire (www.whitehorseyoga.co.uk) drawing a Vesica Piscis on a large piece of calico. It is now taken to sacred symbol courses and workshops so that people can experience the power and/or meditate sitting or lying within this potent symbol. People have reported many different experiences, from feeling a deeper connection to the Divine, seeing the birth of elementals, various ailments disappearing instantly and a greater knowing of Self.

The experience can be further enhanced by the introduction of crystals, lit candles and/or stones, placed on the crossing points. This will bring in yet another dimension to the sacredness of the symbol.

Chapter Eleven

Healing Sacred Spaces

The healing power of place

Adrian visited Milarepa's Cave at Nyalam in Tibet some years ago, during a trip with his 'brother', Subash Tamang, and described the atmosphere as electric.

"As soon as you walked down the steps into the cave you could feel the power of the place. The energy from years of veneration had built up to such an extent that it almost took your breath away," he explained.

"I found it difficult to remain standing, quite apart from the low ceiling which forced me into a stoop. I had to sit on a large stone within the cave. The guide smiled and told me that was where Milarepa sat when meditating!

"I could hardly keep my eyes open due to the energies within the cave, they were so strong that I felt drained and elated all at the same time. Subash and I were almost forced into a meditative state, giving in to the holiness of the site. It was a sublime and humbling experience and we stayed for some time before we, reluctantly, had to continue our journey."

One of the hardest things in common daily life is remembering to treat our home or residence with the respect it deserves. Because of the way we live in this modern throwaway society, many people view their homes purely as an investment. Each move is a stepping stone to a bigger and better house and roots are rarely, if ever, put down.

We so often fail to see the benefits of treating our living spaces as sacred or holy, or to consider them as our sanctuaries, protecting us from the outside world. To value our homes spiritually and not in a monetary way is a huge step up in consciousness. If we could all adopt this thought process (intent) it would help the physical and mental health of our families as a whole. Then there is the spiritual side too: by calling on the full spectrum of energetic vibrations available to us we will be able to maximise the positivity of a space, whether it is one room in a large house or the whole property.

Continuing to focus mindfully on a beneficial outcome, to maintain the spiritual awareness of focused and gentle observation, will help to keep us all in the most appropriate mental state, allowing us to flow with the divine aspects of life.

There is a need and requirement for most of us to believe in something greater than ourselves as human beings and this is programmed into our psyche. It is recognised by psychologists as one of the basic tenets of humanity and it makes us human.

Co-ordinating points for healing

It appears that many holy sites and sacred spaces are built upon triple spirals, energy crossing points, or the meeting of many lines, in other words, the coalescence of earth energies. These are to be considered very special places and, if you are lucky, you may find a coordination point in your home. This can then become your healing centre and a good place in which to meditate.

Earth energy lines have been called many things over the years, including Dragon Lines in some ancient cultures, and the Rainbow Serpent in others. Many sensitives can see all the colours of the rainbow within these lines as they twist and turn across the countryside. Ancient carvings of spirals have been found on rocks around the globe as have those depicting the shape of a labyrinth.

See diagram below:

We believe that the labyrinth evolved from people first walking a large spiral, created either during a special ceremony or on a permanent site. Over time this began to morph into the now familiar labyrinth shape.

This may have taken place over several generations as our ancestors' brains began to expand with increased esoteric knowledge and it is likely that more complex patterns were needed to help to deepen their meditational state of mind as they developed. In fact, the labyrinth can look very brain like, as in the diagram above perhaps this was also a link used by the ancients.

Typical of any labyrinth, is the way a person is drawn to walk towards the centre only to be thrown to the outside before plunging back in again towards the final goal. The labyrinthine shape can be symbolic of so many aspects of our life's journeys and can hold a lot of power.

The energy spirals themselves can also be used as symbols for many of life's processes and revelations over time. These hugely powerful spirals can be felt at both sacred and holy sites. As mentioned previously, altars of churches are often located above them, where water and earth energy lines combine. These spirals are not just created by the Earth alone, they can also be formed by mankind. Planting a standing stone in the ground, for instance, will result not only in water being drawn towards it, but also in a spiral being created that can either be felt or measured through dowsing.

In a circle of standing stones, each stone will have its own vortex which will link to another stone which in turn will link to another stone and so on until the circle is complete.

Interacting with earth energy and the Management

The spiral is one of the most commonly found structures within the context of earth energy and its presence is very significant. It is very common but has such an important role to play in our lives. Earth energy spirals are vortices which affect us far more than we realise.

When two earth energy lines cross or interact with other electromagnetic fields, such as those emanating from water veins, they will form a spiral or vortex. These spirals are basically the two-dimensional, (dowsable) layouts of a three-dimensional shape i.e. the vortex.

Similar vortices are also found in substances like gas or water. So, when we dowse for earth energy, we can often find a spiralling interference pattern, whether due to an earth energy line passing nearby, a crossing water vein, a ley line or an energy channel. When dowsing any spiral, you will find straight radials emanating from the centre hub, very similar to the spokes of a wheel. At the centre of the spiral, or vortex, you should be able to find the infinity symbol or, to give it its full mathematical name, '*The Lemniscates of Benoit*'.

As all these patterns are three dimensional, careful dowsing will often reveal another 'infinity symbol' overlaid at right angles and sometimes, depending on how many water veins or streams are interacting with each other, you will find more. Most commonly you will find two pairs of infinity symbols at right angles to each other. They form loops which pulsate, and they give the impression the Earth is in a relaxed waiting/receptive state. They are rather like a heartbeat from the planet.

These basic earth energy patterns are found at every 'power centre' (significant vortex) in every home in the world. When you begin to interact with this power point in your home, it's really interesting to observe and record how the radials react to you.

You can use dowsing to ascertain how many radials there are before you start to meditate or focus your intent. Adrian always asks to be shown the number at, say, four o'clock in the morning, before the vortex has had a chance to react to any human consciousness in the house, and is at rest.

As you start to focus or begin to meditate, showing or sending love to Mother Earth, the number of radials will begin to increase substantially. When you stop your meditation they will gradually decrease in number, but the more you tune in, the more powerful the centre will become and the more radials will be present at rest.

Hamish Miller never tired of discussing the significance of these power centres as they are hugely important to us as humans. Our thoughts and actions can make such a difference. As our thoughts emanate from us they are collected by the ether at the quantum level of existence; the dimension of pure potentiality from which everything is eventually manifested.

Dowsing is a very simple process for us to use to work with, and interact with, earth energies. It shows us the link between mind and matter, between spirit and earth. Earth energy is the key to unlock many of the mysteries of creation that surround us.

The most useful thing to know is that the behaviour of earth energy radials confirms that there is actually something outside us that reacts to our presence on a purely spiritual level. Earth energy (power) centres are places where connection to the divine can be easiest to achieve. That is why meditation will be at its most effective when conducted at an energy spiral.

The process can work both ways, however. If you meditate in the same location in your home repeatedly, an energy spiral will eventually move to that point and will begin to play its part in a two-way exchange of information.

This is just one of the ways in which the ether (the subatomic field in which these spirals exist) displays signs of awareness. It may be that earth energy knows where you meditate and makes its own decision to relocate the spiral or, equally, it might be a physical process controlled by the physiology of the human energy field that interacts with the electro or geomagnetic energy of the Earth. No matter how it works, there is no doubt that the two fields of energy, human and earth, commune with each other in a dance of life.

In order to get the best from these power centres, it is helpful to still your mind and body, and detach yourself from your everyday, mundane thoughts.

Meditation should bring us into the present moment and allow us to *stop.* When we do, it can enable our brainwave frequency to change, to more closely match the rhythm of the Earth.

Which sites would benefit from reconnection?

If you want to find out which sacred or holy site might benefit from being healed or reconnected, dowse them to find out. Many ancient sites will benefit from being worked on. You can map-dowse an area before you set out on your journey to find which sites need help.

Don't forget the ones that aren't very apparent or well-known, as so many sites have been ploughed, dismantled, or have just collapsed and disappeared. Get the map out and ask if there are any sites in a particular area that need reconnecting.

You might find yourself in the middle of a seemingly empty ploughed field but, although it may be devoid of anything today, it might have been a place of worship in the past, such as a holy well that has dried up or a dismantled stone circle.

Reconnection means lighting up yet another section of the holy grid of earth energies that will eventually surround the planet once again. This reconnecting of sacred or holy sites has been explained using crystals, (see Chapter 6), but can also be brought about by your intent, but please make sure that the Spirit of Place or guardian of site is happy for you to do this work before you start.

We would suggest that you first dowse to see if the site is actually disconnected from other local sites and then, if possible, find out why. It might have been necessary to annexe the sacred site due to a discordant or inharmonious energy for instance. The site, therefore, might need healing before the reconnection is allowed to take place, this is specialised work and we suggest, if you are interested in learning more, that you attend one of our courses on the subject.

Earth energies and what they mean to us

Although research into earth energies has been going on for decades, the terms used to identify these patterns, found either by dowsing or by intuition, need to be clearly defined so all those involved in this fascinating research can understand what they are looking for and what they actually find.

Different labels are currently being used by different people to describe basically the same things. There is a great deal being rediscovered and much of this relates back to either recorded or spoken ancient teachings. Today, however, we are trying to understand how this subtle energy relates both to the development of the human species and the planet and part of that process is to understand what we mean by each label we use to describe what is found.

Earth energy - terms and definitions

We tend to think of earth energy rather like the flow of energy within the human body, travelling along meridians to acupuncture points, but there is no doubt that the Earth and its surrounding planets are far more complex and multi-dimensional than the human body, although of course they have developed in tandem over millennia.

Some aspects of earth energy seem to be linked to features of the human mind, giving credence to the idea that the mind or soul may be partly located outside the body. Research continues in various fields arguing over this concept.

Earth Energy Lines:

These are lines of energy found on the surface of the planet and found by some deep within the ground as well as high in the air, (Hamish Miller famously dowsed earth energy channels while in an aeroplane!) Earth energy lines can be up to 17ft wide and many seem to have been laid down as the planet was formed by the Creator, helping life to exist and evolve.

We can find no bands or other structures within them, other than colour, and have often been described, over centuries, as Rainbow Serpents by those that can see them. The energy usually only flows in one direction, although that can reverse during eclipses, full moons and solstices.

They are part of us and we are part of them. Many people, when standing on an earth energy line, can feel warmth or a vibration under their feet, such is the power contained within them. You will always find them running through sacred or holy sites. They seem to bring in a life force, to energise the area, giving it a special feeling.

Earth energy lines will expand and contract with human interaction. Dowse for the nearest one to you and mark its width. Then walk away from the edge that you have marked (say five feet) then sit and start to think or meditate about the line, in effect, you are tuning in to it. Observe what happens. You often find the line starts to expand, it might move towards you and shortly it will fully encompass you within its energy field.

Ley Lines:

Alfred Watkins wasn't the first man to notice these lines, but he did bring them to prominence in his lifetime. His book, *The Old Straight Track* is required reading for dowsers and anyone interested in exploring earth energies. However, it can be a bit dry and other more modern books have brought his thoughts up to date in a more readable fashion (listed in the Recommended Books list at the rear).

The term 'ley' is Old English, meaning a piece of land laid down to grass (a meadow) or the edge of grass around a ploughed field. However, Watkins used it to describe a line (of sight) linking notable features or alignments of geographical and historical interest, such as ancient monuments, including standing stones and megaliths, natural ridge-tops or notches in hills, water-fords and crossroads etc. Many of the examples that he mentioned or photographed in his book have now disappeared under the development of villages, towns and cities.

In his book, *View over Atlantis* the late John Michell rekindled the term 'ley lines', giving them a more mystical significance, seeing them as a spiritual network of lines running across the country.

We prefer to view them as human intent lines or holy lines, which are present at almost every sacred site. If they are not there now, the chances are they would have been in the past. We believe they would have been created by the shaman or holy man or woman of the village as guide lines for people to follow, perhaps from one holy site to another. Their energies could either be felt or seen by the sensitives and then followed, rather like an early pilgrimage route.

As discussed in earlier sections, the energy found within these lines tends to contain human emotion, which can be quite detrimental to other individuals and animals, especially if we are not vibrating on the same frequency.

Sacred sites can often be dumping grounds for people's emotional problems. These emotional outpourings soak into the ley lines and can be transported for many miles, sometimes affecting people who have never even been to the site. For more information on these complex lines, please read Adrian's book, *Heal Your Home*.

Energy Channels

The famous Michael and Mary lines, plotted and followed over several years by Hamish Miller and Paul Broadhurst, are today what we call energy channels. These energy channels run through and around sacred sites, often crossing and frequently linking to a main ley.

The book of Hamish's and Paul's adventure, mapping these now famous lines, is called *The Sun and The Serpent* and is required reading for anyone interested in earth energies and sacred sites.

Energy channels twist, turn, cross and meet on their river-like paths across the countryside. The crossing points tend to be at, or very close to, sacred sites, holy wells and springs. They are commonly referred to as male or female energy currents and they have a very distinct individual feel to them as you dowse. They are very mercurial and their energy patterns can change quite drastically.

They also react quickly to human consciousness. If you are standing or meditating close to one of these lines they will, just like earth energy lines, begin to expand towards you and again you will soon find yourself enveloped in their energy patterns. It can be an exhilarating experience, especially around the stones at Avebury. There are many different energy channels to be found in the UK, not just Michael and Mary.

When visiting a sacred place, as you start to dowse, ask if there are any energy channels running through it, watch what your rods do and then walk in the direction that they point, until they cross (always ask for the centre of the line). Once they do, you have found yourself standing within an energy channel and if you wish you can dowse the width of the channel too. Then you can start to follow its path by asking the rods to show you the direction it travels and see where it leads you. You will certainly be in for an adventure. You may also like to ask whether the energy channel has a male or female energy associated with it. If it is female, you can search for the male equivalent and vice versa.

If you are lucky to be in a place where the feminine and masculine lines cross (ask the question) you will be standing at a very energetic location, with very holy and special energies.

Energy Spirals (Vortices)

As soon as you find a crossing point of water, fault lines, energy lines or simply varying frequencies of energy, you will come across an energy spiral or vortex.

This whirlpool of energy is, understandably, a very interesting place to stand within. You can find yourself being pulled clockwise or anticlockwise producing a similar effect to riding on a Waltzer at the fairground. These energies have been utilised over generations, providing holy sites with their special feel or buzz.

Some spirals or vortices, however, can be detrimental to us. Sleeping above an energy spiral can produce many symptoms or ailments including insomnia, night sweats, bad dreams and vertigo.

At sacred sites, they will often be found where the centre of human focus is, or where the attention has been in the past. Our ancestors knew how to harness this energy and many churches have been built where they are to take advantage of these power spots. The priests and holy men knew where to stand to achieve maximum impact.

The same will often apply to lecture theatres. An energy spiral or vortex can often be found where the speaker or tutor usually stands, as that is the main focus of the student's attention. In fact, you will often find that people who are giving talks or teaching courses are drawn subconsciously to stand within these vortices.

This is a prime example of the way many aspects of earth energies are intrinsically linked to human consciousness.

Toroids

A toroid is a ring or doughnut-shaped energy field, often found at sacred sites and specifically within henges. One theory is that they are caused by an energy wave hitting the curved side of a henge or bank, being forced upwards and then folding back on itself to form the familiar ring shape.

Another theory suggests that these toroids are a natural geometric shape found at various scales within the all-pervading zero-point (quantum) field, and that the ancients used the circular shape of the henge (excavated ring) to limit the movement of the toroid, keeping it in place as part of the sacred energetic landscape.

It is thought this was to help give the henge (Avebury as an example) a sacred and special feel. It would have given an energetic uplift to anyone who entered the site, enabling a feeling of being elevated to a higher level, helping them to commune with the gods and other devic beings.

The energy patterns produced within a henge can easily be dowsed. But, if you do decide to walk up the steep banks with your dowsing rods in hand, please take care as most can be slippery, especially the wet chalk at Avebury. Also, as you walk away from the bank, ask your rods to show you where the outer edge of the toroid (doughnut) is. This way you will get a better idea of the size of these amazing energy patterns.

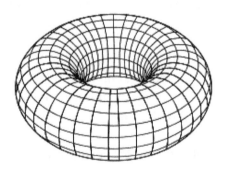

Fault Lines

These are natural lines produced by the movement of the tectonic plates of the planet. The San Andreas Fault is a good example, as is the Rift Valley in Africa, but most of them aren't as massive or dramatic as these two. Take the Craven Fault as an example here in the UK, it includes Malham Cove and Giggleswick Scar, with their exposed, weathered rocks showing a tortuous past of massive upheavals of the Earth.

They cannot always be seen on the ground, but hairline cracks running up the wall of a house can sometimes be a sign of nearby activity.

Many sacred or holy sites will have a fault line either running through them or just skirting their outer edge. Belas Knapp in Gloucestershire is a good example and, going further afield, the ancient site of the Delphic Oracle in Greece.

They seem to have been used by our ancestors to help to energise and enhance the spirituality of the area but, due to their very nature, they can also contain detrimental patterns within them, rather like earth energy lines, capturing human emotional problems as well as the energies from Mother Earth. If you are interested in locating any hidden, lost, ransacked or forgotten sacred or holy sites, dowse to find a fault line then follow it until the rods cross, indicating that you have arrived. You may find that it is worth your while map dowsing the area first. It could save you a long walk.

Ask the question, *'Is there a fault line here that would lead me to a sacred site?'* See what the rods tell you and then walk or drive to the location. Ground work is important to carry out, as much can be seen, especially when the sun is low in the sky. Shadows can suddenly appear to show you where the henge had been before being ploughed over.

How earth energies relate to sacred sites and your home

Purely through man's intent, many of the Earth's energy patterns have been manipulated. This was done to energise sacred sites, to give them the buzz that many people experience when entering. These energies are also responsible for giving each sacred or holy site a special and unique feel. Some can be very beneficial to people, whilst others may not be so good.

Not everybody, however, will be sensitive enough to feel the effects of earth energies, either physically, mentally or psychically, especially if they are not aware of what an energy current is or feels like. These energy patterns operate over a large range of frequencies and vary from location to location as well as differing within the actual site.

Some people entering a stone circle or similar sacred site may experience detrimental effects such as sudden headaches, nausea, blurred vision, actual visions, feeling faint or becoming dizzy, whilst others may feel absolutely nothing. The very same people who felt nothing at a stone circle could then, for example, visit a sacred spring and suddenly become affected by the same unpleasant symptoms.

We are affected in different ways as we are all individual and totally unique. The energies found at sacred sites are usually very strong and these frequencies can be very detrimental to humans and animals, especially if you live near them.

If your home, for instance, was energised to this high spiritual level all the time, the effects could be harmful and debilitating. Your body could start to struggle, as your auric field could be constantly disrupted and this, in turn, could have a detrimental effect on your immune system.

Because we are all individuals, some people can be 'bullet-proof'. These are people that are rarely, if at all, affected by anything. Their constitution is such that they are shielded/protected or immune to anything that might be detrimental to them, whilst other more sensitive souls fall prey to the many energy patterns that we find on planet Earth.

Some of these energies are naturally produced and are commonly referred to as geopathic stress, which is literally illness produced or created by Mother Earth. Others are man-made such as the waves from mobile telephones and masts, microwave ovens, low energy light bulbs, Wi-Fi and other technological equipment. All these can cause massive disruption within your energy field (aura) which in turn can lead to many types of illness.

It is, therefore, a good idea to regularly work on the energy patterns within your home, making sure they are in harmony with you, your family and pets. Geopathic stress affects many people in different ways. If you are interested in learning more about this subject, it is worth your while reading Adrian's book, *Heal Your Home*. This is available via his website www.dowsingspirits.co.uk or see Tim's work at www. knightsrose.com

How do these energies affect sacred sites and holy places?

All holy places and sacred sites will have a special feel to them, this could have come from the chosen location, by intent or by repeated rituals taking place. These energies can be either beneficial or detrimental to you, rarely are they neutral, unless the site has been deconsecrated. These energies at sacred sites are fluctuating all the time and are never still. They will often become more complex as we near a solstice, full moon, solar eclipse, equinox or other major event in the solar system. A large group of people visiting a site can also cause much disruption, especially if they are disrespectful.

Sacred sites were usually designed for a specific purpose, be it worship, Earth healing, spell casting, ceremonies for gatherings of priests or initiates, chanting or singing, even handfasting.

The energy patterns will be enhanced if ceremonies are regularly conducted at these places, especially if that is what the site was originally designed for. These sacred ceremonial activities will create specific energy patterns which can build in intensity and, in time, will feed back to those who are gathered within the sacred site, increasing and heightening the sensations that they will feel during the ceremony.

It is all part of the powerful connection of mind, body, spiritual and earth energies: they all combine in a natural dance within the sacred site.

Sometimes houses and places of work are built over abandoned sacred sites. The land still holds the intention within the earth energy, which is not always a good thing as having this amount and type of energy in your own home might not be appropriate, and constantly living in a heightened state of emotion would be detrimental to many people.

How we can use earth energies

Within the dowsing and Earth mysteries community it is comparatively well known that human beings can affect earth energy lines and water courses with their thoughts and actions. For instance, church builders in the past knew about the acoustic effects underground water features such as blind springs or water domes, could have at surface level. It seems likely, although there is no documented proof, that many of these mediaeval builders would have looked to incorporate these energetic patterns within the confines of the churches they constructed.

The evidence appears in the number of Christian churches that were built on earlier pagan or Druid worship sites and/or altars. A good example of this is at Knowlton Henge in Dorset where a Christian church was built within an ancient pagan henge. By using these early sacred sites, the architects were capturing the high-energy patterns already found there as well as literally building their new Christian belief system upon the foundations of earlier religions.

Many of the stone circles we have visited and dowsed have been energised through human intent, for example by asking the spirit realms and/or Mother Earth to encourage the appropriate energy lines and water courses to be diverted through the site.

At many sacred sites, such as Avebury, people can feel a tingling sensation when they lay their hands upon the huge standing stones. Different bands of energy can be found if they move their hands up or down the stone.

As you look at one of the large stones you are only seeing the top two-thirds, the buried third is the part that reacts or connects with underground water and earth energy lines – they are its power source. It is the interaction of the quartz within the stones and its contact with the water that produces the energetic buzz that can be felt by many people touching the stones at these sacred sites. By tapping into these natural power sources, we can begin to carry out healing of the land, people and animals, but you will find that not all sacred places were designed to be used in this way.

Each site is different. The Thornborough Henges, one of the oldest and most significant sacred sites in Great Britain, is made up of three henges angled to perhaps mimic Orion's Belt in the night sky. When people visit each of the henges they can detect different energy patterns within them, meaning that each henge has a specific feel and vibrates in a different way.

Earth energy is a vastly under-studied aspect of our existence as human beings. We are intrinsically linked to it. Earth energy impacts on every aspect of our lives. We, as humans, have evolved with these earth energies. We have worked with them for millennia. In fact, as soon as we became aware of them, the likelihood is that we would have begun to communicate our awareness to others. The places earth energy was especially strong would have been venerated. Aboriginal peoples such as those in Australia are said to have used earth energy lines to communicate to one and other using telepathy over vast distances. With the ancient widespread building of sacred sites across the world, early humans could have also been linked together in this way.

It's very likely that our ancestors favoured these sites of high energy activity and began to worship there. Eventually they began to erect stones and move tons of earth and rocks to build some amazing structures like Stonehenge, Avebury, the Serpent Mound in Ohio, the Moai statues on Easter Island and so on.

As society developed and became more complex, our ancestors found new ways to enhance the energies within the sites by diverting the many different types of energy flows they found. By doing so they manipulated and increased the energetic influence of the site, presumably to improve their lives or heighten their spiritual experiences.

It would be a mistake for us to give the impression these energies are only present in these flowing lines and vortices etc. that we have described above or purely found at sacred sites. Earth energy is all around, above and beneath us, we cannot escape its influence. The features described here are simply concentrations of the energy fields. It is the life-blood of our planet, the veins and arteries of Mother Earth and as such is sacred and holy.

Sensitive people will feel these energy lines and energy channels in different ways. Buzzing or tingling are words commonly used to describe how they feel when they enter a holy place or sacred site. Another sensation felt as they walk over or move close to an energy source can be the warming of the hands and/or feet. Some people will get goose bumps whilst the hairs on their arms stand on end and, in extreme cases, a mild electric shock.

People's moods can also be affected as they approach or stand close to an earth energy line, especially if they are resonating at a different frequency. Their temperament can change as they come under its influence. You can feel totally ecstatic one minute and then extremely depressed the next, although this will depend on how psychically protected you are and also your level of sensitivity.

This, of course, applies to your home also. If one of these disharmonious energy lines runs through it, it can be very detrimental to your emotions and health.

Certain sacred sites will affect males differently from females. Swallowhead Spring near Avebury is one such site. It is a secondary spring meaning that it only tends to flow when there has been heavy rain. To our ancestors it might have appeared magical, coming to life at certain times of the year, flowing into the River Kennett, giving sustenance to some beautiful trees and shrubs along its banks. Whether they considered it magical or not, it's likely that its sporadic appearance would have made it special in their society.

Energetically, it is a very beneficial place to visit, especially for women, as there is a specific energy there that is uniquely feminine or goddess-like. The stunted trees and unnaturally twisted branches clearly show that this is truly an energetic site. The Mary Line, a highly-charged energy channel full of human emotion and Earth created energies is known to run through the spring. For more information see "The Sun and The Serpent" written by Hamish Miller and Paul Broadhurst .

These earth energies bring a special feel to the spring, but it does have its off days. It can be quite foreboding at times and may feel like human beings are just not wanted there. Both authors have experienced sudden headaches when visiting. However, Allyson appeared very calm and at home, revelling in the cossetted atmosphere she found there.

Perhaps the spring is being balanced, at times, by the West Kennett Long Barrow which lies on the hill above, as that feels uniquely masculine. Adrian has always felt at home when he visits there. The Mary Line also runs through the Long Barrow, linking it inexorably to Swallowhead Spring. A balancing, maybe, of the divine feminine and the masculine. People often refer to the Yin and Yang of the site and this is just another way of describing the feminine and masculine energy patterns produced by Mother Earth.

Overall though, these Earth energies are beneficial and life-affirming. Therefore, taking time out when visiting a sacred site can be very rewarding for your mind, body and spirit.

Sitting still with your eyes closed should help you to unwind, de-stress and eventually connect to the site via the energy patterns there, but please be patient. The connection rarely happens the minute you sit down. However, if you sit quietly with an open heart (and psychic protection) you could be amazed at what you experience.

Grounding yourself and connecting with Mother Earth each day is a good habit to get into. Working with her can bring many rewards; being in tune with, and paying respect to, these energy patterns can also, in time, change your life, but only if you fully acknowledge them and then begin to work with them. Earth healing enables you to achieve a greater understanding of life, yourself and others around you.

Everyday benefit

How can we use the energies of holy sites and sacred spaces in our everyday living? In order to experience the realm just beyond our five senses, as well as attuning ourselves to our external environment, we also need to acknowledge our inner emotions too. In this way, we can connect to and be at one with the physical Earth and also all the sacred sites we encounter.

We know very little about the ceremonies and practices of the ancient

Druids, for instance, since little was written down, relying on the Bards and story tellers to pass on relevant information to the next generation. Consequently, much of their knowledge was lost when they were slaughtered by the Romans.

It is therefore perhaps better for us to look at what these sites can do for us today, not what people used them for in the past. Times change, and therefore we also need to change our outlook.

Just sitting within a holy site can bring a peace of mind that is not achievable when outside. It can depend on how many people are visiting the site but generally you can find somewhere to sit, relax and tune in. You will often find that when you need a period of peace and quiet the Management will provide the solution. People suddenly disappear, and you can have your moment of peace. It might not be for a long period of time, but you will get what you need.

You will need to be aware, when at a sacred site or holy place, that people visiting before you could have deposited a lot of their emotional junk there, as indeed you are probably just about to. So, keep your guard up and psychically protect yourself before you enter the site. You can always dowse to see if today is the right day for you to visit and/or what the best time for you to go is.

Once on the site you can, for instance, ask the guardian or Spirit of Place to be with you and, if appropriate, help bring healing to anything that ails you, both mentally and physically.

Dowse to find out which standing stone is the best one for you to connect with and for how long. Each stone will be different, so keep a clear picture in your mind what you want to achieve from the connection, you might need to sit facing a particular direction and on wet grass rather than a plastic bag, as it is more grounding that way.

It would also be a good time for contemplation and/or meditation as the energies found within the site are normally conducive to your connecting with spirit and also the Earth. This can help you in a myriad of ways, including stress relief, cleansing of your aura, helping you to see your pathway in life a little clearer and so on. It does depend on what you need on the day.

We would suggest that the same healing could be carried out within your own stone circle or Vesica Piscis etc., but by actually visiting a stone circle or dolmen and using its latent energy, you are not only getting healing from the site, but you are adding to it, and keeping it alive.

Sacred sites and holy places are a part of the physical structure that can be used to optimise our connection to the spirit or divine, but we do have to be in a good state of mind to fully utilise them.

Intent

Human intent is powerful, and once directed towards a particular target, person or site, it can produce some remarkable results. Intent can be summed up in the often quoted spiritual platitude *It's not what you do, it's how you do it.* The intent is the 'how you do it' part of that phrase. In order to focus intent for remote healing, for example, one sits in meditation and gathers the feeling of what needs to be achieved, makes contact with the Management upstairs (via a spirit guide or directly to Source or through a collection of spiritual helpers) and asks for the healing to be done by the Management, always for the utmost good and for the best possible outcome to all beings.

Using the power of intent in one's own life is fundamental to 'intentional living', that is living in alignment with the understanding and knowledge that we are co-creators of our realities along with those in the spiritual dimensions (subtle realms), and the Earth itself which provides the mechanism for manifesting in the form of earth energy.

Combining the power of intent, with one's intuitive understanding of the connection to spirit and the Management can be very effective indeed as we hope this book has helped you understand. However, the power of intent at times, needs to be anchored in place. The best way to do that seems to be to exert human energy and move physical mass such as large stones into designated positions. This may be the reason some holy sites were built; they help us to concentrate and/or focus, on a particular task with a particular intent.

If you have a busy mind or a very stressful job, using intent can be difficult. It needs to be focussed in a particular way, especially if it involves sending healing to a person or place.

If the intent isn't strong enough, it can easily be dissolved or diluted. That is why it can be useful to create a holy site or sacred space to work with or within that will act as an anchor point, a place of focus, a site that helps you to exclude outside interference and concentrate on the divine.

Common interest/bond

There are many common interests that tie holy sites together, for example, the furtherance of human knowledge, wealth, health, control of the people, seeking a connection with a higher force (the Creator) or finding solitude from the outside world to experience or live a more spiritual life. The reasons can be many, but each individual thought and hence the combined human intent can add to or build up over many generations to turn, what was perhaps an insignificant site to begin with, into a place venerated and visited by millions.

So, why did our ancestors spend so much of their time and energy building these remarkable sacred sites? Surely the needs of their direct family and tribe should have come first, especially with regard to the planting of crops and general land-husbandry. There must have been a common interest in working on these sacred sites that were perhaps started by an earlier generation that which completed them.

Many people like to congregate or flock together, look at how our towns and cities have developed for example. It may well have been to help complete a sacred site (possibly close to a holy spring) that drew people into an area to settle down As more people congregated in the one place, the feeling of the area would help create a spiritual bond amongst the group or tribe.

As the number of people grew, perhaps they needed a leader, someone who could unite them with a common bond, and that is probably where the need for a Shaman or Village Elder came from. That person would have an innate connection with the people and the elements as well as a direct line to the spiritual realms. The Shaman would then conduct ceremonies as the spiritual leader, the contents of which would have undoubtedly been channelled either directly from above or by them journeying with the help of substances like magic mushrooms or peyote.

Perhaps, as the ceremonies became more complex, a bigger site was needed to hold the energy patterns in place. And so the building began; small to begin with, perhaps a henge, then as the ceremonies became grander and more people attended, something bigger and more ostentatious was needed... like Stonehenge!

Reverence and self-respect

Intent, of course, ties in very deeply with human consciousness. At a holy site, if we are being reverential, it puts us in a mental and emotional state that is open and ready to accept information coming to us from the higher realms.

If we freely accept that there are beings far greater than us and that they are more altruistic, have a greater capacity for compassion and are therefore at a higher level of consciousness, then it stands to reason that we need to be respectful towards them.

We need to be humble in order to allow the relevant and, perhaps, timely information to come to us. However, part of being humble and respectful is also about acknowledging our own self-worth. We are told that we were made in the image of God, and yet we humans often tend to feel that we are not worthy. Or conversely, we can be overly confident and have a self-inflated ego, which can easily lead us to becoming egotistical and/or arrogant.

Both sides of this coin, being self-effacing and lacking confidence, or being arrogant and narcissistic can disrupt the connection with Source.

In that disengaged state when we visit a holy site, we won't feel anything special. Many sacred sites and holy sites will switch on in response to the individual's state of mind and intent as they approach. When they do, that is the time that the most can be gained from the interaction that ensues. Without reverence and a certain degree of humility, this usually doesn't happen.

To those who feel less than confident in their ability to connect to the higher realms, the authors bluntly suggest stop thinking that you are not worthy, as we are all worthy of everything, every second of the day. We just need to adjust or change our current thought patterns, to realise that we are *always* connected to some degree. Even when in ego, there is still a tenuous connection to Source as it is part of life.

With a greater connection we can begin to see, what we refer to as our faults and failings, but we are also able to recognise that this greater being, (Source), also accepts us for what and who we are... warts and all.

And that is liberating.

Altruism, focus, charity

Humans are complex emotional beings. Many of us struggle with life on many different levels, often as a result of early life trauma. Often our struggles are self-imposed through our beliefs about how life should be and our emotional programming.

Through healing and self-development work, deeply disempowering emotional states like shame and self-loathing can be unlearned and gently transmuted into less harmful states of being such as self-depreciation. From there, it in turn can be transmuted into a more self-appreciative emotional state where one can see one's own worth. When this occurs, we are in a much better position to add positively to the lives of those around us. This can eventually lead to an ability to see life in a largely altruistic way, in which we consider other people with true compassion.

If we haven't fully accepted who we are and haven't yet started to see our own worth at all, then it is very difficult to truly help others and that is where many healers can come unstuck. Before you can heal others, you must have the ability, at least to some extent, to love yourself, this is not an egotistical self-love, but a heartfelt inner knowing love, that comes from spirit.

The same seems to be true within the consciousness of the underlying structure of the universe. If we believe we can be guided here on Earth, then we can assume similar guidance exists when we pass over and return to spirit. We can assume that some form of conscious decision-making is maintained by beings greater than ourselves and that they are indeed selfless in their actions, working towards harmony within the whole. That is to say, working towards the advancement of the whole human-based soul-group of the Universe in that dimension. This concept certainly seems to be supported in the many stories told by those returning from Near Death Experiences.

A place to explore the greater meaning

We believe that often sacred spaces can help you explore and think about the big questions of life:

Why are we here?

How did we get here?

Who or what is/was responsible for creating life as we know it?

Often when you receive one answer, it can lead you to another question and so on. Always take a notebook or journal with you when you visit a site, to note how you feel, what you see and, of course, jot down the answers to your questions. You will certainly find it interesting when you look back on these experiences to see how far you have come in your spiritual learning.

When you visit a popular holy site or sacred space, like West Kennet Long Barrow for instance, perhaps wanting to gain deeper insights or to ask spiritual questions, you will be amazed at how often you will be left alone; people will suddenly disappear as if by magic. The powers that be will give you the time that you need to tune in and connect with the site. You will have time alone to experience the same atmosphere and solitude that our ancestors did.

You may also notice that there is a silence associated with a sacred space. Is this created by reverence and veneration, or by design? How did a church feel, for instance, just after it had been built? Were the sacred energies there immediately or did they take time to build?

We need to be reminded sometimes that *Silence is Golden* (a phrase from a longer proverb thought to date back to Egyptian times) and that being still and not talking is important. When the sounds of the outside world disappear, you may start to feel and experience the energy patterns that have been in place for generations.

Generally, we are bombarded by so much noise throughout the day that it makes it difficult for us to hear anything meaningful. Sitting in silence can help you and allow you to perceive messages from the spirit realm.

Gathering of the elders or meetings of counsel

Our forebears here in the UK, as in many places throughout the world, would have gathered in a round house to discuss tribal or holy matters. And before houses were constructed, they would meet in secret glades or clearings in the forest.

There is a location, near Summerbridge in the Yorkshire Dales, called Old Spring Woods that has the sensation of being a past gathering place. It feels full of ancient lore, very still and peaceful. Rocks are placed in a circle beneath an old oak tree. They are covered in a thick layer of moss now, but in the past, who knows what they would have looked like and how they were arranged. There has been a lot of industry in the area, especially in the Iron Age, so the scene may well have changed, but there is still a spiritual energy about this location that can't be ignored. Many of these meeting places were for community decisions or judgement of others (like courts) in which honest communication would have been important. Sacred sites, as we have seen, have the ability to enable higher levels of intuitive interaction and even enable forms of mediumship. At such places, any dishonesty of thought or word would have been much easier to identify. These meeting places would eventually become sacred spaces, treated with respect and reverence and maybe later, with awe and trepidation. These were places to which you were invited for a specific reason or you were summoned.

Some sacred sites were obviously created for a purpose, Avebury (Stone Circle and Henge), Devil's Arrows (Standing Stones), The Thornborough Henges, Stonehenge, Woodhenge and Silbury Hill, but *why* were they built? What was their original purpose? The likelihood is that different sites would have been built for different reasons, but all are based upon the power of human consciousness to change the physical dimension, i.e. working with intent. Whether it was to help with land healing, people healing, sacrifice, worship or secret ceremonies. Or maybe a site could have been used for all of the above? Sites have existed for so many hundreds or thousands of years that through those centuries they would probably been used for many different purposes, even if they were built for one specific reason in the first place.

Man likes to recycle materials where possible, so it's to be expected that many sacred sites have been ransacked over the years, the stone and other sacred objects being used to make new buildings or become part of the scenery. The dry-stone walls in Yorkshire are a prime example of recycling, as are the old sarsen stones creating the foundations of the church in Avebury.

We feel that in many cases these sites were built to help people gain a stronger connection with the higher realms, whether through worshipping the Sun, the Moon, or astronomical constellations such as the Dog Star or the Pleiades. Many sites also acted as a microcosm of existence, mimicking the macrocosm of the heavens. For instance, The Giza Pyramids and Thornborough Henges echo the off-angle shape of Orion's Belt and the henge at Avebury echoes the surrounding hills of the Marlborough Downs.

It is also possible that the hallucinogenic effects of certain plants ingested by our ancestors helped to put them into a trance-like state, helping them to connect with the gods or their Creator. Interestingly, in modern times, one of the best places to gather magic mushrooms can be at sacred sites such as stone circles.

Many of the world's holy and sacred sites can now be found on the internet, and Google Earth is a wonderful app to use when looking for hidden or lost places.

The good news is that you do not have to visit these sites in person to get a feeling for why they were built, by whom and how they are currently being used. Download a photograph of, for example, the Serpent Mound in Ohio, U.S.A. or The Hurlers Stone Circles in Cornwall, UK and begin to ask questions either via dowsing or psychically. As you tune in, you will, very quickly, start to build up a picture of the place and often begin to experience the energies found there.

Adrian will often distance dowse from the comfort of his home before he visits a site. That way, he can fully concentrate on the task without any interruption or disturbance. He will build up a picture of what awaits him when he arrives on site. This is particularly advantageous when visiting a church, as dowsing isn't always welcome within the hallowed walls.

There was one memorable occasion when remotely dowsing a church in Ledbury, he mapped out several important water courses running beneath the building which crossed some sixty feet behind the church. When he visited the church and went to where the streams crossed he found the remnants of a holy well, which was probably why the church was built in this location.

Chapter Twelve

Healing

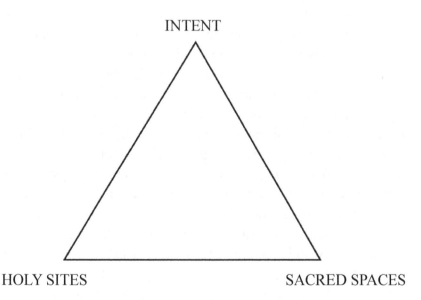

INTENT

HOLY SITES   SACRED SPACES

Interconnectedness for harmony

Humans are amazing beings. Like other animals, our bodies and minds have self-healing capabilities that work to maintain our optimum health. It is when our bodies and minds are overwhelmed, that disease and poor health occurs. In order to help our natural self-healing it is important to live a healthy and self-supportive lifestyle, that of course includes good diet and exercise for both mind and body.

If we are drawn to healing then it is very important to incorporate as many sources of energy to draw upon as we can. There are many ways of healing, but here we are referring to it as healing between humans and/or Mother Earth using the subtle energies of our realities, rather than any physical pharmaceutical or natural remedy.

By drawing upon the ever-present subtle energies around us, we can engage with a patient/client remotely or in their presence, to aid to their recovery or wellness. In this sort of healing it is vital that we recognise we are only the channel for the healing to take place. It is the universal loving energies of creation or Source that are carrying out the actual supportive work enabling the body and/or mind of the patient to heal itself.

However, that doesn't fully portray the complete complexity of this very deep, sometimes dramatic, and fast healing that can occur for some. Increasingly, mainstream disciplines such as ecology and environmental sciences that study the sustainability of biodiversity on this planet, see how the health of the overall system depends upon the intricate interconnectedness of everything. All types of living systems actually contribute in some small way to the overall health of the planetary system in which we thrive as a species. The same is true when we look at small aspects of each diverse living system, from the populations of certain animals in specific environments down to the health of cell colonies in our bodies. Everything can be seen to depend upon a vast network of balanced harmonious interconnected elements. The spiritual world is a part of the overall balance of the eco-system's wellness on Mother Earth.

Much of our reality on Earth is informed from spirit, as we have tried to illustrate throughout this book. The intelligent creative forces of consciousness, such as those in the angelic realms, permeate into our dimension and co-exist alongside our physical one.

Our relationship with those spiritual dimensions is fundamental to the sustainability of this physical one. We live in a time where action is required in order for balance on Earth to be restored. This in turn will sustain the necessary biodiversity required to aid the continual evolution of consciousness in all dimensions. Our physical dimension is not an isolated singular entity, it is intrinsically connected to many others.

What we have tried to illustrate in this book is the power that an individual holds to affect the reality around them. Everybody has this power and everybody can change the world around them. That work is done by changing our inner space first. Part of that change is in growing our relationship with the energies of other dimensions, those of the Management.

Developing a relationship with the Management for healing purposes is not a passive process, it is one founded on discussion, exploration, testing, and development based upon results and individual progress. In many ways, it is much like any logical developmental process used by large corporate organisations and individuals to effect change. Healing is often seen by those who experience it as a passive process by the healer (the channel or conduit for healing). We suggest, however, that some forms of healing are less passive than others. Some forms of healing which can be very simple in their application, allow a greater active influence from the Management on our physical dimension and we have tried to illustrate how we can all begin to be more proactive in bringing healing in our daily lives throughout this book.

Mother Earth: a connection with the Creator

Connecting to a higher energy source from the subtle realms of spirit, such as angels, is important in any healing activity, but we should not forget about our important connection with the Earth. The Earth will help ground us as well as adding to those powerful subtle energies.

We believe that it's important to ask for the help of Mother Earth as well as the higher energies or God when we carry out healing. Combining these forces makes the healing so much more powerful.

For example, before starting to give healing, Adrian always sets his intention to connect with The Highest of the High and Mother Earth.

He also includes our Life-giving Sun (for without it we would not be here) and, of course, the all-important Moon. Connecting these four important aspects of life together brings about a whole new aspect to his work. By connecting these four modalities he is covering all the bases. Many of our past cultures worshipped this way and we believe it is now time to do so again.

By connecting Mother Earth, the Sun, the Moon and the Creator, we become a conduit capable of carrying out powerful healing, not just on people, but also on animals, the elementals and of course, on Mother Earth herself.

A word about healing

Without meaning to, some healers often use their own energy, rather than connecting to an external source and using universal healing energy to help others. In effect, they are draining their own batteries, using their own internal magnetic healing, to give to others rather than tapping into the Universe.

In order to keep their own energy intact, and to not become exhausted, healers need to ensure that they are channelling healing energy from spirit, and as mentioned above, also include Mother Earth, the Sun and the Moon. Many healers call upon the archangels to help them, using their endless universal energy to help transmit healing to others, either through their hands or over distance via intent. This channelling of Universal Energy is far healthier for both parties as it maintains a pureness during the healing, and the healer is not passing on any of their own thoughts, emotions or illnesses onto the client during that time.

Mikao Usui (the founder of Reiki Healing) was one of the first to bring channelled healing to prominence here in the West. He was a highly-educated man and, later in his life, became a Buddhist monk. He felt that Zen Buddhism was very much about healing the mind (mental) and, through his research of the Buddhist scriptures and texts, he could not find anything relating to the healing of the body (physical). It was during one of his fasting periods that he received divine inspiration, giving him the foundations for Reiki. Perhaps this was the archangels at work.

Knowledge of how to heal effectively can be gained by reading a book, talking with others, attending workshops and courses, travelling, general life experiences, or we can allow the channelling of information from above in order to learn. Everybody can link into the angelic realms given a little practice. Try it and let it flow. The angelic realms are there to help, but remember they have to be asked with respect and with the belief that they will respond.

Connect with Mother Earth, the Sun and the Moon

In our current reality, we are all children of the Earth and we have a role to fulfil on the planet, whether we know it or not. In order to thrive, we need to maintain our physical, mental and spiritual connection with Mother Earth or Gaia.

She is a living and breathing world. This notion of a living Earth is not just New Age rhetoric as there are aspects of its life that even science can detect. For example, the hum known as the Schumann Resonance (known by most as a frequency of 7.83 Hz) can be heard and felt almost like the Earth's heartbeat or breath. It is harder to detect these days, as our modern world is so full of man-made Electro Magnetic Frequencies. However, it is still there and can sometimes be heard as a distant background rumble or vibration. The Schumann Resonance is one of the few aspects of life, often associated with our spiritual connection, which the scientific world can confirm. Even NASA has acknowledged these vibrational waves exist and it is rumoured that this background resonance is so integral to our survival as a species on Earth, that it is transmitted to the Space Station for the welfare of the astronauts.

The Schumann Resonance is a tangible auditory resonance of waves that is literally on the edge of usual human perception and forms a direct link between us and Mother Earth. During the latter part of 2016 and into the early months of 2017, the Schumann waves were spiking at hitherto unseen heights. This led to many sensitive people feeling out of sorts and in some cases made them feel much more connected to the spiritual realm than to planet Earth herself. Which makes sense, as we are not only children of the Earth, but we are also children of the stars. Many of the trace elements in the galaxy can be found within our bodies, giving us a direct connection to the Divine or Creator and this is so important to remember when we meditate, give healing, or start to dowse as it draws us closer to the healing power of the Universe.

If it wasn't for the Sun we would not be able to survive on this planet for very long, so when connecting with the Earth, consider doing the same with the Sun; visualise how you might do that or feel it as you begin to meditate. Use its powers for self-development, self-healing and/or understanding. It is all energy and we are all able to utilise it on some level.

The Moon's energy also influences all that we do and can be utilised for healing. Without it, we would not have tides and our weather patterns would certainly be different. We, as human beings, are all made up of around 60% to 75% water so is it any wonder that people are also known to suffer from the influences of a full, new and dark moon. It is also well known that many women's menstrual cycles are linked to the phases of the Moon.

Connecting to all these heavenly structures, the Moon, Mother Earth, our life-giving Sun and the divine or universal energy enhances our healing, psychic and mental abilities. Most people, when in healing mode and working on a client, agree they feel a connection with something outside themselves. In fact, all healing, apart from magnetic healing, which uses our own internal and emotional energy, comes from somewhere outside us. Our ability or desire to tune into this external source enables us to enhance and prolong healing sessions. By channelling this external and extraordinary energy, we can accomplish much more than by purely using our internal energy.

Case Study

In early April 2017, during a Dales Healing and Meditation Group meeting, Adrian decided to do something very different. Before starting a healing session, he always connects with Mother Earth as well as spirit. He also includes the energies of the sun and moon as they are vital to our daily wellbeing. However, most healers are taught to connect with spirit only and Adrian wanted to find out how people would react, both healer and recipient, when they linked firstly with the Earth and then afterwards with spirit, separately.

"I explained the process to the group and they split into pairs," explains Adrian. "Each chosen healer then placed his or her hands directly onto the shoulders of their partner who was sitting in front of them. I then talked them through how to connect with the Earth and only the Earth," Adrian continues, "Most of the healers sat down shortly after the healing started and stayed that way until the end of the session. They then swapped over and became the recipient. Again, most healers sat down during the ten minute healing. We then cut the connection and sat quietly for a few minutes."

During the discussion that followed, almost everyone said how heavy they felt when giving or receiving the healing. Most agreed that it took time for the energies to kick in but, when they did, they were very powerful. Most said that they enjoyed the experience, but that it felt very different from what they were used to.

"We then connected with spirit, hands on shoulders as before, but this time most healers stood for the ten minute healing. We all, then swapped over and, once finished, I asked each in turn how they felt. 'Much lighter,' was the main comment. Another was, 'It was totally different from the Earth connection' and finally, 'The healing came through instantaneously unlike the Earth healing which took time to manifest itself.'"

The group then sat in a circle and connected with both Earth and spirit to send the appropriate healing to everyone in the room, and also friends and family. Then they sent the energies out into the Universe to help others.

Healing from Mother Earth is bound to be heavier than spirit. The vibration level is going to be lower on the planet compared to the heavens. Our ancestors would have, undoubtedly, used this earthly connection for their healing. It is just that we have forgotten to do so, or perhaps it is now instinctive to only connect with spirit.

When you start out on establishing a connection, as with anything new, you will need to practice. Practice will strengthen your abilities. The stronger your abilities, the stronger your connection will become; the stronger your connection, the greater your abilities. The better your abilities and understanding become, the stronger your connection will grow... the cycle goes on and on in a development of positive improvement.

Adrian always starts his connection process with The Lord's Prayer, but he chooses to make the following additions: 'Our Father who art in Heaven, our Mother who is on Earth, our life-giving Sun and heavenly Moon hallowed be your names...'

This sort of prayer at the start of a healing session, sets up your intent, indicates to all the assembled beings and to your physical body what you are about to do, that is, to work with an external source. Once bonded, it is time to start healing, dowsing or perhaps tapping into your psychic abilities.

Belief systems and how to work with them

Belief systems are important. They give us firm foundations on which to build, but that is not to say that our thoughts can't change as we look, listen, learn and gather experience and knowledge. In fact, it is very important that we do adopt new ideas and build them into our lives as we grow. Learning is partly what we are here to do; as is using what we have learned to help others.

Most belief systems are built upon the notion that there is *something* out there which (or who) oversees our planet. This external source is called many things from God to the Universal Library and the Akashic Records or simply the Highest of the High. The Akashic Records are thoughts, events, and emotions believed to be encoded in a non-physical plane of existence known as the Astral Plane.

Within most basic belief systems there also exists free will for us here on the planet. In this understanding, we are left to our own devices, making mistakes and hopefully learning from them, until we stop and physically ask someone, (or the Management), for help.

Our advice would be to avoid being too focused on following one set of beliefs. You have an ability to learn and to then build your own set of beliefs. *Choose what works for you.* All you need to remember is that working with the Universe is simple – you only have to ask.

Are you an introvert or an extrovert?

When embarking upon a spiritual path it is quite common to feel inadequate, especially if we compare our progress to somebody else's progress or abilities. This comparison is a natural part of being human, but it is not very helpful for us individually. Always remember that you are you and you were born to be uniquely you. Try to see your own gifts and develop those wonderful abilities and talents that you have, rather than compare yourself to others.

Bottom line: everybody is different and our differences should be celebrated. Often, although not always of course, it is the sensitive introvert who is most affected by these comparisons to others.

Our experience of life, of our reality in each moment, is presented to us through a vast array of energetic fields. These emanate from other humans, animals and plants as well as those naturally occurring from Mother Earth.

We will each experience spirituality and a spiritual awakening in different ways. Some will actively seek a guru or teacher to learn from, preferring to attend courses and workshops, whilst others will remain solitary and seek their own form of enlightenment via meditation, peace and creative inspiration.

Those who receive a boost of positive energy by sharing their time with their peers, are usually classified as extroverts. Those who prefer being alone, away from what they perceive as the stress of interaction with other people in order to restore their batteries, are classified as introverts. Of course, everybody is a mixture of each personality type, but often we can see general themes of type in our lives. That is not to say that you don't find sociable introverts, it is just that, as a defining personality type they will be happier and more energised spending time alone. An introvert, for instance, is more likely to be inclined to access a spiritual experience that, they feel, is created purely for them and they will shun any interaction involving another human energy field. This may ultimately lead them towards periods of deep introspection. We can, of course, use psychic protection to exclude or lessen other people's influence over us. Or we can limit the intrusion of others in our lives by living in the middle of nowhere and not mixing with or connecting with other people's energy fields or auras.

This is what some introverts are attempting to do when living in solitude. They are trying to rid themselves of any outside interference and concentrate purely on connecting with spirit. A retreat will often enable an extrovert to quickly get into a mind frame that is similar to that of the hermit so we are not saying that, as a natural extrovert, you cannot connect with the divine equally well. It is just that you will do it in a different way.

When we become intensely focused on the experience of our subtle energy fields and we observe our emotions and experience of daily life, we can see that frequently, other people's interaction in our realities changes the way we feel, and subtly changes our reality. Some Shamans declare themselves careful of who they closely associate with for this very reason.

As soon as two people come face to face, they are automatically engaging and connecting energetically via their individual auric fields. These human energy fields intertwine and mix, exchanging information. If another person joins them then their energy field will also interact with the original pair.

Our human energy fields are always, at some level, enmeshed with others, including those of the natural world, but the more intimate the relationship, the greater the influence will be upon our aura.

In just the same way that having physical contact (kissing for instance) with someone who has a cold will give you a greater chance of catching their germs than if you just sat in the same room as them, the interaction of those around you will have a subtle effect on you.

Knowing ourselves, knowing what is *our* energy and what is somebody else's, and knowing that when things come into our reality that they can affect us, will protect us from confusion and emotional stress. To repeat, these affects from other people can be very subtle, but can also be quite insidious in a detrimental way. If we are aware, then we can take action or simply be content in recognising the change and know that the feelings will pass. We can also delight in understanding why.

By removing much of the detrimental emotional baggage found in other people's thoughts from our daily life, (maybe from within our house or from a mobile phone, for example,) we can all focus more clearly on a spiritual connection with greater intent and effect. One of the aspects that enables us to function effectively in the real world in a calm and confident way, is to actually know who we are, to know ourselves intimately, inside and out. In truth, most people don't know who they are and in some cases, just don't care. However, trying to discover this information is one of the biggest and most rewarding challenges we can face in our lifetime.

But knowing yourself is not as easy and straightforward as it may sound. You have to start by looking at all your prejudices, how you view life and your current values and then be willing to change. So, what do we mean by *knowing yourself*?

To us it means knowing how you would react in a variety of circumstances and knowing that the life that you lead is built upon your own belief systems and not the belief systems of others. It means living your own truth, being totally honest in your actions and the words you use, being transparent in all things you do, and perhaps even living by a set of strict rules or values that you have identified as yours.

When we do not have this confidence, it is easy to react from fear, especially if we think someone is confronting and questioning what we perceive to be long-held beliefs. If our beliefs are weak and shaky we can become defensive and possibly aggressive in response.

We each have a role, or part, to play in the two-way relationship between ourselves and another person, but when we lack confidence, it is difficult to have an open, honest and true conversational exchange. The same can apply when we enter into a spiritually-based conversation within, or with a guardian of a sacred site.

Honesty is the key here. The site reacts not only to our brains but also to our hearts. It reacts with our subconscious as well as our conscious awareness and in order to receive insights and a magical experience, our subconscious and conscious thoughts need to be aligned in honesty. To be honest and true to ourselves, and to live from the heart is very difficult for many people because of a lack of self-respect and self-love.

As children, we are rarely taught to love who we are, as it is often believed to lead to egotism. We more often than not, adopt our parents' emotional patterns; we are hardly ever taught to build our own. Careful, detached observation of our inner selves can assist us in getting rid of much of the emotional junk that we carry within us. In order for us to progress on our spiritual path we need to be as clear of this baggage as possible.

Spirit, Earth and human being

There is a well-known statement that says: *We are not human beings on a spiritual journey, we are spiritual beings on a human journey.*

Fundamentally, the problem with being a human on a spiritual path is twofold. First of all, as we have seen, the subconscious rules our lives and by its very nature we are rarely aware of what our emotional trigger points are, or indeed what motivates us to believe the things that we do.

And second, our egotistical self will fight tooth and nail to stop our soul-selves from developing. If the soul-self develops, it means the egotistical self will have to change and it doesn't want to.

The egotistical self (more commonly called the ego-self) is the part of us that runs on automatic pilot. It is this subconscious behaviour that feeds our habitual daily responses to situations and life in general. It is this aspect of us that stops us from experiencing the new, it controls the filter in the brain which only allows certain information to permeate into our conscious minds.

When we walk into a sacred site or tune into the sacredness of our homes with respect and honesty, we put our ego selves to one side. But to say that we should abandon our ego selves completely as some spiritual teachers suggest, is, in the opinion of the authors, not very constructive.

Our humanness is created by our ego selves. It is what makes us unique, each with our own baggage and principles to deal with. So, instead of trying to squash or expel the ego, a more useful process is one in which we acknowledge all the hard work and effort that the ego-self has expended in getting us to this point in our lives.

Acknowledge and congratulate your ego, be kind to it, thank it and tell it that you will respect it as an integral part of you, but from now on, you want your soul-self to be at the forefront of your life. You want your inner soul-self leading and showing you the way to lead the rest of your life.

This process needs to be done with specific intent, ideally a short ceremony, that connects you to Mother Earth via the earth energy power centre in your own home or perhaps at a more public ceremony when visiting a sacred site – it is entirely up to you.

To communicate with the higher realms, we have to lift, or raise, our vibrations. To do this we clear ourselves of our emotional and mental baggage which helps to lift our spirits. The connection therefore becomes easier to achieve.

It is the lower emotional vibrational energies that drag our spirits down, keeping us in a state of depression or unease. These low states are caused by such negative thoughts as:

'I am not worthy'

'I do not deserve to be happy'

'I cannot do (XYZ) because I have never been able to'

'I am not allowed to do this'

'I do not deserve to be successful at this'

'I must not do things differently because bad things will happen if I do.'

It is this mindset that keeps us tied to the lower vibrational level of physicality. Unfortunately, this is where ego feels comfortable and it is very happy for us to stay that way. There are many of us who want to achieve a higher vibrational state of emotional being, to access the magical realms of the spiritual self. The very fact of wanting to achieve this is the first big step along a beautiful, but testing pathway. We need to heal ourselves in order to climb that vibrational scale of wellness by identifying our thought patterns, both good and bad.

But this is not always as simple as you think and external help is sometimes necessary to enable you to move forward, to help you release your angst and change the parental patterning, in short, to allow you to be you. Once achieved, you are likely to be drawn towards healing of others and in doing so, will change the world around you.

What of the future?

There is lot of fear about the state of the world; yet it is quite common for those who have passed into spirit, or our spirit guides, to reassure us with comments like, *'The world and humanity will be all right in the end'* and *'Everything is as it should be'*.

Tim's guide Myrddin, also goes along with this sentiment. One of the most striking things he has said is, *'The Earth is here because of humanity, not the other way around!'* Myrddin says the population as a whole has been taught to believe that Earth, a massive lump of rock hurtling through space, is here to enable our species to evolve and grow.

Now that may well be the case, but let us consider a 'WHAT IF...' scenario. What if... that lump of rock was here for us *because* we, as a species, *had to exist* in order to fill a vital and missing role in the development of the multi-dimensional existence of the Universe as a whole? What if we were created out of necessity and the dimension in which we "live" was made for us to live in by beings far greater than we could possibly imagine? It's a possible, philosophical viewpoint that might help us to think of ourselves as spirits being human: the Earth could be here because it was necessary for us to have something to live on. In this sense, we refer to the complete universe in all its facets in the seen and unseen realms.

There is no doubt that humanity, with its ability to be both objective and subjective, has an important role to play in the inter-connectedness of everything in many dimensions.

If we look further into our role amongst the elementals and the angels, we may, hopefully begin to see humanity's importance in the overall scheme of things (the bigger picture) and begin to believe that we and the archangels, angels, elementals and all beings in the universe are all as equally important.

At this point in time (*time* being a human concept), we appear to be coming to terms with the idea that we act as an interface between the subtle realms and physical world. By that we mean that we are a species acting as a bridge between spirit and earth.

So, it is possible, for a reason that we are not yet aware of, or perhaps couldn't even begin to comprehend, that we had to exist as a species for this very purpose: to bridge the realms and co-exist with angels, archangels and elementals. If that is the case, then all we need to 'do' on an individual level is continue being human be observant, aware and mindful and enjoy our lives. We don't need to be 'doing' anything specific with our lives to fulfil a supposed specific destiny or course of action. Destiny as a concept need not exist, we are instead transmuters of emotional energy from one state to another in our search for spiritual enlightenment. We are changing negative low vibrational energies within us to a higher level of more altruistic and positive emotion. In healing ourselves and others we find ourselves inextricably moving on a path towards the ultimate goal of unconditional love, and that is a place of peace and joy. The Earth might actually be here for us, as our playground and place of learning; a place where we simply enjoy being human.

About Tim

Tim attended film school at the age of eighteen, where he found himself to be exemplary at being ordinary and utterly average in most achievements. The only aspect of his life in which he excelled was the ability to be stressed by almost everything around him. As a result he was also a somewhat cynical individual. He continued that way until decades later he found himself running a small film and television production company while also working as a video production consultant for the world's largest life assurance company. With more pressure in his professional life, his levels of stress only increased. For many years, it seemed that the whole of Tim's life was to be dedicated to the world of film, television and high blood pressure.

However, all that changed with the decision to relocate from the busy South East of England to the comparative calm of the Welsh borders. He and his family moved into an old Georgian townhouse house in The Forest of Dean, and it was there that they met what would commonly be called a ghost. But 'Jane' was no ordinary ghost, and over the fifteen years the family lived with her, Tim's attitude to life changed completely.

Today, Tim works as a life coach and geomancer, helping people through life-crises or helping them to learn the power of their intuition. Currently renovating his home in the Yorkshire Dales, he is also developing a keen interest in the healing power of gardening and nature.

He loves helping others to change their lives by enabling them to find peace and harmony through mindfulness, meditation, dowsing and the power of focused intent. Tim is still a very ordinary individual, but is somewhat less cynical and stressed…

About Adrian

Dowsing has featured in Adrian's life since he was seven, but it never dawned on him that it would have such an impact on him later in his life.

Owning a busy Estate Agency in Surrey inspired him to look at the repeating patterns of divorce in certain homes, and from that Dowsing Spirits was born. To help people be healthy and happy and have harmonious relationships, Adrian checks for detrimental energies in people and their homes, and then heals them. His clients have included several royal families, a number of well-known film stars and many successful businesses throughout the world.

For three years, he was the Vice President of the British Society of Dowsers and was chair of both their Earth Energies and Health dowsing groups.

His self-help book, 'Heal Your Home', has been described as the bible of geopathic stress and has a worldwide readership. His friendship with Tim brought about the filming of 'Intuition', a DVD on dowsing and how to access your inner knowing. Both the book and DVD are available from his website.

One of his missions in life is to bring dowsing into the 21st century and is fulfilling this by teaching various courses and giving talks around the UK and Europe.

He lives with his wife, Allyson, and springer spaniel, Annie, in a small village near Ripon in the Yorkshire Dales.

Also available from the authors:

Heal Your Home - Book

Often referred to as 'the bible of geopathic stress' this best-selling book is the 'go-to' for anyone interested in, not just earth energies but many other noxious problems that affect their home, office or workspace. The book describes, in down to earth terms, how to locate and then deal with the detrimental energies that can affect us in our daily lives, including spirits, earth energy lines, inherited human emotions, attachments, psychic attack, curses and much more. Importantly it has been written as a self-help book with a detailed section on how to carry out a healing yourself.

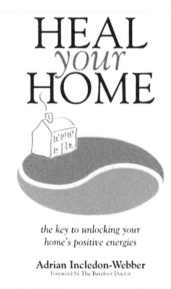

the key to unlocking your home's positive energies

Adrian Incledon-Webber
Foreword by The Barefoot Doctor

Intuition – Your Hidden Treasure – DVD

A treasure house of information on how to develop your sixth sense through dowsing. Many subjects are covered from how to make and use dowsing rods, what to look for at ancient sites, working how detrimental your household products can be, horse racing, how psychic protection helps a rock band, how vibrations can help enliven sacred sites and more.

Get your copy now from Adrian's website: www.dowsingspirits.co.uk

Diverse Dowsing - DVD

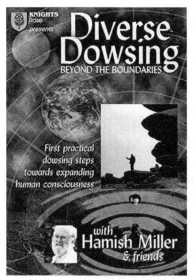

Hamish Miller gives an earthy, honest, practical demonstration of basic dowsing tools, instruction on dowsing techniques, a "potted history" of their various developments and takes you quickly and expertly beyond the popular perception of dowsing as "just a way of finding water". Dowsing skills have developed to sophisticated levels which require practitioners to specialise in a particular field so that they can provide confident and competent solutions to problems as they arise. These diverse specialities are explored in this film with expert practising dowsers. They talk knowledgeably and demonstrate their skills in this fascinating, colourful and intriguing film.

Hamish on The Parallel Community - DVD

This is a remarkable portrait of an amazing man, who after a mid-life Near Death Experience became determined to make a difference in the world and to live from his heart. Hamish Miller in "Hamish on the Parallel Community" introduces a way of living that many of us have been searching for; a life that provides peace, insight and wisdom on earth where humanity is a collection of caring souls functioning as part of a much bigger universal picture. "Hamish on The Parallel Community" was made 2 years before Hamish died, even then he knew his days on this earth were coming to a close.

Get your copy now from Tim's website:
www.knightsrose.com

Recommended Reading Material

Books that have helped Adrian's development:

The Shining Ones by Christian and Barbara Joy O'Brien
The Light in Britain by Grace Cooke *
The Ancient Secret of the Flower of Life I and II by Drunvalo
Melchizedek
The 72 Names of God by Yehuda Berg
Cosmic Consciousness by Richard Maurice Bucke
The Tibetan Book of Living and Dying by Sogyal Rinpoche
Autobiography of a Spiritually Incorrect Mystic by Osho
Talking to Heaven by James Van Praagh
Celt, Druid and Culdee by Isabel Hill Elder

Mythos Press:

Sun and the Serpent by Hamish Miller and Paul Broadhurst

Tom Graves series of books:

Needles of Stone Revisited
The Diviner's Handbook
The Dowser's Workbooks
The Disciplines of Dowsing by Tom Graves and Liz Poraj-
Wilczynska
Elements of Pendulum Dowsing
Inventing Reality

General Dowsing Reading:

Dowsing: A Path to Enlightenment by Joey Korn
Dowsing One Man's Way by Jim Scott Elliot
Pendulum: The psi Connection by Francis Hitching
Earth Radiation by Kathe Bachler
Dowsing by Robert H. Leftwich *
Dowsing for Beginners by Richard Webster
Dowsing by Naomi Ozaniec *

Complete Guide to Dowsing (Water) by George Applegate
Earth Currents by Gustav Freiherr von Pohl *
Places of Power by Paul Devereux
Points of Cosmic Energy by Blanche Merz *
Ley Lines and Earth Energies by David Cowan and Chris Arnold
The Old Straight Track by Alfred Watkins
Spirals by Geoff Ward
Dowsing in the 21st Century by Elizabeth Brown
Powerpoints by Robin Heath
Ley Lines by Danny Sullivan
The Diving Hand by Christopher Bird
The Divining Rod by Sir William Barrett and Theodore Besterman

General Reading on Earth Energies and other esoteric matters:

Silbury Dawning by John Cowie
Lines on the Landscape by Nigel Pennick and Paul Devereux
The Lost Magic of Christianity by Michael Poynder
The View Beyond (Francis Bacon) 978-1-905398-22-5
The Modern Antiquarian by Julian Cope
The Megalithic European by Julian Cope
Men Amongst Mankind by Brinsley Le Poer Trench *
The Creation of Health by C Norman Shealy and Caroline Myss
Lost Secrets of the Sacred Ark by Laurence Gardner
Stukeley Illustrated by Neil Mortimer

Other books of interest:

The Powerwatch Handbook by Alasdair and Jean Philips
The Elphite by Michelle Gordon
The Earth Angel Training Academy by Michelle Gordon
The Doorway to PAM by Michelle Gordon

Those marked with an * are now out of print, you will need to scour second hand bookshops or internet to find them.

Books that have helped Tim's development:

The Self Aware Universe by Amit Goswami
Physics of the Soul by Amit Goswami
The Tao of Physics by Fritjof Capra
The Cosmic Code by Heinz R Pagels
The Biology of Belief by Bruce Lipton
Spontaneous Evolution by Bruce Lipton and Steve Bhaerman
It's Not Too Late by Hamish Miller
The Wee Book of Dowsing by Hamish Miller
The Wave by Jude Currivan
The Field by Lynn McTaggart
The Power of Now by Ekhart Tolle
Living Energies by Callum Coates
The Souls Code by James Hillman
Jonathan Livingstone Seagull by Richard Bach
Illusions by Richard Bach
Seven Days in New Crete by Robert Graves
The Hitch Hikers Guide to the Galaxy by Douglas Adams
Mindfulness - A practical guide to finding peace in a frantic world
Mark Williams and Danny Pelman
Seed of Knowledge, Stone of Plenty: Understanding the Lost
Technology of the Ancient Megalith Builders by John Burke & Kai
Halberg

Many of these books can be ordered from The British Society of
Dowsers bookshop (www.britishdowsers.org)The British Society of
Dowsers
01684 576969
www.britishdowsers.org

If you would like to get in touch

You can follow us on the usual social media platforms or email us directly:

Email: adrian@dowsingspirits.co.uk
Website: www.dowsingspirits.co.uk

Email: tim.walter@knightsrose.com
Website: www.knightsrose.com

Both websites give up-to-date information and details on workshops and dowsing courses which include:

Spiritual Earth workshops presented by both authors together and...

Adrian's workshops:

Introduction to Dowsing
Dowsing for Health I and II
Earth Energies I
Dowsing for Health and Healing I, II and III
Healing Your Home I and II
Healing with Sacred Symbols

Tim's workshops:

Discovering your Intuition I
Discovering your Intuition II
Dowsing earth energy for wellness
The creative living landscape

If you would like to discuss Paul Gerry's research into mindsets and work with the Mind Mirror, Paul welcomes emails to: brainwavedowser@hotmail.com

Independent Publishing Services were provided by Michelle Gordon:
The Amethyst Angel
theamethystangel@hotmail.co.uk
theamethystangel.com